TOMORROW'S COM

Lessons for Community-based Transformation in the Age of Global Crises

Edited by
Henry Tam

P

First published in Great Britain in 2021 by

Policy Press, an imprint of
Bristol University Press
University of Bristol
1-9 Old Park Hill
Bristol
BS2 8BB
UK
t: +44 (0)117 954 5940
e: bup-info@bristol.ac.uk

Details of international sales and distribution partners are available at
policy.bristoluniversitypress.co.uk

© Bristol University Press 2021

British Library Cataloguing in Publication Data
A catalogue record for this book is available from the British Library

ISBN 978-1-4473-6110-7 hardcover
ISBN 978-1-4473-6111-4 paperback
ISBN 978-1-4473-6112-1 ePub
ISBN 978-1-4473-6113-8 ePdf

Cover design: Robin Hawes
Front cover image: MARTÍ SANS Stocksy.com
Bristol University Press and Policy Press use environmentally responsible
print partners.
Printed in Great Britain by CMP, Poole

Contents

List of tables and figures

Tables

Figures

Notes on contributors

Rosalind Beadle is Adjunct Lecturer at the Centre for Remote Health, Flinders University, Australia; and a University Fellow at Charles Darwin University. She developed an expertise in community development and participatory action research through her work in culturally diverse contexts. Her PhD dissertation describes how a group of Ngaanyatjarra women in a remote Aboriginal community in Western Australia framed their work in ways compatible with the social and cultural context of their lives.

David Boyle is Policy Director at Radix Think Tank for the Radical Centre, UK; an advisory council member of the Schumacher Centre for New Economics in Massachusetts, US; and a fellow at the New Economics Foundation, UK. He was the UK government's independent reviewer of Barriers to Public Service Choice (2012–13). He is the author of a number of books about history, social change and the future, including *Tickbox*, *Authenticity* and *Broke* (which looked at the slow destruction of the middle classes).

Mary Brydon-Miller is Professor in the Department of Educational Leadership, Evaluation, & Organizational Development at the College of Education and Human Development, University of Louisville, US. She is a participatory action researcher who conducts work in both school and community settings. She is the editor, with David Coghlan, of the *SAGE Encyclopedia of Action Research*. Her latest book, which she edited with Sarah Banks, is *Ethics in Participatory Research for Health and Social Well-Being: Cases and Commentaries*.

Gabriel Chanan is a social researcher, and formerly Director of Research & Policy at the Community Development Foundation, UK. He was seconded as an adviser on community involvement to the UK's Home Office and Department for Communities and Local Government (2005–08). He directed pioneering EU research projects on urban regeneration. Recent work has included running the Health Empowerment Leverage Project (HELP), and a series of projects with Community Places in Northern Ireland. He has published widely on social and literary issues, and also writes and produces plays.

Pat Conaty is co-founder of the Synergia Institute; and an Associate of Co-operatives UK. His work at the Birmingham Settlement and New

Economics Foundation in the 1990s led to development funding for the establishment of the Community Development Finance movement. At Community Finance Solutions he co-led development work to establish the Community Land Trust (CLT) national demonstration project and the founding of the National CLT Network. He is co-author, with Michael Lewis, of *The Resilience Imperative: Co-operative Transitions to a Steady-state Economy*.

Alison Gilchrist is an independent practitioner, writer and researcher; and formerly Director of Practice Development at the Community Development Foundation, UK. She has also been research fellow at INLOGOV at the University of Birmingham, UK, investigating the impact of 'community connectors' in urban innovation. She has mainly worked in inner-city neighbourhoods and has a long-standing commitment to shared learning, through training, publications and conferences. She is the author of *The Well-Connected Community: A Networking Approach to Community Development* and co-wrote the *Short Guide to Community Development*.

Neal Lawson is Director of the good society pressure group, Compass, UK. He serves on the advisory board of the social democracy journal *Renewal*, which he helped found; is an adviser to public ownership campaigners, We Own It; and a member of the Commission on a Gender Equal Economy. He writes for *The Guardian*, *New Statesman* and *Open Democracy*. He has also worked as a trade union researcher, and an adviser to Gordon Brown. He is the author of *All Consuming* and co-editor of *The Progressive Century*.

Ed Mayo is Chief Executive of the social enterprise, Pilotlight, UK; and formerly Chief Executive of Co-operatives UK, the National Consumer Council and the New Economics Foundation. He has been Chair of Involve, the democracy charity, and Jubilee 2000, the campaign on global justice. He is the author of *Values: How to Bring Values to Life in Your Business*, as well as books on economic co-operation and marketing.

Marjorie Mayo is Emeritus Professor of Community Development at Goldsmiths, University of London, UK. Her research has included a focus on community action and development, community–university engagement, learning for active citizenship, and access to justice in disadvantaged communities. Her recent publications include *Community-based Learning and Social Movements: Popular Education in a*

Populist Age and *Changing Communities: Stories of Migration, Displacement and Solidarities*.

Colin Miller is a writer, theorist and researcher on democratic and constitutional issues; and Compass Associate. He is a founder member of the Deeper Democracy Group, which focuses on the role that participatory practice can play in helping transform democracy. He has previously managed a local government community development team, and was seconded as an adviser to the Civil Renewal Unit at the UK's Home Office. His publications include *Participation at 45°: Techniques for Citizen-led Change* and *Rethinking Community Practice: Developing Transformative Neighbourhoods* (with Gabriel Chanan).

John Restakis is British Columbia Program Director at the Community Evolution Foundation, Canada; and co-founder of the Synergia Institute. He was Research Co-ordinator for the FLOK (Free/ Libre Open Knowledge) Project in Ecuador on Social Knowledge and the Social Economy; and co-founder and Co-ordinator of the Bologna Summer Program for Co-operative Studies at the University of Bologna, Italy. He also advised Syriza on the development of the social and solidarity economy in Greece. His books include *Commons Transitions*, *Co-operative Advantage* and *Humanizing the Economy: Co-operatives in the Age of Capital*.

Philip Ross is a founding member of the Association of Independent Professionals and the Self Employed (IPSE), UK and served on its first board as External Affairs Director. He is a member of the CRSE think tank and a Research Associate for Co-operatives UK, for whom he co-authored the influential report *Not Alone: Trade Union and Co-operative Solutions for the Self-employed*. He is the former Mayor of Letchworth and a writer on the Garden City movement. As a freelance IT professional, he specialises in digital transformation projects.

Martin Simon is the founder of Fair Shares; formerly Co-Director of Asset Based Community Development, Europe; and Chief Executive of Timebanking UK. He has advised governments and worked with communities in the UK, the US, India, Croatia and Spain. He teaches, mentors and writes about community-led approaches to positive social change. His publications include *Your Money Or Your Life: Time For Both*, *Community Connectors* and *Connecting People and Place*.

Henry Tam is a political writer; Director of Question the Powerful; and formerly Head of Civil Renewal, UK government. He was Director of the Forum for Youth Participation & Democracy in the Faculty of Education at the University of Cambridge, UK; and Visiting Professor at Birkbeck, University of London, UK. He has advised a wide range of government ministers on policy areas such as community empowerment and social inclusion. His published books include *Time to Save Democracy*, *Whose Government Is It?* and *The Evolution of Communitarian Ideas*.

Diane Warburton is a founding Trustee of Involve; and Evaluation Manager of the UK government's Sciencewise programme. She has published widely, including two books: *Community and Sustainable Development* and *From Here to Sustainability*. She has completed 20 evaluations of major national deliberative and community initiatives for government departments and non-governmental organisations, and overseen more than 40 more as Evaluation Manager for the Sciencewise programme. As a local activist, she has been involved in a traffic campaign in Hackney, in a neighbourhood council in Hammersmith, and in community and street improvement groups in Brighton.

Alice Willatt is a lecturer in the School of Management at the University of Bath, UK. She is interested in alternative food spaces and community wealth-building initiatives that emerge in response to social crises. She brings together feminist ethics and action research practice to co-generate knowledge on the ethico-political practices of the organisations involved and the changing nature of voluntary work. She is co-author, with Mary Phillips, of 'Embodiment, care and practice in a community kitchen'.

Steve Wyler is an independent consultant, researcher and writer in the social sector; and co-founder of A Better Way. He was a panel member of the Inquiry into the Future of Civil Society; Vice-Chair of Social Enterprise UK; and Chief Executive of Locality (previously the Development Trusts Association), the national network of community organisations dedicated to community enterprise, community ownership and social change. His publications include *Community Responses in Times of Crisis: Glimpses into the Past, Present and Future* and *In Our Hands: A History of Community Business*.

Preface

Can a society truly govern itself for the common good? Until 2016, the prevailing view was still that a basic voting system with no means for adjudicating between true and false claims would be sufficient. Then came the twin shocks of Brexit and Trump, and many realised belatedly that mass deception and the promotion of prejudice could easily subvert democracy and defeat their opponents. By 2018, when my book *Time to Save Democracy* was published by Policy Press, there was intense interest in finding ways to protect our collective self-governance from abuse and manipulation.

I decided to follow up on the strategic analyses and recommendations set out in *Time to Save Democracy* with more detailed exposition of why and how a number of policies and practices should be introduced. This involves showing what governments and communities could do to complement each other in strengthening our civic cohesion and capacity for collective problem-solving. The first part of this task was completed with the help of a team of leading experts on how governments can develop more informed and collaborative relations with citizens. The result was *Whose Government Is It?* – a critical guide to what changes should be pursued, what pitfalls to avoid and how obstacles could be overcome.

The second part of the task is to show how, in parallel with changes to the way governments operate, communities themselves can play a critical role in tackling the problems they face and improving everyone's quality of life. That is the aim of this book. With *Tomorrow's Communities*, I have again been fortunate in being able to bring together prominent researchers and practitioners to explain what evidence points to as the key changes that can make a difference in initiating and sustaining community-based transformation.

The contributors to this book possess an unrivalled track record in examining what works and what does not in enabling communities to advance their wellbeing. From them, there is no idealisation of 'community', just evidence-based analysis of why certain routes are more likely than others to help people collaborate, with each other and with public institutions, in attaining a better future.

I would like to share a collective sigh of relief with all the contributors to this book that whatever else the COVID-19 pandemic stopped us doing in our own lives, it did not prevent us from producing this book together. I am most grateful to them for their steadfast work throughout these unsettling times.

Thanks must also go to our colleagues at Policy Press: the ever-helpful Sarah Bird, Emma Cook, Amelia Watts-Jones, Ruth Wallace, Millie Prekop and, of course, Alison Shaw, a beacon to us who write in pursuit of social purpose.

Finally, I should add that, politics aside, 2016–18 were memorable years for me, for 2016 marked the arrival of Fabian and 2018 introduced us to his brother, Elliot. In many ways, this book will be of particular importance to them, for their future will be much affected by the paths taken by tomorrow's communities.

Henry Tam, January 2021

Introduction

1

The challenges for tomorrow's communities

Henry Tam

Communities under threat

There is a new mantra in town. Communities must become more resilient. It is imperative that they can withstand the shocks and strains that are increasingly coming their way. What has brought this about? The short answer is that global crises have, of late, been arriving like proverbial buses. During the decade after the 2008 banking crisis, the world was confronted in 2016 by the fervent unilateralism of Brexit and Trump – and its disruptive impact on trade relations and economic stability. Then came the COVID-19 pandemic in 2020, causing social as well as financial havoc. In the meantime, the climate emergency has only worsened; in 2018 inequality widened to the point that the world's 26 richest individuals possessed as much wealth as the 3.8 billion people who made up the poorest 50 per cent on the planet (Elliott, 2019); the worldwide surge of anti-liberalism is escalating hatred and discrimination against vulnerable groups; and job insecurity everywhere has been intensified by the rapid advancement in automation and artificial intelligence.

But how are communities (which in this context generally refer to the people who live and/or work in a broadly defined geographical area at a level below the country or region) to attain the capability to cope, let alone thrive, in the midst of all these challenges? It is vital to remember that small-scale communities have for centuries moved towards being integrated into larger units of governance such as empires, nations or federal unions. In nearly all cases, they have either found it beneficial to be part of a greater political entity, or discovered that they could not realistically resist being absorbed into a more powerful regime. Indeed, as development in transport and communications led to ever-more cross-border interactions – peaceful or otherwise – it became widely recognised that international rules and institutions were necessary to deal effectively with the threats and opportunities arising from proliferating global connections.

Thus, when we hear that communities should be made stronger in safeguarding themselves from worldwide vicissitudes, we must unpack what is meant by this. One possible interpretation would posit some idealised community of the past – small, bound by traditional expectations and hierarchies, proud and self-sufficient, and shielded from any 'outside' authority – and hail it as a model to which we should aspire. This fits with the ideas of thinkers such as Ferdinand Tönnies, whose notion of *Gemeinschaft* (often translated as 'community') denotes a communal form of life, where people have a strong sense of subordination to the group, conform to customs that have been handed down to them, and are inclined to keep out opinions and practices (even people) that have come from elsewhere (Tönnies, 2003). This outlook permeated initiatives such as the 'Moral Majority' movement in the 1980s in the United States (US) and the 'Big Society' rhetoric in the 2010s in the United Kingdom (UK), which exhibited a number of similar features: governments should not intervene in the social and economic practices that have come to prevail in communities; society should respect and reinforce 'traditional values' (as defined by those who declare themselves the custodians of these values); and individuals and their communities should take responsibility for looking after themselves, rather than asking for external help.

Tönnies' vision of *Gemeinschaft* and its echoes in the various conservative attempts to roll back progressive public policies have been subject to extensive communitarian critiques (Tam, 2019b). In essence, the idealisation of *Gemeinschaft* is flawed on three levels.

First, it is presented in a false conceptual dichotomy as the only alternative to *Gesellschaft* – a type of social existence wherein individuals only care about the group in terms of what they can personally get out of it, and their adherence to laws and procedures has little to do with traditional values and much more to do with the extent to which they facilitate the pursuit of their own interests. What does resemble *Gesellschaft* in practice is the impersonal market society promoted by laissez-faire advocates. However, as Durkheim pointed out, *Gemeinschaft* and *Gesellschaft* are not the only options – people can develop strong bonds of solidarity without blindly following rigid customs (Durkheim, 1984).

Second, the *Gemeinschaft* model celebrates the cohesiveness of traditional compliance, and overlooks the ignorance, oppressiveness and inflexibility that that very compliance can bring. The prejudicial views and treatment of women and minority ethnic groups, the reluctance to experiment and innovate, and the inertia in the face of changing circumstances, generate countless faultlines for tradition-bound communities.

Third, the argument that any deviation from *Gemeinschaft* would lead to some *Gesellschaft*-like superficial and self-centred form of human association is, as we will see in this book, flatly contradicted by the evidence. Many communities – neighbourhoods, villages, towns and cities – have undergone development that takes them away from outmoded thinking and practices to attain a higher degree of common wellbeing; and most significantly, the improvements are not achieved at the expense of close, committed relationships, but on the basis of building such relationships through mutual respect and thoughtful co-operation.

If tomorrow's communities are to find a way to become more effective in attaining the wellbeing of their members, we need to learn and apply the lessons from a range of developmental approaches that have transformed lives for the better. Instead of trying to reconstruct inward-looking traditional communities, or expecting deregulation-obsessed market societies to engender inclusive unity, we should explore diverse methods and models, and identify the practices that are most likely to bring about the changes we seek.

What can communities do?

The alternative practices we will be examining in this book have emerged in the wake of growing scepticism about a model of societal governance that was broadly accepted by all democratic governments for around three decades following the Second World War. According to this model, people of diverse communities can trust their democratically elected government to secure high levels of employment, reconcile conflicting interests and protect them from ill-health and poverty; in return, those voted into public office will be held accountable for how well they carry out their social as well as economic responsibility for the country by means of media scrutiny and periodic elections (Birnbaum, 2001). Years of rising prosperity, decreasing income inequality, action against discrimination and improvements in health and life expectancy sustained general support across the political spectrum for the post-war model.[1] But during the

---

[1] This period has been described as 'The Golden Years'. See Chapter 9 of *The Age of Extremes* (Hobsbawn, 1994).

1970s, anti-progressive currents (labelled variously as the 'New Right' and 'neoliberalism') gained momentum in attacking it for being too 'social' (too much public spending), too 'liberal' (too much tolerance) and too 'unresponsive' (bogged down by too many checks and balances) (Harvey, 2005).[2] Notably, what were then prescribed as better options were none other than the old *Gemeinschaft* and *Gesellschaft* duo, except that unlike Tönnies' notion, the proposal was not to have one or the other, but to have both – a revival of traditional community attitudes and relations *and* an acceleration of deregulated and socially indifferent market activities. Its outlook can be summed up as: 'political correctness is bad; privatisation is good'.

The dominance of the New Right formula since the 1980s has played a key part in exacerbating economic inequality and instability, while dismantling the societal infrastructure needed to protect people from threats and hardships beyond their control. When turbocharged with a heavy injection of demagoguery in the late 2010s, it has – in the name of enabling people to 'take back control'/'become great again' – gone on to destabilise economies, polarise communities and endanger the environment at all levels. It could be tempting to think that we should revert to the model of the socially responsible government that prevailed up until the late 1970s, but that would be to ignore a critical weakness of that model: its disconnection from community life. In assuming that electoral victories once in a few years would give them a comprehensive mandate to do what they deem best for the country, political leaders overlook the need to engage communities in working out how to respond to their diverse concerns. This leads to three far-reaching problems.[3]

First, with the electoral focus on securing a majority (indeed, often it is simply a large-enough minority) of the votes across the country, the different socioeconomic conditions of varied communities do not all get the same attention. This in turn means that many communities in need end up being neglected (because they are ignored as unwinnable constituencies by one side or taken for granted as cast-iron safe seats

---

[2] These attacks were facilitated, ironically, by the largely unregulated global market system through: (a) supply racing ahead of demand in a world where the poorer countries could not afford to buy the output of the richer ones; and (b) the surge of oil prices that threatened all oil-import-reliant economies.

[3] The three problems related to the disconnection from community life all played a significant part in engendering public dissatisfaction with the status-quo politics of the post-war era, and drew many towards the New Right's sweeping rhetoric and radical policy proposals.

by the other), and the systemic deprivations afflicting them make a mockery of any suggestion that they can overcome their predicament if they would just stop looking for external support.

Second, we have the problem of fragmentation when a centralised state acts in a manner that causes intra- and inter-community distrust, because the state appears to have favoured some at the expense of others (which may or may not be the case, but lack of involvement can give rise to suspicion). Distrust, in the absence of healthy community relations, can fuel tension, and the state ends up not tackling a range of problems for fear of offending one group or another, or pushing ahead with plans that widen social divisions even more.

Third, even where a government, buoyed by technocratic confidence, delivers policies that fit with its own defined objectives, the outcomes can prove to be a disappointment to communities when the latter have been treated as passive recipients of top-down intervention. Without communities being given a chance to deliberate on the issues or having any meaningful say about the appropriate policy options, it is not surprising that intricate community perspectives are missed out at the planning stage, the implementation phase is then vexed by mistakes that local input would have helped to avoid, and the eventual outcomes fail to address the real concerns of the people affected.

If we are to avoid these three interrelated problems, communities must become active agents in shaping and pursuing their priorities in collaboration with their members, other communities and public institutions.[4] In this book, we will accordingly set out the ideas and practices that have had a notable impact on the community-based transformation of:

- socioeconomic relations at the local level;
- collaborative behaviour in and across communities; and
- policy outcomes that meet people's needs and concerns.

Experts who have studied these forms of transformation and/or helped to make them happen possess in-depth understanding of why they are needed, how they can be brought about and what has to be done to overcome the likely obstacles. For this book we have brought together a team with such expertise, to draw from their knowledge and experience

---

[4] Conversely, government bodies should become more inclined to co-operate with citizens and more adept at doing so. How this can be done is explained in *Whose Government Is It?* (Tam, 2019a).

of development in the UK, the US and other parts of the world, to set out how communities can achieve social, economic and environmental improvements by working collaboratively among themselves and in partnership with state bodies.[5] The community-based approaches to be considered will range from mutual support, community development and organising, and participatory decision making, to co-operative enterprise, the co-production of public services and civic activism. For our present purpose, however, we will leave out options that are premised on the cessation of dialogue and co-operation (for example, those involving direct confrontation, or retreats into self-sufficiency groups cut off from wider society). It is possible that such measures may become necessary in some circumstances, but we will keep our focus in this book on what we should pursue when there is still scope for collaborative working.

Corresponding to the three areas where communities most need to reconnect internally and externally, the chapters in this book are grouped into three categories: the transformation of socioeconomic relations in communities; the transformation of collaborative behaviour with communities; and the transformation of policy outcomes by communities.

The transformation of socioeconomic relations in communities

It is often assumed that when communities need resources to tackle problems, they have three choices: state-directed funding; revenue from standard business transactions; or charitable donations. However, there are other ways that can significantly boost communities' socioeconomic capacity, especially when one or more of these more conventional options is not forthcoming.

In Chapter 2, 'The case for community economic development', Ed Mayo and Pat Conaty examine how community-based practices can bring about a virtuous circle that connects social inclusion with economic progress. Lessons on what works and what does not are drawn from a range of case examples, from the work of the Highlands and Islands Development Board in Scotland; and the Asset Transfer Programme in England and Wales; to the Fisherman's Community

---

[5] The UK and the US have been where the dominance of the New Right has been most sharply felt, and examples of how communities can develop a different path under these circumstances are therefore of particular importance.

Interest Company in Sussex; and the impact of the Community Land Trust in Vermont. We learn more about how untapped resources in communities can be used to create value, why community economic development is still not yet a recognised component of public policy and what should be done to mainstream it.

In Chapter 3, 'Reciprocity and alternative mediums of exchange', Martin Simon points to how the development of decentralised and reciprocal arrangements can reduce the disparities and exclusion created by an overreliance on conventional economic transactions. He explains that, in conjunction with a wider public safety net, time banking and asset-based community development can enhance neighbourliness and co-operation in communities and utilise their existing strengths as the basis to build a stronger future. By enabling people to decide for themselves what it is that they care about enough to commit their time and energy reciprocally to help each other, a non-monetary resource can be readily translated into a practical source of community wellbeing.

In Chapter 4, 'Regeneration in partnership with communities', Gabriel Chanan examines the attempts that have been made to regenerate communities over the decades, and assesses how local people can be involved in improving their socioeconomic circumstances. Lessons to be considered include: approaches to bridge the gap between stated regeneration objectives and ground-level concerns; what needs to be done to advance equality, diversity and social inclusion; how to reflect residents' experiences holistically in formulating programmes' goals; and ways to keep communities informed and involved in reviewing the outcomes. The author proposes a comprehensive national plan to support the regeneration of deprived communities, taking on board the importance of local strategic partnerships.

In Chapter 5, 'Worker co-operatives and economic democracy', Pat Conaty and Philip Ross consider the challenge of generating and developing better employment opportunities. In response to the increasing poverty and damages to communities caused by the gig economy, they draw inspiration from the lessons offered by economic democracy in the past and the successes of current development work with worker co-operatives to set out a new path for workers to join forces to secure their economic future. By examining examples such as Smart in Europe and Green Taxis in the US, the authors explain how the application of WorkerTech – pro-worker platform technology – can enable individuals, who would otherwise be too powerless to defend their economic interests, to become part of a wider co-operative organisation that can offer them more cost-effective support and long-term protection.

The transformation of collaborative behaviour with communities

With many communities alienated from public institutions and divided themselves by social and economic factors, it is easy to be sceptical about the prospect of community co-operation at any level. However, the experience from the work done with a wide range of communities would suggest that people with diverse backgrounds can learn to become more confident and prepared in identifying and pursuing common objectives.

In Chapter 6, 'Four factors for better community collaboration', Steve Wyler examines how practices such as community organising, cross-sector partnerships and community anchor organisations can engender effective collaboration. At the same time, he explains why it is often so difficult for those who work in formal institutions (national, regional or local), and those who operate at the community level, to find common cause and to build effective alliances; and he suggests what can be done to bridge the gap. The author assesses a range of place-based collaborative experiments (for example, New Deal for Communities, Our Place, Big Local) for their impact and puts forward recommendations for how funders, investors, policy makers and community practitioners can lay the foundations for better collaboration.

In Chapter 7, 'The importance of community-based learning', Marjorie Mayo discusses how enabling communities to learn about the problems they face and options for dealing with them is vital to building long-term co-operation. Through such learning, diverse members of communities can develop shared understandings of the underlying issues, work towards shared agendas for solidarity and social justice, formulate strategies for collaborating across differences and divisions, tackle discriminatory attitudes and behaviours rather than blaming 'the other', and build democratic alliances and movements for social change. Drawing on research and case examples from around the world, the author highlights the approaches that have been effective in bringing communities together across their differences, to deal with their shared anxieties and overcome mutual distrusts.

In Chapter 8, 'The 45° Change model for remaking power relations', Colin Miller and Neal Lawson consider the issue of power and its impact on collaborative behaviour. In place of the dominant local state model of command and control, they put forward the '45° Change' model to explain how deliberative engagement can be fostered through state institutions and communities being able to interact as equal partners. The authors draw on case examples from the Co-operative

Council Learning Network, the Fearless Cities Network and areas such as Madrid and Frome to examine the extent to which local authorities and communities have managed to democratise power relations, and succeeded in collaborating with residents in making important decisions, tackling cross-cutting problems and devising transformative solutions.

In Chapter 9, 'Connecting at the edges for collective change', Alison Gilchrist explores how the use of a complexity-informed approach to the development and evaluation of community action can improve joint working. In addition to reviewing the adoption of this approach by public agencies and funders such as the Lankelly Chase Foundation in the UK and the FSG consulting firm in the US (with their emphasis on trust-based partnerships and evaluations that are open, flexible and oriented towards collective learning), the author looks at a project grant-aided by the National Lottery Community Fund, which uses a complexity-informed approach to strengthen the connections within and between communities, and promote neighbourhood evaluation that endeavours to identify optimal levels of interaction and inclusion that allow 'order' to emerge from 'chaos' through the co-production of sustainable outcomes.

The transformation of policy outcomes by communities

After looking at how community-based actions can increase socioeconomic capability and enhance collaborative working, we will then turn our attention to how communities can attain greater efficacy over public policies and become more informed and influential in shaping decisions and outcomes that critically affect their quality of life.

'Co-production' is often cited as something that can transform communities from being passive recipients of (flawed) services from remote public agencies, into active co-producers of policies and services that more closely reflect their needs. But it can be interpreted in different ways. In Chapter 10, 'Co-production and the role of preventive infrastructure', David Boyle contrasts co-production as conceptualised by Elinor Ostrom, with degraded versions of the concept applied in some public service reforms. Drawing on a range of research findings and case examples, he sets out how co-production should be carried out in practice, what can be done to overcome the main obstacles and how it can help to strengthen communities in terms of resilience, inclusiveness, equality and satisfaction with public service outcomes.

In Chapter 11, 'Humanising health and social care', John Restakis focuses on how community-based models are required to place the public interest and citizens' needs above the commodification of care for profit. Core features of community health and social care include: democratic structures and inclusiveness, which ensure more affordable, accessible and accountable forms of care; and engagement with the people it serves, which helps to protect services from re-privatisation by governments and exploitation by corporate interests. The author examines these with examples from Europe and Asia; and identifies key risks and opportunities to inform the future development of such alternative provisions.

In Chapter 12, 'Reshaping the food-aid landscape', Alice Willatt, Rosalind Beadle and Mary Brydon-Miller look at the problem of hunger and malnutrition and how it can be tackled when public funding and charitable donations are not sufficient by themselves. They draw attention to issues of difference and diversity in relation to poverty and wider social injustice; and make use of extensive research on a range of community food initiatives to explore how they can generate more ecologically and socially just food-provisioning practices. Lessons from participatory action research point to how communities can work together with shared resources; supplement this with their own food growing; and promote healthy eating, environmental responsibility and cultural diversity.

In Chapter 13, 'Sustainable communities for the future', Diane Warburton looks at how communities can become a driving force in protecting and enhancing their environment. Drawing on a range of case examples, she sets out five types of impact that can be achieved by community-based action that takes into account issues of disadvantage, race and class. These cover: the tackling of pollution with community projects and organised challenges to environmentally unfriendly proposals; enhanced communities' role in influencing the development of land and buildings; local engagement to improve green spaces; the development of neighbourhood environment with the help of community architecture; and climate change-related actions, from community energy projects to campaigns directed at wider climate policy.

Lessons for tomorrow's communities

As the chapters in this book will show, communities can become stronger in tackling the problems they face, and more inclusive in improving their quality of life. Given the challenges posed by one global crisis after another, it is imperative that communities learn and apply the relevant lessons as quickly as possible.

These lessons are not derived from any single theoretical model, let alone tied to a particular ideological position. They come from examining practices that exemplify the ideas of many different thinkers, such as community learning (Freire, 1972), co-production (Ostrom, 2015), participatory democracy (Gutmann and Thompson, 2004), neighbourhood involvement (Gibson, 1998), community economics (Schumacher, 1993), time banking (Cahn, 2000), associative democracy (Hirst, 1993), deliberative engagement (Fishkin, 2009) and a range of communitarian reforms (Tam, 2019b).[6] While they do not have an established designation in common, they share at least three important principles:[7]

- Communities should be built on and orientated towards reinforcing mutual responsibility and equal respect.
- Communities should develop a shared understanding of what warrants belief through co-operative enquiry that is grounded on reason and objectivity.
- Communities should facilitate citizen participation and rectify power imbalances to ensure that everyone can have an informed say about decisions that affect them.

Because there is hitherto no common platform for promoting these ideas and practices, or even a generic name to refer to them, their complementariness is often overlooked. Practitioners can become attracted to advancing one particular approach without recognising the valuable roles that other methods can play. Policy makers, meanwhile, tend to view them as disparate tools and not as mutually supportive elements of a holistic action plan.

With this book, we aim to show that there are many tried-and-tested ways that can be brought together to enable community-based transformation. Our contributors will share both their specialist knowledge of research findings and practical experience of what helps or hinders in seeking progress. From their reviews and recommendations, we will see that a range of approaches need to be

---

[6] This is not an exhaustive list. For a more extensive listing of writers who have made relevant contributions, consult the references cited in the individual chapters that follow.
[7] For a historical account of how many of these ideas and practices relate to each other and wider intellectual and policy development, see Tam (2019b).

deployed, and that to achieve the desired impact, we must be able to anticipate and respond to the obstacles ahead. By its very nature, any change strategy premised on respecting the needs of all members of diverse communities has to engage people inclusively. While there will be different techniques involved in engaging people with contrasting backgrounds in terms of, for example, ethnicity, gender, socioeconomic situation, culture and health, they all have to be guided by the same underlying concern with understanding the distinct needs as well as common interests of members of overlapping communities.

Anyone interested in what options are available and how to take the most promising ones forward to empower communities to become fairer and stronger tomorrow, will find in the chapters that follow, explanations of why certain approaches are worth implementing, what pitfalls and limitations need to be dealt with, and how improvements can be brought in despite the relentless challenges we have to face. In the concluding chapter (Chapter 14), the key lessons will be summarised, and a nine-point policy agenda will be set out to help us meet these challenges. It is now vital for the fostering of community-based transformation to be recognised as a top priority for civic activists and policy makers alike.

References

Birnbaum, N. (2001) *After Progress: American Social Reform & European Socialism in the Twentieth Century*, Oxford: Oxford University Press.

Cahn, E. S. (2000) *No More Throw-away People: The Co-production Imperative*, London: Essential Books.

Durkheim, E. (1984) *The Division of Labour in Society*, Basingstoke: Macmillan.

Elliott, L. (2019) 'World's 26 richest people own as much as poorest 50%, says Oxfam', *The Guardian*, 21 January.

Fishkin, J. S. (2009) *When the People Speak: Deliberative Democracy and Public Consultation*, Oxford: Oxford University Press.

Freire, P. (1972) *Pedagogy of the Oppressed*, Harmondsworth: Penguin.

Gibson, T. (1998) *The Doer's Guide to Planning for Real*, Telford: Neighbourhood Initiatives Foundation.

Gutmann, A. and Thompson, D. (2004) *Why Deliberative Democracy*, Princeton: Princeton University Press.

Harvey, D. (2005) *A Brief History of Neoliberalism*, Oxford: Oxford University Press.

Hirst, P. (1993) *Associative Democracy: New Forms of Economic and Social Governance*, Cambridge: Polity.

Hobsbawn, E. (1994) *The Age of Extremes: The Short Twentieth Century*, London: Penguin Books.

Ostrom, E. (2015) *Governing the Commons: The Evolution of Institutions for Collective Action*, Cambridge: Cambridge University Press.

Schumacher, E. F. (1993) *Small is Beautiful: A Study of Economics as if People Mattered*, London: Vintage Books.

Tam, H. (2019a) *Whose Government Is It? The Renewal of State-citizen Cooperation*, Bristol: Bristol University Press.

Tam, H. (2019b) *The Evolution of Communitarian Ideas*, Basingstoke: Palgrave Macmillan.

Tönnies, F. (2003) *Community and Society*, Mineola: Dover Publications.

PART A

Transforming socioeconomic relations in communities

2

The case for community economic development

Ed Mayo and Pat Conaty

Every generation of people looks for ways in which they can prosper in the settlements and localities in which they live out their lives; and arguably every generation ends up rediscovering the tools of community economic development. This chapter looks at the field of community economic development, to understand how that process of rediscovery could be eased and conversely why it might repeatedly be obscured.

There is no better introduction to community development than the story of Tony Gibson, who made his name on the Meadow Well Estate in Tyneside in the United Kingdom (UK), which was constructed in the 1930s. Starting with a talent survey of random houses in 1991, residents came together to respond, with the idea of 'a new heart for Meadow Well' in the form of a development centre built on a discredited youth centre. The response, though, was inertia. Despite the efforts of one sympathetic local employee from the council, a senior officer was heard to say: 'those fuckers couldn't plan a pram shed'. A decision was taken, instead, simply to close the youth centre (Gibson et al, 1997).

As this dragged on over five hot summer months, the residents started to drop out and then a group of local young people burned the youth centre down. What followed was two days and nights of riots, with fires, a burnt-out corner shop and pot shots at a police helicopter cruising above. The riots forced everyone to think again. The working party held estate-wide elections to form a group that could negotiate with outsiders. They used Tony Gibson's Planning for Real approach – which creates a mock-up of the neighbourhood, from litter on the ground to buildings up high – on a table that people could then walk around, explore and together discuss options for improvement. This led to the development of a new community building, launched with a fun day. The first of many community-led improvements, it was the first building scheme in the borough that had taken shape from day one to completion without a single case of vandalism or theft.

Founded in 1994, Meadow Well Connected operates a community café, a free-to-use technology suite that supports local people to acquire the skills to get the jobs they need, as well as a community garden, joinery workshop and after-school club. In 2020, the charity was given a Garfield Weston Small Charity Award, with strategic support from Pilotlight, the business skills charity, to build the organisation and its services for the community going forward.

On the Meadow Well Estate, some of the key developments included the formation of a credit union and a community store. The community was also able to influence regeneration works on the quays in North Shields, bringing access to employment. Neighbourhood inspector, Neil Armsworth, of the Northumbria Police, has said that 'the changes to the Meadow Well estate as well as the role and work of the police has [sic] been simply transformational over the past 25 years' (Sharma, 2016). This is reflected in the ability of the community to take action in crisis. During the national COVID-19 lockdown in 2020, working through the Cedarwood Trust, residents played a key role in delivering information and food to neighbours across the estate.

What characterises successful community economic development is a virtuous circle, in which there are positive outcomes both in terms of community development and in terms of sustainable economic progress, broadly understood (Morris et al, 2013). Of course, what communities want is not static. It expands with confidence. As with the individuals who make them up, communities of place can be diagnosed as being in a state of self-determination or one of 'learned helplessness'. The one factor that seems to make a significant difference between these two is the ability of people to work together over time – community co-operation (or collective self-efficacy in academic terms). As this rises or falls, the appetite for local control over local matters rises or falls. The quality of community co-operation shapes the collective sense of what is possible and it also makes what is possible more achievable.

In the US, community economic development grew out of the civil rights movement and the War on Poverty programmes of President Johnson and Robert F. Kennedy. In his 1967 book, *Where Do We Go From Here: Chaos or Community?*, Martin Luther King championed economic empowerment for African Americans, citing the example of Operation Breadbasket, a church-led programme to open up jobs through boycotts of companies with poor employment records and to promote savings with Black-led credit unions and market access for Black-led enterprise (Luther King, 1967). Luther King's economic agenda was a radical one, including arguments at a national level for a citizen's income and for land value taxation.

In South West Georgia, work led by Slater King (Luther King's cousin) and Charles and Shirley Sherrod turned from restoring burnt-out churches to creating rural land trusts for African American farmers. The work was inspired by the success of the Bhoodan and Gramdan movements in India. Bob Swann – co-founder with Ralph Borsodi of the Institute for Community Economics – had close contact with the Gramdan movement and worked closely with the organisers to set up the pathfinding US 'Community Land Trust' (CLT), New Communities Inc in 1970, on 5,735 acres of farmland (Davis, 2010).

As ever, the formation or promotion of institutions – community enterprises – to advance local services was core to the field of community economic development. One key vehicle for the early programmes in the US and championed by Kennedy was the community development corporation (Perry, 1987). These corporations evolved to become multi-purpose anchor organisations that were locally based, delivering affordable housing and enterprise workspace. Alongside these, over time, emerged a range of specialist community development finance initiatives, benefiting from community reinvestment legislation first passed in the 1970s after campaigns led by Gale Cincotta and others against 'redlining' or discrimination on grounds of race or place, which placed an affirmative obligation on banks to serve the entire community in which they were licensed (Mayo et al, 1998).

The connections between community protest and community building were not accidental – many of the key people and networks saw themselves as organising a social movement, at different levels and with different interventions oriented to a common goal of social justice. Ted Wysocki, for example, was a graduate student who started working as an intern in 1974 with Gale Cincotta (the 'mother' of the Community Reinvestment Act) at National People's Action (Rosenthal, 2018) and continued working on staff until 1984. Drawing on this and learning from Saul Alinsky's 'community organising' activist manual, *Rules for Radicals* (Alinsky, 1971), he went on to direct the Chicago Association of Neighbourhood Development Organizations (generating the evocative acronym CANDO) in 1984, which played a catalytic role in uniting community economic development organisations and providing policy advocacy and technical assistance.

The agenda, as Wysocki described it, was one of opposition and proposition and the organising behind it drew on existing community networks and civil rights activists in Chicago such as John McKnight, a co-founder with Cincotta of National People's Action and a pioneer of asset-based community economic development.

On 6 March 1984, the most impressive agreement in the short five-year history of the federal Community Reinvestment Act [CRA] was announced when First National Bank of Chicago committed to $100 million over five years, for loans at below market rates to revitalise and redevelop Chicago neighbourhoods (Wysocki, 1984). This extensive Neighborhood Lending Program with new loan products was designed over two months through productive negotiations, community tours and discussions between bankers and community leaders associated with Gale Cincotta, the Chicago Rehab Network and CANDO (Marchiel, 2020). Barry Sullivan, bank chairman, stated at the joint press conference, "The community groups have been instrumental in helping to analyze the needs of our city and developing a program that will address the credit needs of our Chicago neighborhoods." (Wysocki, 1984, p.1).

Some of the initiatives that emerged in the city can now be seen as pioneering examples of community economic development, replicated widely in other US cities, such as the National People's Action-inspired Neighborhood Housing Services and the city-wide Neighborhood Lending Service community development finance fund – which by 2011 had advanced more than $419 million to 169,000 low-income homeowners and attracted an additional $1.1 billion of finance to underinvested neighbourhoods (Mayo et al, 1998; Lewis and Conaty, 2012).

What we can see is that there is a system in play that operates at different levels, with different actors and different roles (see Figure 2.1). Alongside the dominant forces in the economy and society of the state and private sector, citizen action and community enterprise interact in ways that have the potential to change power relations in favour of community economic development to meet local needs.

In the US, the bootstrap efforts over 20 years to establish CLTs from 1968 got more traction in 1979 with the setting up of the Institute for Community Economics' revolving loan fund (the first community development loan fund) by the Dorothy Day-inspired Catholic worker activist, Chuck Matthei, whose innovation was to show how to practically overcome the investment exclusion of land trusts by banks (Rosenthal, 2018). As Matthei (Rosenthal, 2018) recalled:

Figure 2.1: The context for community economic development

The context for community economic development

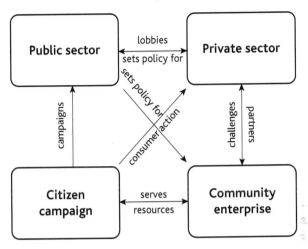

I didn't set out to be a banker. I didn't have a bank account or a steady income of my own … We began to go to individuals, religious institutions and others whom we knew and began to say: if you have savings beyond your immediate personal needs, lend it to us and we'll use it to finance projects like these.

This led to funds to prove that the CLT solution could work, but a bigger breakthrough came from an imaginative politician. In 1984, Bernie Sanders, the newly elected mayor of Burlington, Vermont, provided municipal support to community efforts to provide long-term affordable housing through CLTs.

On its land, the Burlington CLT (now the Champlain Housing Trust) supports 2,000 homes (some for rent and others for part sale), five housing co-operatives, a day centre for older people, a children's nursery, managed workspace and the community development credit union for the region. The CLT is a community-owned mutual with more than 2,500 members, including resident leaseholders (tenants and shared homeowners) and community investors.

Periodic long-term evaluations of the Burlington CLT have shown that its shared ownership housing has in fact become more affordable over time. In 1984, the first homes were affordable to households earning 62 per cent of area median income and by 2009 they were affordable to households earning 53.4 per cent (Lewis and Conaty, 2012).

It is perhaps natural that land emerges as a site of protest and as a prompt for community enterprise in this story so far. In the UK, we could trace similar roots in 1903, when First Garden City Limited gained its land by an Act of Parliament and began developing Letchworth Garden City. Today, the Letchworth Garden City Heritable Trust, a community benefit society, owns £56 million worth of offices, shops and business units, the rent from which is used for the foundation's community development and charitable purposes for the benefit of the community (Lewis and Conaty, 2012).

Those roots could also be found along the banks of the River Thames in the 1980s. After a long campaign by local residents against an office development that would replace their neighbourhood, Coin Street Community Builders were given control of a large development site of 13 acres on the South Bank by the municipal authority, the Greater London Council, as one of its last acts in 1984. The sale to the community was for a below-market price of £1 million on the basis that they would develop the land asset in the most effective ways and with community benefit as a clear objective. And judged by that, they have succeeded handsomely: the development trust site now includes artist studios in and around the Oxo Tower, street markets, restaurants and affordable, co-operatively managed housing. It has sustained an active community, valued the area's heritage, shaped a physical infrastructure that remains convivial and human scale, and become a major contributor to the revival of both the area and its residents. Just as Letchworth had done, Coin Street Community Builders and Champlain Housing Trust have retained the freehold and will therefore be able to continue to shape the development of the area into the future and generate funds for community benefit.

The stories of community economic development travel far from the communities they are born in. Just as post–independence India influenced the efforts of those following Martin Luther King in the US, so experience in the US has influenced efforts in the UK, such as in Northern Ireland with work after Bloody Sunday by Paddy Doherty and the Derry Inner City Trust to rebuild the 'Bogside'. This work built on earlier success in 1960 with the co-founding with John Hume and others of Derry Credit Union (the first credit union in the UK and one of the most successful with more than 30,000 members). In the context of division, the inspiration came in part from the US civil rights movement and its shift from challenging segregation to promoting economic justice such as through practical community economic development, focused on meeting needs. The US slogan of 'rebuilding neighbourhoods, one home and one business at a time' captured this ethos of grassroots repair and renewal of streets and livelihoods.

But it is in Scotland that we can see that community economic development is operating at scale. The Highlands and Islands Development Board under the distinguished economist, Sir Kenneth Alexander, after 1976 was the first UK state body to recognise the relevance of the community-led approach, focusing on the needs of the Hebrides (*Na h-Eileanan a-Staigh* and *Na h-Eileanan an Iar*). Conventional thinking had been that the islands were on the periphery of the periphery, distanced both from mainland Scotland and from wider Europe, so that what was needed was to connect up the island economies with a wider national economic agenda – in short, to reduce the pace of falling behind. Alexander saw it differently. He decentralised development support and planning and gave backing to community initiatives, including enterprises for service provision and cultural events and programmes designed to give confidence and identity to a region long seen as on the fringe.

Over time, the population outflow from the islands was stemmed and new initiatives gave life to the local economy, from the University of the Highlands & Islands through to community enterprises such as Skye and Lochalsh Enterprise Company. Community-owned land has become commonplace, with pioneers such as the islanders of Eigg following the example of the Assynt crofters of north-west Sutherland who, in 1993, had jointly purchased the North Lochinver Estate.

The Isle of Eigg was purchased by the community from a private landowner in 1997. Before this, the islanders had little say in how the island was run, but after the purchase, efforts were made to attract newcomers, to improve the housing stock, to encourage enterprise and to invest in renewable energy, for security of supply, lower costs and energy efficiency (Mackenzie, 2010). Compared with a decrease in the Scottish islands' population over the ten years to 2001, the number of Eigg islanders grew by 4 per cent between 2001 and 2011. Since then (the time of the ten-year Scottish Census), evidence points to further population growth and the reason, according to one workshop set up to explore this in 2019, is a policy framework that is 'founded on community ownership of the development process' (Islands Revival, 2019).

Today, half the land mass across the Western Isles is now under the control of residents – and some three quarters of people live on community-owned tracts, where they have a say in the running of the estate (*Hebrides News*, 2014). More widely across Scotland, there has been a tenfold increase in community groups owning assets over the past decade. This has been helped by a progressive policy environment in the form of Community Right to Buy legislation and financial support through the Scottish Land Fund. Even so, of the 209,810 hectares of land in total across Scotland that is now in community ownership, the largest proportion of this land (70 per cent) is located in the Western Isles (Scottish Government, 2019). More widely, Scotland's Highlands and Islands, which are home to less than 10 per cent of the country's population, account for 22 per cent of its social enterprises. An example of this is transport, including the Skye ferry in Glenelg, which provides residents with a transport link to the mainland but is also a huge tourist draw that brings much-needed visitors and income, as well as community bus services in places such as Badenoch, Tongue and Lochinver.

The language of community action is fluid, unstable and often contested and different terms come in and out of favour. And yet in the case of the Western Isles, there clearly is sufficient overlap and consensus over time around three defining pillars of community economic development, that:

- a process of purposeful economic development operates over time within a specific geographic area and that focuses on making the economy in that area work well for that community;
- the voice of people living, working and running businesses in that area plays a key role in shaping decisions around that process; and
- they become over time a key actor, with their participation, individually and collectively, shaping what emerges in terms of practical action.

At its best, community economic development is a system in which institutions have both the capabilities but also the accountabilities that allow for effective, multifunctional activity, with partnerships that reinforce rather than marginalise the power of local people. It is not an individual project or an isolated programme for community improvement. In cities with a long track record of community economic development, such as Chicago, what you find is a complex array of institutions and partnerships that are able to blend and match the social and financial resources to sustain action over time.

The UK research base for community economic development solutions was developed in particular with leadership by the Joseph Rowntree Foundation, championing work by Professor Stephen Thake and colleagues (Thake, 1995, 2001; Aiken et al, 2008). On community finance intermediaries for community development, we would add our own work for the Joseph Rowntree Foundation, published in 1998 as *Small is Bankable* (Mayo et al, 1998).

There are caveats, of course, that emerge from this research. In terms of tackling disadvantage, community economic development has a role to play but it is a role with limits. People on low incomes tend to live in neighbourhoods with others of the same class or circumstances as themselves, leading to areas of concentrated deprivation (Pike et al, 2016). The primary causes of that deprivation are unlikely to be local. They will tend to originate in the wider regional, national and global economy, and it is at that level that they need to be addressed.

Even so, there has been a re-emergence of the concepts of 'place' and 'community' in the policy agenda on disadvantage. This has included a set of policy initiatives over time to build the asset base of intermediaries such as the Phoenix Fund for community finance, the Scottish Community Land Fund and the Asset Transfer programme in England and Wales, which has looked to bring into community ownership underused assets and facilities previously in local public ownership. In recent years, there has been a re-emergence of place-based initiatives. One in 2015 was a two-year programme in England on community economic development, launched by the government, the first official national programme for a generation, which aimed to support 50 neighbourhoods to draw together their own community economic development plans. The partners in this work were Co-operatives UK, Locality, the New Economics Foundation, the Centre for Local Economic Strategies and Responsible Finance.

The results of the programme were published in 2017, with the conclusion that successful plans needed to:

- encourage interventions in the local economy in a way that helps it generate a better balance of social, economic and environmental outcomes – and to do so, it needs to target a strong set of 'triple-bottom-line' outcomes at the outset; and
- rebalance power at the local level and achieve greater community control – and to do so, this involves having an understanding of local power structures and how those might act as a barrier or enabler to achieving their objectives (Co-operatives UK, 2017).

Of these two, the second proved more challenging and the groups involved saw themselves as less able to tackle the dynamics of local power structures. What did make a difference was where there was a strong participatory process, and where the anchor organisation had a clear framework of accountability to the community that gave it added legitimacy in speaking for their needs. The model of 'community shares', for example, was used by some to raise the vital, patient equity capital they needed to start or grow a community business. But they also used it, with low entry barriers for new members, to enfranchise the local community, given the democratic, co-operative framework of 'one member, one vote' they were using. In other cases, the work was rooted in a wider programme of community development, notably work by the charity, Local Trust, which helped to resource the level of engagement needed from a wide range of stakeholders and to give their shared voice more weight in local decisions.

In the case of the Safe Regeneration programme in Liverpool, UK, the community economic development partnership entered the programme with ambitions to push beyond the project work they were already delivering on their business incubation hub, in order to make a much wider impact. What emerged as plans were transformative, including taking on ownership of a derelict pub to create a homeless transition hostel upstairs and a gastro pub downstairs, coupled with partnering a national body to regenerate the canal towpath that borders it, to generate more footfall and make more of it for the local economy.

More widely, many plans returned to the challenge of business development, using a very wide portfolio of initiatives (see Table 2.1), often with links to supportive institutions such as universities, but more rarely with support from mainstream local enterprise partnerships. These included:

- promoting access to capital, including social investment and community shares;
- skills development for entrepreneurs;
- support with market studies;
- demand-side schemes such as 'buy local' or complementary currencies;
- business parks or incubators;
- facilitating network development;
- a focus on women's entrepreneurship;
- micro-enterprise;
- community business development; and
- community or worker co-operatives.

Table 2.1: Community economic development toolkit – illustrating forms of action

Social participation	Anchor organisations, culture, participatory decision making, equalities and human rights, co-production and organisational development for small charities and social enterprises
Resource development	Land in common ownership, asset transfer, community housing, permaculture, renewable energy, energy conservation and planning
Value chain development	Buying local loyalty schemes, enterprise networking, local food systems, complementary currencies and plugging the leaks
Infrastructure development	Micro-grids, micro-renewables, community broadband, public social partnerships and community transport
Labour market interventions	Local apprenticeships, local hiring, equalities action, intermediate labour markets and skills development
Access to capital	Community development finance initiatives, social investment, community shares, mutual guarantees and credit unions
Innovation	University/community partnerships, 'intrapreneuring' and social innovation prizes
Enterprise development	Accelerators, business advice, leadership development, skills and knowledge transfer and co-operative and social enterprise development
Productivity	Employee and worker ownership, cluster development and export advice

Many of these are seen to have strong local multipliers (Conaty, 2011, 2015). For example, Responsible Finance estimates that every £1 invested through a community finance initiative – essentially here a revolving loan fund – yields a net contribution of £8 to the local economy (New Economics Foundation, 2017).

In Eastbourne, a Sussex town of 101,000 residents, the work on community economic development was led by people who had been invisible in the plans of the town authorities – fishermen:

'Fishermen have never occupied a particularly powerful position when it comes to local decision-making ... we need community economic development as previous development strategies have not delivered the changes needed for the local fishing fleet and the community it supports. Fishermen need to be better able to plan for the

future and contribute to the area they live and work in'
explained Eastbourne Fisherman's Community Interest
Company. (Co-operatives UK, 2017)

Eastbourne has a higher rate of unemployment than other Sussex towns
or the national average, a higher average age of population and a higher
proportion of people with long-term health problems or disabilities.
The local fishing community has a long history, providing employment
today for 72 fishermen (which, using industry multipliers, equates to
around 200 direct and indirect local jobs linked to the fishery). Around
90 per cent of the fishing vessels are 'small-scale' fishing boats (under
10 metres in length).

In 2013, local fishermen formed the Fisherman's Community
Interest Company, to be able to purchase and work from the land by
the waterfront in Sovereign Harbour, with a community economic
development plan to develop the land as a Fishermen's Quay, with
traditional net huts, wet fish sales, offices, workshops and a heritage/
visitor centre. Working with the New Economics Foundation, the
analysis behind this initially focused on opportunities for 'plugging
the leaks' – a popular and educational community economic
development strategy for import substitution that the Foundation
had borrowed from the Rocky Mountain Institute in the US in
the 1990s.

The five measures of success that they evolved through the planning
process combined local value creation through shorter supply chains,
reducing the reliance on third parties for processing and distribution,
together with new sources of revenue and greater competitiveness
through higher productivity. These were:

- residents eating local, seasonal and sustainable fish;
- more money spent on seafood circulating locally;
- fishermen/the fishery being more visible in the life of the town;
- residents/local business being more engaged in the fishery; and
- there being stronger links to local heritage/local fishing history.

The example of Eastbourne is a reminder that community economic
development has to combine practical action, meeting contemporary
needs, with visionary action that can inspire people to come together
to create a more positive and sustainable future. The needs vary from
area to area. In cities at times of unemployment, work has been at

the core of community economic development, such as in Glasgow through intermediate labour markets – meeting social need and nurturing skilled workers – and in Bristol, where Ambition Lawrence Weston operates effective skills development and recruitment pathways that link good employers to community-led partnerships in deprived neighbourhoods (Boyle, 2014).

And what happens when the vision starts to be realised? The classic dilemma of community economic development is where success in terms of economic development leads to dispersal and displacement in terms of community development – in class terms, gentrification. So, for example, local jobs need local people but rising house prices can have the effect of driving exactly those people out. This outcome is not, however, an inevitable one, and there are examples of community economic development that safeguards access and inclusion for local people.

In the UK, the first CLT, the Stonesfield Trust, was set up in rural Oxfordshire in the mid-1980s – in an area where house prices were becoming unaffordable but no one was building new, affordably priced homes (Conaty and Large, 2013). Cornwall has become the most effective region for CLTs, with the input among others of Bob Paterson. In one case, St Minver, average house prices in the village were higher than in London. A CLT was kicked off at the prompting of a parish councillor after a local farmer had offered land at a low price to those in local need willing to join a community of self-builders with a local contractor. The North Cornwall District Council provided a start-up grant and an interest-free loan to underpin the development of new housing on community-owned land, taken forward through work in partnership with the Cornwall Rural Housing Association and with an expert county-wide network, Cornwall Community Land Trust in support. With these partners in place and with the model gaining recognition, Cornwall has benefited from a range of CLTs, developed in a proactive way with action to identify appropriate sites and link local community support with affordable finance and technical expertise.

Since 2007, Cornwall CLT has supported the development with local communities of 12 local CLTs and more than 250 affordable homes (Cornwall CLT, 2019). A structured six-step method, the 'Commonwealth Wheel' (see Figure 2.2), has emerged for building the social and financial capacity to grow CLTs in the UK.

Figure 2.2: The Commonwealth Wheel

The Commonwealth Wheel

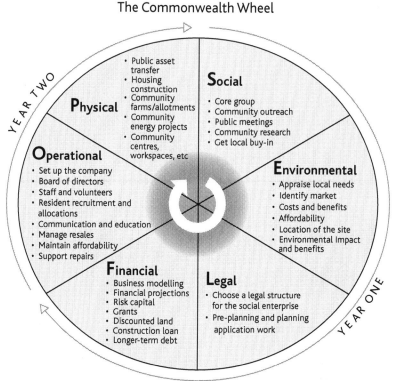

Conclusion

There can now be some hope for renewal. The case of the Western Isles in Scotland represents a domestic exemplar, no less inspiring than the regions so often recycled in writings on the social economy, of Mondragon in the Basque Country or the co-operatives of Emilia Romagna. There is a range of place-based programmes gathering pace, such as Empowering Places in England and the rural spread of initiatives such as CLTs. The lesson of ensuring patience in the framework is one that appears to be validated in the formative work of the charity, Local Trust.

There is a growing network of effective community anchor organisations across neighbourhoods of both wealth and disadvantage. Even at a time of low interest rates, it is extraordinary that 140,000 people have invested around £140 million in community-based co-operatives and societies across the UK over the past decade, from co-operative pubs to community energy – a renewal of the co-operative form in the UK that is genuinely a world-leading practice. There has been a crackdown on the worst forms of US-style predatory lending and, despite constant policy change, renewable energy at the community level is on the rise in the UK, in particular in Scotland, as across the European Union more widely. Alongside these, there is a renewed confidence to take municipal action on sustainable economic development, with progress on 'community wealth building', with notable leadership in Preston from Councillor Matthew Brown, now spreading more widely across the UK (O'Neill and Guinan, 2019). Although in the UK this approach tends to have strong municipal rather than community leadership, it has been influenced by community economic development principles such as plugging the leaks and it recognises participation and community ownership (for example through worker co-ops) as an aspiration, not least as a key part of the 'Cleveland model' from the US that inspired the work.

But despite such signs of progress, no community economic development operates in isolation; it sits within a wider context. And that wider, macro context, unfortunately, is an uncertain one. While the case is increasingly heard for more localised economic activity, more in balance with environmental limits, with wider ownership and more human in terms of its impact on health and wellbeing, the thrust of economic development since 2007 has been the opposite, encouraging a more financialised economy, with greater inequalities and more restricted economic ownership.

While devolution has reshaped the pattern of governance and administration across the UK, with some positive examples of regional/national economic action, such as food and drink in Scotland and renewable energy in Scotland and Wales, it has not shifted decision making in ways that either systematically empower local communities or reverse the decline of local authorities. The idea of 'double devolution' is sometimes cited, but less often the principle of subsidiarity, which is a different framing, one that can be understood as giving legitimacy to the lowest level, the level of communities, with power flowing up where there is consent for that to happen, rather than starting from the nation state and looking to pass power down (Hirst, 1994).

Yet economic policy priorities will turn again, following the 2020/21 COVID-19 pandemic, and there is no question that the imperative of encouraging greater economic resilience, in the context of any shock, whether health related or in the shudders of adjusting to a changing climate, will put a premium on the forms of inclusive economy, bootstrap economic development and local co-operation that characterise the best community economic development (Schumacher,

1970). Climate adaptation represents an imperative, the response to which must include community solutions as a necessary part.

Anyone who works on neighbourhood development knows that the local economy shapes and defines what you can achieve. If there are no jobs, you are playing catch-up. If the bank closes, businesses close as night follows day. If you have no business, you will have no life on the streets, but the siren hoardings of payday lenders. There are a great many small businesses that live and die in deprived neighbourhoods and overshadowed towns, which are not well served by local enterprise partnership models and their equivalents across the UK. These businesses are critical parts of their communities and would be better served through community economic development type approaches. Some of the most inspiring examples of neighbourhood renewal are those that have turned the local economy from vicious spiral to virtuous circle.

At the heart of community economic development is the concept of 'shared agency' – that people can act together and in taking action find that they are expanding the constituency of collective self-belief (Nutshell, 1997; Restakis, 2011). As we have seen throughout this chapter, ideas have a motivating power and, at times, they can run ahead, prompting innovation, motivating people to take action at a community level to challenge and change their circumstances in line with trajectories that the wider world needs to shift towards. Whether we can change the world or not, we can have some confidence that, with effort and belief, we can change our community.

In the spirit of Tony Gibson, the best place to start is always here and the best time is always now and the best people to do it is always you and me and kindred spirits. The case for community economic development is strong. We just need the confidence to challenge those who stand in the way. For as Tony Gibson concluded in the report, *Taking Power*:

> For every starting point, there are many premature end points, marked by the failure of those with power outside to let go. The change in mindset also has to work for the people who are, in Tolstoy's words, sitting on the backs of the poor, decrying their condition, and willing to do anything but get off their back. This includes letting people make mistakes and giving the time needed for a participative local democracy to develop great deeds by small steps. (Gibson et al, 1997)

References

Aiken, M., Cairns, B. and Thake, S. (2008) *Community Ownership and Assets*, York: Joseph Rowntree Foundation.

Alinsky, S. (1971) *Rules for Radicals*, New York: Random House.

Boyle, D. (2014) *Ultra-Micro Economics*, Manchester: Co-operatives UK and partners.

Conaty, P. (2011) *Co-operative Green Economy: New Solutions for Energy and Sustainable Social Justice*, Manchester: Co-operatives UK.

Conaty, P. (2015) *A Collaborative Economy for the Common Good*, Cardiff: Wales Co-operative Centre.

Conaty, P. and Large, M. (2013) *Commons Sense: Co-operative Place Making and Capturing Land Value for 21st Century Garden Cities*, Manchester: Hawthorn Press.

Co-operatives UK (2017) *Community Economic Development: Lessons from Two Years' Action Research*, Manchester: Co-operatives UK.

Cornwall CLT (2019) *Annual Report for 2019*, Truro: Cornwall CLT.

Davis, J. E. (2010) *The Community Land Trust Reader*, Cambridge: Lincoln Institute.

Gibson, T., Mayo, E. and Thake, S. (1997) *Taking Power*, London: New Economics Foundation.

Hebrides News (2014) 'Stronger voice for community estates', *Hebrides News*, 11 September, http://www.hebrides-news.com/stronger-voice-for-western-isles-community-estates-12914.html.

Hirst, P. (1994) *Associative Democracy: New Forms of Economic and Social Governance*, Cambridge: Polity Press.

Islands Revival (2019) 'Islands Revival Declaration', https://islandsrevival.org/the-islands-revival-declaration.

Lewis, M. and Conaty, P. (2012) *The Resilience Imperative: Co-operative Transitions to a Steady-state Economy*, Gabriola Island: New Society Publishers.

Luther King, M. (1967) *Where Do We Go From Here: Chaos or Community?*, Boston: Beacon Press.

Marchiel, R. (2020) *After Redlining: The urban reinvestment movement in the era of financial deregulation*, Chicago: University of Chicago Press.

Mackenzie, F. (2010) 'A common claim: community land ownership in the Outer Hebrides, Scotland', *International Journal of the Commons*, 4(1): 319–44, DOI: http://doi.org/10.18352/ijc.151.

Mayo, E., Conaty, P., Doling, J., Mullineux, A. and Fisher, T. (1998) *Small is Bankable*, York: Joseph Rowntree Foundation.

Morris, J., Cobbing, P. and Leach, K. with Conaty, P. (2013) *Mainstreaming Community Economic Development*, Birmingham: Localise West Midlands & Barrow Cadbury.

New Economics Foundation (2017) *Community Economic Development: A Literature Review of Constraints, Enablers and Outcomes*, London: New Economics Foundation.

O'Neill, M. and Guinan, J. (2019) *The Case for Community Wealth Building*, Cambridge: Polity Press.

Perry, S. E. (1987) *Communities on the Way: Rebuilding Local Economies in the United States and Canada*, New York: SUNY Press.

Pike, A., MacKinnon, D., Coombes, M., Champion, T., Bradley, D., Cumbers, A., Robson, L. and Wymer, C. (2016) *Uneven Growth: Tackling City Decline*, York: Joseph Rowntree Foundation.

Restakis, J. (2011) *The Co-operative City: Social and Economic Tools for Sustainability*, Vancouver: Co-operative Association.

Rosenthal, C. (2018) *Democratizing Finance: Origins of the Community Development Finance Institutions Movement*, Victoria: FriesenPress.

Schumacher, E. F. (1970) 'The economics of permanence', *Resurgence*, 3(1).

Scottish Government (2019) *Community Ownership in Scotland: 2018*, Edinburgh: Scottish Government, https://www.gov.scot/publications/community-ownership-scotland-2018.

Sharma, S. (2016) 'Meadow Well riots twenty five years on', *Chronicle*, 8 September, https://www.chroniclelive.co.uk/news/north-east-news/meadow-well-riots-25-years-11848759.

Thake, S. (1995) *The Effect of Community Regeneration Organisations on Neighbourhood Regeneration*, York: Joseph Rowntree Foundation.

Thake, S. (2001) *Building Communities, Changing Lives: The Contribution of Large, Independent Neighbourhood Regeneration Organisations*, York: Joseph Rowntree Foundation.

Wysocki, T. (1984) '$100 million CRA victory', Disclosure Number 83, National Training and Information Center.

3

Reciprocity and alternative mediums of exchange

Martin Simon

As a social innovator, I have for many years explored new ways to connect people and bring forth the kindness, consensus and confidence necessary for them to generate the value of collective acts of caring and take control of transforming their neighbourhoods in an inclusive and sustainable manner. In this chapter, I will review a variety of strengths-based approaches to community development and illustrate how they have created the space for in-person convivial connections and enduring relationships to grow, even in the most difficult of circumstances.

We should begin by questioning the failure of conventional economics to recognise that commerce cannot function without a sub-strata of unpaid care provided by families, neighbourhoods and communities. This sub-strata has been described as the 'core economy' and it runs on self-organised, decentralised, reciprocal mediums of exchange. The chapter will show how a mix of money and reciprocity might raise the value of collective action and go on to look at ways in which the relationship between the state and the community could change to strengthen the core economy and better protect tomorrow's communities. It will explore some of the personal attributes and types of approaches required for bringing in the required changes. Two case studies then demonstrate the importance of whole-system collaborations and the power of connectivity and collective action.

A more humane way to measure growth and prosperity

Conventional economics

Currently, economic planning is driven by the goal of increasing Gross Domestic Product (GDP), based on a narrow measure of monetary gain. The monopolisation of money as a medium of exchange and the disparities and exclusion this creates throughout society make it imperative that we revise our understanding of growth and prosperity.

> Monocrops do not grow naturally, so in order for them to flourish we have to make changes to the entire ecosystem. In the same way a monocrop extracts critical nutrients from the soil, a fixation on the pursuit of money drains personal relationships, depletes informal support systems, commercialises professional callings and contaminates democratic processes. (Cahn, 2018, p 3)

Alternative mediums of exchange such as sharing, swapping, doing favours, gifting, bartering and 'community currencies' are ignored by mainstream economists. Indeed, families and members of a community who control their consumption and limit their carbon footprints (for example, by keeping themselves healthy and fit; growing and cooking fresh food; avoiding addictions to gambling, alcohol, drugs or cigarettes; mending and repairing things; playing at home with their children without gadgets and screens; or breastfeeding their babies) are deemed to have a negative impact on GDP. Yet responsible consumption and sharing communities contribute to sustainability, equality and wellbeing. And healthy families bring huge potential savings for public services.[1]

The core economy

The sub-strata of connections, skills, local knowledge and practical support provided by families, friendships, kinships, neighbours, citizens, affinity groups and civil society is called the 'core economy' by the ecological economist, Neva Goodwin. Not only is it essential at times of austerity or crises, it also preserves many of the social and moral aspects of a well-ordered society without which the business world could not function: by passing on cultural norms, creating an infrastructure for rearing healthily socialised children and providing the majority of care for people who are marginalised.

The core economy favours co-operation, caring, spontaneity and trust and is fuelled primarily by *reciprocity*, whereas the market economy operates around competition, scarcity, contracts and specialisation and

---

[1] Some local authorities in England have begun to focus on wellbeing to measure progress; while in Scotland, New Zealand and Iceland it is at the centre of government decision making.

is fuelled primarily by *money*. A combination of reciprocity and money can achieve great things. But, if we continue to let money colonise everyday life and allow reciprocity to diminish, we will seriously undermine the potential for mutual aid. It is in our nature as human beings to reciprocate, to answer in kind for any support we receive. Reciprocity is owned by no one, but can be used by everyone; it is a living example of a social commons. Reciprocity offers us incentives to be trustworthy and dependable: if you are good for a favour you are more likely to get one back, whereas money is only real to each of us because it is enforced legal tender.

New technologies

> Many people think that what's missing in order to move societies towards a new economy is just a set of ideas and policy proposals that are better than those we have already. But that's not the case. We also need new structures and technologies that enable groups to move from their habitual thinking and practices to co-create an eco-centered economy. (Scharmer, 2013)

The monetary system has worked well for an elite who enjoy unrestricted levels of luxury, privilege and power. As Jason Hickel informs us, 'only 5% of new income from global growth goes to the poorest 60% of humanity' (Hickel, 2019).

The organisation Positive Money campaigns for a monetary system that works for society rather than against it and for a citizens' dividend (sometimes referred to as a 'universal basic income'). It argues that the current system is riddled with anomalies: banks are bailed out by typing numbers into a computer, food banks proliferate as stock markets register record highs and politicians claim that the economy is fine in order to win votes. A positive step would be to decouple money from debt and transfer the power to create money to a transparent, democratic and accountable body and away from banks. However, as the chief executive of Positive Money says, this is unlikely until 'expert opinion and public opinion collide' (Boait, 2014).

In theory, the internet can bring us numerous options for alternative mediums of exchange but, in practice, all the new 'essential features' have come under the control of monopolies (for example, Google, Facebook, eBay, Apple and Amazon). Equally worrying are privatised monetary systems, which could introduce and rely on extremely intrusive systems of surveillance over all financial transactions. Blockchain was originally championed as a force for social good, but Bitcoin – the largest of the cryptocurrencies – functions, in part, on the darker side of the web and is moving towards monopolisation and away from democratisation.

However, new, localised community currencies could move us along a trajectory towards platforms that form connections, power local exchanges of goods and services and where resources are governed democratically (Community Currency Alliance, 2020). Some community currencies have pricing systems that are linked to state currencies and all seek to complement rather than replace conventional money. They range from mutual credit systems where 'communities of businesses' trade with each other, to time banks that stimulate mutual aid among older residents. Particularly interesting are 'community inclusion economies', which run parallel currencies to exchange goods and services and incubate small businesses without having to rely on scarce and volatile national currencies, such as Bangla Pesa in Kenya (Ruddick, 2017). Some of the largest software platforms that power local currencies around the world want to pass on their knowledge and share online tools with millions more people. Community Exchange Alliance (2020), for example, facilitates conversation and action to help raise the value of the unpaid economy, reciprocity, solidarity and community currencies, both locally and internationally.[2]

More time for social money

Time banking, combining time and technology as a medium of exchange, is now happening in 33 countries. It contributes to the preventative infrastructure and generates multiple acts of individual and collective caring. It is driven by reciprocity and sometimes a little money to employ a coordinator and is at its most creative and inventive when it is informally structured and run by and owned by local people. Its key features include the following:

- An hour's contribution to the wellbeing of another member of the time bank or the community earns the giver one 'time credit', a community loyalty point.
- Time credits are deposited at the time bank and can be spent on tasks supplied by other members, an hour for an hour.

---

[2] Any assessment of the impact of the internet on civil society has to acknowledge the massive contribution made to communication sharing and to mobilising social action by, for example, WhatsApp, Meetup, Facebook and TikTok, but also remember the existence of a digital divide.

- A computer holds information about who is available, when and with what skills, and a time broker builds relationships and matches members and assignments.
- The time bank provides a broad-based framework for people of all abilities and from all backgrounds to participate and functions as a safe 'letter of introduction'.
- Everyone can make contributions to the wellbeing of others and all are welcome.
- Exchanges can be one to one, one to many or many to one.

Time banking sets in motion a chain reaction that brings people together to form unpredictable friendships and every supportive act enhances the overall social capital. The real value of each time credit is in the promise it signifies to pay back to the community at some point in the future for the help received. Everyone's skill is valued equally, there is no pricing system and one hour is always one credit. In the United Kingdom (UK), there are around 300 local time banks connecting more than 40,000 members across the country who have exchanged more than five million hours of mutual aid (Timebanking UK, 2020). It feels good to be useful and to be known as a helpful person, to become part of something bigger than oneself – to be part of a community.

Reyaz Limalia from Fair Shares, the original UK time bank, telephoned all 350 of his time bank members in a multi-racial area (many of whom have disabilities and are elderly) at the beginning of the COVID-19 pandemic to offer them support. Ninety-five per cent of them thanked him but said they had already self-organised and were exchanging the emotional and practical support they needed. They were already well connected. Reyaz was able to cast his net wider, check out more residents and connect the 5 per cent who needed help from the time bank. Coping with emergencies has proven to be an important and celebrated role for time banks. As first responders in the aftermath of disasters such as earthquakes, hurricanes and floods from Florida, US, to Lyttelton, New Zealand, they know the area and can mobilise very quickly.

Changes in the relationship between the state and communities

The public servant must be trusted and respected by senior management to be given the autonomy and skills to develop a collaborative relationship with service users in ways that often cannot be predetermined by rules and procedures. Equally, the service user must be trusted and respected by the public servant to have insight into their own needs and freedom to develop solutions for themselves – less of a beneficiary or customer, now an active 'partner'. (Lent and Studdert, 2019, p 49)

Institutions and local action

There are growing calls on public services to hand power over to communities. This is a welcome shift from doing things *to* people (the medical model) and doing things *for* people (the charitable model) to doing things *with* people (co-production). However, for community empowerment to gain traction, whatever happens has to be *of* the people; it has to be decided and acted on by local people themselves. This requires a culture change in public services, for example the adoption of the recently updated *Route Map to an Enabling State* – 'put wellbeing at the centre – give people permission to take control – help people to help each other – support people to participate fully – move upstream – build in radical kindness – tell an authentic story of change' (Davidson et al, 2020).

Moving away from a monetary model

A decade of austerity measures in the UK has led to a disproportionate number of cuts to the funding of mental health and social care services. Systems are focused on saving money while delivering safe, unilateral transactions as efficiently as possible to those most in need. As has been discovered in the National Health Service (NHS) during the COVID-19 pandemic, bureaucratic processes and box-ticking targets can inhibit the effectiveness, spontaneity and creativity of frontline staff (Boyle, 2020). The questions we should be urgently asking are: Who picks up most of the burden when cuts are made to frontline services? Who can best strengthen social and community support networks? The answer to both these questions is the same: the core economy of family, friends, neighbours and communities. But, no one is compensating people for the extra unpaid work they do or supporting them to self-organise. We need to resource people directly to stay in control and accept that their efforts need to remain *small, slow and local.*

42

Trusting in the common good

The public sector believes that, if collective acts of caring were resourced and were to proliferate, it would be necessary for someone in authority to exercise controls over the activities and scrutinise the use of any money. So, funds targeted at combatting social issues are routinely channelled through local authorities and agencies, with only a small percentage being passed to the communities concerned for them to manage the funds directly. This reticence of the public sector to put its trust in people echoes an influential article by Garrett Hardin, who claimed that 'freedom in a commons brings ruin to all' (Hardin, 1968). But the Nobel Prize-winning economist, Elinor Ostrom, has disproved this myth and showed how a commons can effectively regulate itself for the common good (Ostrom, 2015). However, the misplaced pessimism remains and amounts to a denial of the primary drive that makes us human: our empathetic nature. It also flies in the face of everyday experience; people are sensitive to inequalities and things need to feel fair. 'Humans are hard-wired to co-operate' (Bollier, 2009) – it gives us pleasure.[3]

Helping people to help each other

Our experience of building communities has exposed the question that those working within the system, who want to help with community empowerment, should ask themselves: What is it that I can *not* do to be helpful? Carrying on claiming to have effective preventative strategies in hand with the knowledge that adequate resources will not be made available is de-motivational. Without a prior commitment to participate from significant numbers of the local population, there can be no co-production or collaboration, just promises and policies. The first move is to find out what it is that enough people care enough about to take action to change and then help them develop their plans for a way forward. This requires *everyone* to be clear and honest about what it is that local people can do best for themselves, what they might need assistance with and what they might need outsiders to do for them. Any idea that has a community behind it has a real chance of success and will generate more activity and inspire others. The key insight to keep in mind is that the people who will build and sustain a community are the ones who live there.

---

[3] Acts of solidarity are as potent as physical exercise in enhancing mental wellbeing and once experienced they are not given up lightly.

Table 3.1: Traditional versus developmental evaluations

Traditional evaluations	Developmental evaluations
Render definitive judgements of success or failure	Provide feedback, generate learnings and support changes in direction
Design the evaluation based on linear cause-and-effect logic models	Design the evaluation to capture system dynamics, interdependencies, models and emergent interconnections
Accountability focused on and directed to external authorities, stakeholders and funders	Accountability centred on the innovators' deep sense of fundamental values and commitment (Gamble, 2008: 62)

A framework for new learning in the community

Traditional evaluators act as impartial third parties who gather data and assess the efficiency of projects. This is useful for measuring progress towards predetermined outputs such as the number of volunteers recruited and activities organised. Community-led development, however, is part of life; the people involved are not to be viewed as volunteers or participants in activities designed by outsiders. They are families, neighbours and citizens working together on what they have determined to be important to them. Progress is better measured using 'developmental evaluation' techniques that show how effective the activities undertaken are at facilitating more space for the community to co-create what *they* value. For comparisons between traditional and developmental evaluations, see Table 3.1.

Lessons learnt on how to facilitate the exchange of support

'They often say to us, "you are inadequate, incompetent, problematic or broken. We will fix you." We ignore these voices and strive to be citizens, people with vision and power to create a culture of community, capacity, connection and care' (McKnight, 2009).

The iron rule of community organising is this: *Never, never do for others what they can do for themselves.* That is to say, stop doing the things for people that they can do for themselves if they had the opportunity and the tools because 'given the opportunity, people tend to do the right thing' (Chambers, 2004, p 104). Over recent years, asset-based community development (ABCD, 2020) has inspired community builders and neighbourhood connectors in the UK. They have, in general, adopted a less confrontational stance than the community organisers in the United States (US), and unlike their American counterparts, have been prepared to take public funding in carrying out local projects.

There are lessons we can learn from projects such as 'Looking Out for Others' Potential' (Gloucestershire Gateway Trust, 2019), involving street-level conversations, led by local people who are trusted and enjoyable to be with, to invite households to become a welcoming neighbourhood contact point in their street.[4] A small team of 'neighbourhood connectors' were trained so they could positively re-enforce collective acts of caring wherever they find them and ask people what they care enough about to act on, what skills they have and who else might be interested in changing the neighbourhood for the better. To form authentic connections, the neighbourhood connectors are **A**vailable, **R**esponsive and **E**motionally present **(ARE)**.

Available

The part-time neighbourhood connectors are local people with a deep understanding of their neighbourhood, who are ready to explore new ways to meet up with and motivate people. They work in the public spaces where local people naturally gather. They walk the streets and knock on doors. They aim to be accessible, recognised, respected and tuned in. They look out for 'local hosts' who will act as informal and friendly contact points – to spread news, talk about issues and organise social events – and listen. Neighbourhood connectors want people to know that if they feel insecure or uncertain, there are people around who care and can be reached easily.

Responsive

The neighbourhood connectors ask questions and listen carefully and non-judgementally to the answers. Then they create space for people to make decisions and choices and to take whatever action they think is appropriate. Neighbourhood connectors are positive and passionate about home-made social change. When things go off course, they are responsive and comforting but do not take on the responsibility for fixing the situation. They help people learn from their mistakes and shift the focus onto what has gone well in the past and what could go well in the future.

---

[4] I am proud to have been associated with this project myself.

Emotionally present

Neighbourhood connectors nurture relationships that are life-affirming and mutually supportive. They believe that everyone has the capacity to think for themselves. They are open hearted, talk straight and are as honest as they can be at all times. Being emotionally present means that they form quality relationships that endure. When they find isolated local people, they make sure that they stay found. When they discover a common purpose, they help other possibilities to emerge.

This approach has evolved from practical experience over many years and from guidance distilled in the following:

- *Asset Based Neighborhood Organising: The Method of the Abundant Community Initiative in Edmonton, Canada* (Hopes et al, 2015);
- A universal set of human values: '• People want control over their own lives for as long as possible • People strive to maintain or improve their own quality of life • People seek social interaction • People seek "warm" relationships with others' (Buurtzorg, 2020); and
- *Participatory Community Building Guidebook, Building Community Capacity* (Jeder Institute, 2020).

Two case studies

Let us now look at two case studies, both in England, that will illustrate what is involved in practice. The first comes from Croydon and shows the importance of real collaboration: being prepared to change to enhance each other's performance, take risks and make a stand on common ground. The second, in Torbay, shows how ageing was reframed from being a personal problem into a community opportunity. Both case studies demonstrate what can be achieved through reciprocity and the exchange of support.

Croydon

In response to the London riots in 2011, Croydon Council commissioned the 'Social Recovery' project, hosted by Croydon Voluntary Action (CVA) and guided by the organisation Nurture Development. While young people had been falsely portrayed in the media as being responsible for the rioting, local residents had famously picked up their brooms and cleaned up the area themselves. My colleagues at Nurture Development, Cormac Russell, Paul Macey and Jennine Bailey, had prepared the ground for more asset-based community development (ABCD) work by running a pilot project that had mobilised significant numbers of people from the Black, Asian and minority ethnic community and impressed Croydon Council and NHS Croydon in relation to their prevention and self-care agendas. Three part-time community builders were employed to work in Thornton Heath, Selhurst and Broad Green. In brief, the approach was to focus on what was strong, what was possible and what worked (not on what was wrong) – and then to combine the strengths we had found to tackle what was wrong (Russell, 2020).

Among the strengths, assets and hidden treasures the Social Recovery project aimed to uncover were:

> The practical skills, capacity and knowledge of local residents. The passions and interests of local residents that give them energy for change. The networks and connections – known as 'social capital' – in a community, including friendships and neighbourliness. The effectiveness of local community and voluntary associations. The resources of public, private and third-sector organisations that are available to support a community. The physical and economic resources of a place that enhance well-being. (Foot and Hopkins, 2010, p 7)

Over the first 18 months, the project linked up with more than 60 'natural connectors' who set up 77 community action groups, and connections were made with more than 240 neighbourhood-based clubs and associations.[5] (The project won a Community Empowerment Award for Croydon Council.) A community of practice (CoP) group was set up. Every month, welfare professionals, business people, community leaders, local people and politicians had lunch together in a safe and neutral environment, to help establish common ground, deepen practice and share information. The compassion and positivity shown by the CoP group when they stood behind and opened up opportunities for young people and the collective action by residents were an impressive example of the power of collectivism.

---

[5] As a Director of Nurture Development, I mentored the community builders and convened the community of practice. Of the 77 new community action groups set up, several received matching funds from the council (Diers, 2004).

Under the Croydon project, when a group of residents had an idea for an activity that would contribute to the common good and that was not dependent on long-term external funding, they could pledge so many hours of their time and skills to make it happen. The time pledged would be matched with start-up money if needed (for example, £200 for 20 hours). The mix of reciprocity, passion, local skills and a little money was a powerful recipe. The relationships and connections that evolved were inspiring. Examples include: Food for Thought – Greet & Eat; CRIS (Croydon Renewable I.T. Skills); GP Partnership Tool; The Young Chef's Academy; Saving our Lollypop People; Personal Development Workshops; Women in Action; Overcoming Isolation in the Asian Community; Community Cricket; and many others (Community Connectors, 2014).

Torbay

'Ageing Well Torbay' is part of the 'Fulfilling Lives: Ageing Better' programme of the National Lottery Community Fund. With 6,000 isolated 'over-50s' in Torbay, new ways were needed to bring people together (Torbay Community Development Trust, 2020). Working in 30 neighbourhoods, 20 community builders took an ABCD approach, combined with time banking. They were not there to 'fix' older people or to take charge of their lives. Whatever was to be done was to be decided on by the people themselves, at a pace they were comfortable with, without the use of jargon and in ways that made sense and mattered to them. The team looked for isolated older people and also for natural connectors and good neighbours, local people who knew what was happening locally and believed in connecting with people. Many of them initially resisted the impulse to get involved as the message they had sometimes received from professionals in recent years had been: *leave it to us, you are not qualified, you may be unsafe*. The team almost had to give them permission, with the full support of the authorities, to act as 'animators', to find out what people were passionate about and prepared to do to help themselves. They connected up those with similar aspirations, helped them to get organised and then stepped back so they could stay in the driving seat of any change. As a result, new relationships and connections were made between 1,500+ neighbours and connectors and 1,600+ isolated older people and more than 250 new citizen-led activity groups were set up. They are all widely appreciated as long-term neighbourhood assets; they are growing neighbourliness and modelling active citizenship.

The formal evaluation of the first four years by SERIO, University of Plymouth, exceeded all expectations:[6]

- The proportion of people who agree with the statement 'I am able to utilise my skills, knowledge and/or expertise for the benefit of my community' has increased from 23 per cent to 56 per cent.
- Thirty-eight per cent say they do social activities 'more than most' people of a similar age, compared with 16 per cent on entry to the programme.
- Talking to neighbours has increased from 19 per cent to 35 per cent.
- Eighty-three per cent are involved in providing unpaid help to others, up from 59 per cent on entry to the programme.
- More than 250 new grassroots social activity groups have formed.
- General practitioner (GP) visits have decreased from an average of 6.9 times a year to 4.7.
- Non-elective hospital stayovers have decreased from 42 per cent to 16 per cent.
- Fifty-three per cent now report that they are *not* anxious or depressed, compared with 28 per cent on entry to the programme.

While knocking on front doors in a low-income estate, Nina Cooper, a community builder, met three older women interested in starting a community café. She brought them together and they ran some pop-up cafés on the green space in front of the shops to test local support. The core group grew to 20 people and with a little help they leased and converted an unused office into a café called the Crafty Fox Café and Hub. The café is now the main connection point for more than 100 residents every week. It is a much-appreciated source of refreshment, friendship, information and advice and the GP refers isolated patients to it. A diverse mix of local people share their skills, make all of the decisions and run the place themselves voluntarily. A whole range of services and activities are now available and people's self-confidence and mental wellbeing have vastly improved. Prior to the COVID-19 pandemic, over a 12-month period, 96 residents of varying ages used the employment service at the café (34 developed new skills, 34 were involved in activities to increase employability, 27 accessed training, 22 were involved in activities promoting mental health, 21 got new jobs and 18 took work experience). The ripple effect from the café includes a Sunday Lunch Club

---

[6] A full summary of the resulting *Community Building* report is available (see Ageing Well, 2020).

and an informal transport service. It is genuinely resident-led and their solidarity is infectious and helps them involve many more residents who were previously regarded as 'hard to reach'.

Conclusion

Throughout history, small conversations have grown into big ideas and communities have lined up behind them in support. Mass unpaid collective action, social movements, such as the suffragettes, and civil rights activists devoted their social capital and expertise to protect the freedoms we enjoy today. They imagined a better world than the one they inhabited. We must not let them down and allow money alone to define for us what it is that we value in future. Today, there should be a community builder/neighbourhood connector/time broker in every neighbourhood to fulfil a connecting role as opposed to delivering a service.

However, we all depend for our survival on profits accumulated in the form of capital and distributed as wealth. 'The existential question of our lives – what we value – cannot be separated from the economic organisation of our society' (Hagglund, 2020). We need to transform (and localise) how we produce, exchange and consume what we need to survive and use a variety of mediums of exchange. We could even collectivise the distribution of wealth by introducing a citizens' dividend (basic unconditional monetary support for everyone). That would make it possible for everyone to live without ongoing insecurity, to grow individually and collectively as citizens, and to do the things in life that they value most. By providing an economic platform that ensures everyone receives what they need to survive and with the power of enlightened self-interest to direct the rest of us, a more co-operative society would have a fairer chance of emerging. Our activist forebears would approve of that; seeing how the advance of social responsibility is being inspired by their past achievements. Even Adam Smith, an originator of capitalism, admitted: 'How selfish soever man may be supposed, there are evidently some principles in his nature which interest him in the fortune of others and render their happiness necessary to him though he derives nothing from it except the pleasure of seeing it' (Bregman, 2020).

Ultimately, people care about how their neighbourhood responds to the challenges they face – from pandemics to the climate change crisis. Every neighbourhood is unique but they all have the inventiveness and generosity to make them places where the practice of collective acts of caring and kindness can improve the quality of life and wellbeing for all. We need the culture of our public services to change and for them to intentionally connect with communities and help them tap into what is already there and self-organise. When we build inclusive networks of relationships, then reciprocity and supportive connections will inevitably spread and lead to a better future for all communities.[7]

References

ABCD in Action (2020) http://abcdinaction.org.

Ageing Well (2020) *Community Building*, Torbay: Ageing Well, https://ageingwelltorbay.files.wordpress.com/2020/03/community-building-summary-pdf-1-10th-march-update.pdf.

Boait, F. (2014) 'How does the money system affect inequality?', *Housing & Environment*, https://positivemoney.org.

Bollier, D. (2009) 'Hard-wired to cooperate', *On The Commons*, 1 December, http://www.onthecommons.org/hard-wired-cooperate.

Boyle, D. (2020) *TICKBOX*, London: Little Brown Book Group, https://www.littlebrown.co.uk/titles/david-boyle/tickbox/9781408711866.

Bregman, R. (2020) *Humankind: A Hopeful History*, New York: Bloomsbury, pp 249–59.

Buurtzorg (2020) 'The Buurtzorg model', https://www.buurtzorg.com/about-us/buurtzorgmodel.

Cahn, E. (2018) *The King Midas Monoculture: Why We Need Other Kinds of Money*, Durham: Duke University Press, p 3, https://doi.org/10.1215/08879982-6817889.

Chambers, E. (2004) *Roots for Radicals: Organising for Power, Action and Justice*, New York: Continuum International Publishing Group, pp 103, 104.

Community Connectors (2014) 'Asset based community development pilot', https://www.croydon.gov.uk/sites/default/files/articles/downloads/abcfull-report.pdf.

Community Currency Alliance (2020) www.currency.community.

Community Exchange Alliance (2020) http://www.communityexchangealliance.org.

Davidson, S., Wallace, J. and Ormston, H. (2020) *The Enabling State: Revisiting the Route Map to an Enabling State*, Dunfermline: The Carnegie UK Trust, www.carnegieuktrust.org.uk.

---

[7] Two books that are sources for the medical and philosophical foundations of this chapter are Mittelmark et al (2017) and Rosenblum (2016).

Diers, J. (2004) *Neighbor Power: Building Community the Seattle Way*, Washington: Washington University Press, http://www.neighborpower.org/book.html.

Foot, D. and Hopkins, T. (2010) *A Glass Half Full: How An Asset Approach can Improve Community Health and Wellbeing*, London: IDeA, http://www.assetbasedconsulting.net/uploads/publications/A%20glass%20half%20full.pdf.

Gamble, J. (2008) *A Developmental Evaluation Primer*, Montreal: J.W. McConnell Family Foundation, https://mcconnellfoundation.ca/wp-content/uploads/2017/07/A-Developmental-Evaluation-Primer-EN.pdf.

Gloucestershire Gateway Trust (2019) 'What is the LOOP Project?', www.gloucestershiregatewaytrust.org.uk/loop.html.

Hagglund, M. (2020) 'What should we value', *New Statesman*, 28 August – 3 September, p 29.

Hardin, G. (1968) 'The tragedy of the Commons', *Science*, https://www.garretthardinsociety.org/articles/art_tragedy_of_the_commons.html.

Hickel, J. (2019) 'A letter to Steven Pinker (and Bill Gates, for that matter) about global poverty', 4 February, https://www.jasonhickel.org/blog/2019/2/3/pinker-and-global-poverty.

Hopes, K., McKnight, J. and Lawrence, H. (2015) *Asset Based Neighbourhood Organising*, Chicago: ABCD Institute, https://www.tamarackcommunity.ca/library/paper-asset-based-neighbourhood-organizing.

Jeder Institute (2020) *Participatory Community Building Guidebook, Building Community Capacity*, Wagga Wagga, Australia: Jeder Institute.https://www.jeder.com.au/wp-content/uploads/2021/03/Participatory-Community-Building-Guidebook-2020_v2-1.pdf

Lent, A. and Studdert, J. (2019) *The Community Paradigm*, London: New Local Government Network, p 49, www.nlgn.org.uk/public/about-nlgn.

McKnight, J. (2009) 'From clients to citizens forum', opening remarks, Coady International Institute, Nova Scotia, https://coady.stfx.ca/wp-content/uploads/pdfs/ABCD_ConferenceMaterials/John%20McKnight%20Opening%20Remarks.pdf.

Mittelmark, M., Sagy, S., Eriksson, E., Bauer, G., Pelikan, J., Lindström, B. and Espnes, G. (2017) *The Handbook of Salutogenesis*, Cham, Switzerland: Springer, https://link.springer.com/book/10.1007%2F978-3-319-04600-6.

Ostrom, E. (2015) *Governing the Commons: The Evolution of Institutions for Collective Action*, Cambridge: Canto Classics.

Rosenblum, N. (2016) *Good Neighbors: The Democracy of Everyday Life in America*, Princeton: Princeton University Press, p 248.

Ruddick, W. (2017) Documentary on Will Ruddick and community currencies in Kenya, https://www.youtube.com/watch?v=ojFPrVvpraU.

Russell, C. (2020) 'ABCD trainers', www.nurturedevelopment.org.

Scharmer, O. (2013) 'From ego-system to eco-system economies.' Open Democracy, 23 September, https://www.opendemocracy.net/transformation/otto-scharmer/from-ego-system-to-eco-system-economies.

Timebanking UK (2020) National Umbrella Network Organisation. UK. www.timebanking.org.

Torbay Community Development Trust (2020) Torbay Community Development https://www.torbaycdt.org.uk/

4

Regeneration in partnership with communities

Gabriel Chanan

Taking possession of revival

The phrase 'community-based transformation' signals a progressive approach to change with its feet on the ground. It draws on a rich tradition of local practice and theory, prioritising local action and empowerment of the most disadvantaged in order to overcome inequality and achieve sustainability. But it also conceals some big uncertainties. Can progress to equality and a sustainable society really be led by communities when inequality, attacks on democracy and unsustainable growth are driven by national and multinational forces?

We generally use the term 'community' as code to mean disadvantaged sections of the population or the residents of poorer neighbourhoods. But it can also mean people anywhere with shared values of equality and participation. We have to keep juggling these meanings. On the one hand, action is needed to overcome concentrated disadvantage. On the other, some changes are needed throughout society and government. Changes in communities will only be part of the picture, but a vital part, and one that illuminates the whole. This chapter reflects on the situation in the United Kingdom (UK), especially England, but the issues we will be looking at apply to many other countries where the post-war political consensus has been undermined by the rise of neoliberalism and right-wing demagoguery.

Throughout the coronavirus pandemic, there has been much talk of getting back to normal. This seldom reflects the complexity of the public mood – a mixture of grief, fear for health and jobs, and amazement that it is possible to stop modern life in its tracks (which may not be entirely for the worse). A return to normal is a return to jobs and social life where possible, but also to the feeling that we cannot go on like this: with a galloping climate crisis, widening inequality, worldwide threats to human rights and debased political discourse.

The regeneration trajectory

Some of the most relevant community-level experience we can call on in the UK lies in the regeneration programmes of 1970 to 2010. Starting with a small number of local economic experiments, these policies eventually became, for a time, a carrier wave for widespread community involvement in social and economic development.

It cannot be accidental, although it was not very clear at the time, that the rise of regeneration schemes paralleled the rise of globalisation. As heavy industry, mining and manufacturing moved increasingly to India, China and elsewhere, the economy of the UK became ever-more dependent on financial services, high-tech industries, leisure and service industries. The social cost was most visible in the hollowing out of parts of our once-thriving industrial cities. These were among the foremost target areas for regeneration.

A similar pattern was evident across Europe. The European Union's (EU) response played a considerable part in regeneration in the UK and elsewhere. Based on comparing regions within as well as across countries, the EU allocated 'structural funds' to assist 'lagging' regions to 'catch up' with the richest. These metaphors bolstered the idea that there was nothing wrong with global development, only with the failure of ex-industrial areas to get on to the hi-tech, financial services, leisure and tourism bandwagon fast enough.

Of course, 'lagging' regions never could 'catch up' with the 'advanced' ones because the 'advanced' ones continued to multiply their advantages. But the poorer regions did nevertheless benefit from regeneration. Behind the EU rhetoric was an understanding that it was in the interests of the richer regions to assist the poorer ones. It was no secret, at least to finance ministers and big companies, that a proportion of the substantial sums transferred to the poorer regions would flow back to the richer ones through contracts to build social and industrial infrastructure. Competition rules ensured that contracts had to be advertised across Europe and awarded on the criteria of cost and efficiency, which could be best met by companies in the richer areas. At the same time, a degree of genuine economic improvement in the poorer areas would also help to build longer-term markets for the richer areas. This pattern can also be seen in international aid as a whole, showing that capitalism is not merely a free-market system but a combination of free-market and state action.

The extent to which one might regard this system as either viciously deceptive or a relatively virtuous compromise with the realities of power might depend on a number of factors. Were the grants well spent in the poorer areas or did they create 'white elephants'? Were projects targeted where they were most needed and beneficial? Did they consist only of short-term job creation or did they improve long-term conditions for the whole local population? Above all, were local people involved and influential in the projects, ensuring maximum effectiveness for the intended beneficiaries? Patchy results left an inconclusive legacy, but during the Thatcher period, EU funding was a lifeline for a variety of progressive local UK projects, which would not have survived her regime otherwise. And continuing until even after the Brexit vote, networking with local projects across Europe was an important source of comparison, learning and improvement.

From scattergun to coordination

With Thatcher's departure in 1990, the (still Conservative) government of John Major was more favourable to local experimentation on a variety of social issues. Indeed, there was a confusing proliferation of separate local projects. In a study of Birmingham in the mid-1990s, Collinge and Hall (1997) found 53 different executive bodies operating in the city, each with its own social projects, some covering the whole city, some specific areas and neighbourhoods.

As Deputy to John Major, Michael Heseltine introduced a more concentrated form of regeneration. City Challenge (1992–98) created partnerships of local authorities and private sector developers to improve disadvantaged inner-city areas in England by linking job creation, education and other social issues. There were 31 partnerships of five years each, using about £80 million per area to lever in double that amount in the form of private investment (a total government cost of about £2.5 billion).

Research on City Challenge (Robson et al, 1994) showed that projects had delivered considerable benefits but that these tended to 'leak out' to surrounding areas, bypassing some of the communities in greatest need. The successor Single Regeneration Budget (SRB) (1994–2002), a major expansion of government commitment, made greater efforts to empower local residents by involving them in the regeneration process. A total of £26 billion was spent across about a third of local authority areas in England and eventually supported more than a thousand projects for up to seven years.[1] The word 'single'

---

[1] £5.7 billion came from central government, with the rest from sources such as local authorities, European funds, and voluntary and private sectors.

in the oddly-titled scheme indicated the integration under one plan of issues covered by different departmental budgets, from which the money was 'top sliced': an obligatory pooling of a segment of resources to drive a more integrated approach to localities.

There was much rhetoric about community involvement, not always borne out in practice. But the government accepted advice from the Community Development Foundation (CDF, 1999) that community strengthening needed to be an explicit objective of the scheme, with a specific budget allocation and criteria parallel to those on the 'hard' issues of job creation, education, housing and health. As a result, the SRB channelled money to tens of thousands of local community groups.

Incoming New Labour in 1997 phased out the SRB in order to invent something more comprehensive. The National Strategy for Neighbourhood Renewal (Chanan and Miller, 2013) actually did much the same sort of thing as the SRB, in much the same sorts of places, but in the end went further, creating a model for comprehensive community participation in all local authorities. The government at last appeared to grasp what communities had been trying to tell it for years – that improving life in a given area meant looking at the whole spectrum of social, economic and environmental issues together. An essential component was responding to what local residents themselves were already trying to do about their shared problems in the locality, and had been doing for decades without recognition in policy.

The culmination of New Labour's attempts to develop a comprehensive participative framework for local development was the creation of local strategic partnerships (LSPs). These were a forum for interaction between all public services, all issues, all groups and all neighbourhoods across a local authority. This was no longer merely regeneration of disadvantaged areas, it was a standard model for all local authorities, although only the most disadvantaged got regeneration money to back it up (see Chapter 6).

Success and dissolution

Evaluation of LSPs (for example, Geddes, 2007) showed, unsurprisingly, mixed results in these early years of such a major innovation, but with strong indications of the positive potential of the model. The members of most LSPs felt they were making progress on the development of a collective vision and a coordinated local strategy, widening the range of interests involved in local decision making and creating a stronger local voice. Substantial numbers of LSPs claimed to have made some progress towards service improvement on crime, education, training, employment and health.

Labour's new frontiers in regeneration were obscured by problems in higher-profile policy areas, especially the Iraq war. By the time evaluation was delivering quite favourable long-term verdicts, no one was listening:

> Official evaluations of the Decent Homes, Neighbourhood Renewal Fund and New Deal for Communities programmes show that between 1997 and 2010, 90% of social housing was brought up to a decent standard, there was a fall in vacant housing rates in unpopular estates; domestic burglary rates and worklessness fell in the 'worst' neighbourhoods; and user survey data suggested clear jumps in resident satisfaction about cleaner streets and parks, lower crime, and better schools, crèche and day-care provision (though) there was still a 15% gap between the 'worst' areas and the national average on burglary, vandalism, litter and resident satisfaction. (Nathan, 2016)

With the eruption of the financial crisis in 2008, there were signs of rowing back even before Labour lost its majority in 2010. The advent of the Conservative–Liberal Democrat coalition government initiated a decade of austerity, and regeneration underwent a steep decline. The notion of a unified approach to localities with major input from the full spectrum of community groups disappeared from government discourse, replaced by an ersatz version, 'Big Society', claiming to be a new idea.

Anecdotally, many community representatives on LSPs had found the experience difficult but much of the dissatisfaction was surely the difficulty of learning to operate for the first time in a comprehensive local policy-making environment. Given the large size of UK local authorities, especially after the introduction of unitary authorities from 1973 onwards, there was a big distance, both geographically and psychologically, between the local authority/LSP level of governance (covering populations upwards of 200,000) and individual neighbourhoods of 5–10,000 people.

It had been easier to take an integrated view of social issues at district level (around 60–100,000 people). An example from Northumberland shows what had been possible: Blyth Valley achieving a remarkable turnaround of conditions and morale between 1995 and 2005. Following a period of shocks resulting from high unemployment and the deaths of a number of young people through drug abuse, the council reshaped itself as a 'community-based council'.

Although only a district council with limited resources, it invested £1 million out of its £10 million budget in community development. Twenty community development workers were employed to build up the capacity of the community in terms of its own socially productive activities and its engagement with the council and other authorities. In parallel, the council built up a 'hub and spoke' network of 25 community centres, at least one in each ward, to generate greater capacity of the community both to solve its own problems and to draw in extra resources. Other staff of the district council were trained in the principles of community development, which they then cascaded through the authority and its partnerships (Communities and Local Government, 2006).

In Blythe Valley, the result over ten years was a doubling of the number of voluntary and community organisations from around 300 to 600, with a corresponding doubling of volunteers. The danger of Blyth becoming a stigmatised area after industrial decline and the emergence of major social problems was averted. It changed from a low housing demand area to an area with demand for new housing and consequent investment by property companies. The council used the levy on house building to create further community amenities, while the growth in the voluntary and community sector also enabled it to bring in an extra £6.5 million from external resources.

Blyth Valley as a district council was abolished in 2009, being absorbed into Northumberland County Council unitary authority. Ironically, it was the first of the 'red wall' areas to fall to the Conservatives by a slim margin in the 2019 'Brexit' general election, after decades with a strong Labour majority.

By 2016, the UK could be seen as having entered a 'post-regeneration' era (O'Brien and Matthews, 2016). The building of new housing continued with little or no reference to notions of community and participation, although communities continued to press for influence on the plans, sometimes with signal success (Sendra and Fitzpatrick, 2020).

In Wales, the devolved government's flagship programme 'Communities First' continued for some time into the new era. Applied to around 150 disadvantaged neighbourhoods and small areas, it was conceived as a grassroots approach to addressing issues caused by poverty. After 17 years it was closed in 2018 on the grounds that poverty still persisted, although the scheme had not promised to overcome poverty itself (Pearce, 2020).

Deleting the community: an ill omen

The conditions of the 2020s may unexpectedly provide an opportunity to revive the stream of comprehensive community involvement. In the wake of the COVID-19 pandemic, governments again face crises in employment and all the related issues of poverty, physical and mental health and social tensions. Nor is there any let-up in the pre-existing crises in environment, housing and policing. There is a manifest need for a regeneration-type approach to link all the issues, and it is essential that lessons from the earlier regeneration period and since are brought back into play. Reducing the environmental and climatic threat must be a dominant consideration, not an afterthought. There is a need for a degree of de-linking from globalisation, with restoration of national self-sufficiency in certain basics such as food, utilities and health products, which can provide some new jobs. But full international co-operation must be maintained on environment, science, health and human rights. There is a sense of ferment in communities and civil society, looking for profound change.

But at the time of writing there is little sign that government is recognising or responding to the issues. On the contrary, in August 2020 the Ministry of Housing, Communities and Local Government published its intention to review planning rules in a way that would eliminate the ability of local authorities to obtain the best possible deal for local infrastructure from property developers (MHCLG, 2020). The attitude of the Housing Minister, Robert Jenrick, to the Community Infrastructure Levy (CIL, also known as planning gain or Section 106) was already suspect from alleged attempts by him only two months before to assist property company Northern and Shell to evade a £40 million levy on a £1 billion development in the London Borough of Tower Hamlets (Pogrund, et al, 2020).

The national media were interested for a time in the whiff of sleaze but did little to elucidate the underlying issue. The way in which the CIL process is conducted, and the entire language in which it is couched, present it as a penalty that developers incur, not an opportunity for a creative, participative way to develop communities. Developers are assumed to want to pay as little as possible towards the quality of the place where they are building houses for sale, and local authorities are assumed to have to squeeze what they can out of them for this purpose on behalf of local communities, who may or may not be consulted. Ominously, the new version will not be called the Community Infrastructure Levy (CIL) but the Infrastructure Levy (IL) – 'Community' will be deleted.

The shift to health

Ironically, the question of participative local development has nevertheless come back onto the policy agenda via the National Health Service (NHS), in part because massive cuts to local authorities have displaced many social problems onto doctors' surgeries and hospitals, including Accident & Emergency (A&E) departments. Having struggled for decades to shift a proportion of its effort from individual treatments to community-based prevention, the long-term plan of the NHS (NHS, 2019) institutes a place-based model of primary care. Local networks of general practitioners (GPs) and other health professionals are required to take a holistic view of the health of the population across a cluster of neighbourhoods totalling around 50,000 people. With an increased emphasis on prevention (although treatment is still by far the dominant element), the aim is to improve health proactively through the 'social determinants of health', including housing, employment, environment, education and safety – all the social issues that concern communities.

A particular mechanism in the community health armoury is the use of 'social prescribing', that is, referring patients wherever possible to community activity rather than medical treatments, or alongside them. A new profession of social prescribing officers has been created, to be the bridge between patients and the local community and voluntary sector. But this innovation does not go so far as to recognise that the community sector itself needs a major boost if it is to accommodate the substantial traffic of referrals being generated. 'The community' is seen as a mysterious infinite resource that can absorb whatever is thrown at it, much the same as 'the environment' used to be treated before policy makers grasped that it too was a limited resource.

It is unclear how far the need to combat the current and future pandemics will compromise the growth of community involvement in health. In a worrying move in August 2009, Health Secretary Matt Hancock set out to replace Public Health England, which has been instrumental in promoting community involvement, with a body tasked with concentrating solely on pandemics.

The development of the place-based health approach is far from complete, but the direction of travel suggests that the NHS is potentially a major player in any new wave of regeneration. A glimmer of the sort of vision needed is the Healthy New Towns scheme funded by NHS England from 2016 to 2019 (TCPA, 2016). Ten three-year projects brought together action on the built environment, new models of care and community activation.

One of the ten projects that I was able to evaluate in detail was in Barton, a disadvantaged area of 7,400 people on the north-east edge of Oxford, cut off from the city by the permanently busy ring road as well as major disparities in income and conditions (Chanan, 2019). Surveys of residents in 2017 revealed high levels of poor diet, low levels of exercise, poor mobility and high levels of cardiovascular disease, liver disease, asthma and hypertension. Although few complained of loneliness, 16 per cent had suffered from depression. Of the working population, 4.5 per cent were receiving mental health-related benefits. Problems in the locality included lack of activities for young people, poor shopping facilities, closure of the only post office and closure of a church hall, the British Legion and pubs.

In Barton, action began with a small grants scheme for local voluntary and community organisations, but this was more about the use of the sector than building it up: five of the eight grants went to organisations from outside the neighbourhood. The neighbourhood centre, however, generated additional activities and fostered crossover between health and other community issues. Many residents spoke positively of benefits through both physical activities and socialisation. There were clear signs of reductions of outpatient appointments, admissions to hospital and demands on GPs.

A major contribution of the NHS to 'place' should be to drive more precise thinking about neighbourhoods. Statistics used for local health planning show that virtually *all* cities and *all* local authority areas contain dramatic contrasts of wealth and poverty. This is most vividly seen in variations in longevity of up to ten years between one neighbourhood and another in the same city or area. This confirms the misguided nature of the original regeneration language about helping poorer areas 'catch up' with the most prosperous ones. Prosperity and poverty grow in tandem at the hyper-local level. The need for redistribution is permanent. But this is not just about jobs and income. It is also about improving the life and conditions of the locality as a whole, and much can be done on this even when the national economy is not buoyant.

The decimation of community infrastructure

Support for community action needs a comprehensive and permanent basis. The ability of communities to respond, be involved and be influential depends not on isolated, occasional short-term projects but on the cumulative strength of the community sector over time. The baseline question is: What is the condition of the existing community sector in the place as a whole? So one can ask: How strong is it? How many groups are there? How much interaction is there between them? How much volunteering takes place? How much involvement in community activity? How much influence does the sector have on public services and local policy decisions?

During the austerity period, 2010–20, there was a shocking loss of community amenities, depriving tens of thousands of community groups of places to meet and carry out activities (Gregory, 2018). A number of local authorities valiantly sought to protect their community support role despite the losses. But what was – and is – needed is provision of community infrastructure and support everywhere.

Drawing together a variety of sources, Corry (2020) finds that there are fewest registered charities in the localities that need them most. The average for England is 1.8 per 1,000 people. But it is much higher in well-off areas, for example 5.5 in the Cotswolds; and lower in disadvantaged areas, for example around 0.7 in Blackpool, 0.8 in Knowsley and 1.0 across Manchester. The pattern for community groups (unregistered charitable organisations) is likely to show an even more acute differentiation, except where there may have been a sustained community development strategy. Most of these groups create themselves 'from the bottom up' but, contradicting 'Big Society' assumptions, are still very much affected by the availability of institutional support. For example, few will have premises of their own, so their ability to carry out activities will often depend on a local community centre or similar amenity. The community centre will be a registered charity, so in places where there are few community centres or similar amenities, there is likely to be a dearth of community groups. And where community centres are under pressure to wholly fund themselves, they inevitably put up hire prices and concentrate on weddings and commercial events, which squeeze out many community groups.

Can community practice handle it?

Some of the people who are in the best position to argue for a national policy on community support – community practitioners – are themselves uneasy about it and hold back. A government plan, with government funding, would entail some level of government-type control, which is seen by some as anathema to the culture of community empowerment. The result, ironically, is that community practice hobbles along on patchy, spasmodic project funding, which prevents strategic development and effectiveness. The fact that community practitioners fail to put forward a strategic case for public investment in community development does not prevent some practitioners from blaming government for the dearth.

Some commentators are fatalist about the role of the state and posit a diametrical opposition between the state and the interests of communities:

> Municipalism rejects seizing state power ... The state, whether capitalist or socialist, with its faceless bureaucracy, is never responsive to the people ... the question is, in whose hands will power reside – in those of the state, with its centralized authority, or in those of the people at local level? ... When we confine ourselves to voting for ... social democracy, we play into and support the centralised state structure that is designed to keep us down for ever. (Bookchin, 2019)

But the majority of case studies (including some within the collection introduced by the quotation from Bookchin, 2019) show that the valiant and very real achievements of community-based projects almost always involve some negotiation and co-operation between communities and state agencies. This is often achieved by individuals within one service or another going the extra mile, improvising collaboration between the service and a community initiative, as in the case study of a Bristol-based Single Parents Action Network (SPAN) (Cohen and McDermot, 2016).

Like many other locally created social projects, SPAN grew and survived by dodging and weaving among the constant shifts of public policy and fragmented funding. This was only possible because of a combination of determined community initiative, partial public funding and the personal support of individuals within or close to the public service system. These individuals – a primary school head, a council officer, an architect, a head of libraries and the director of a major local charity – acted beyond their strict professional role. The lesson is that community action needs allies in and around the local public and professional services – and the services they are working in need to give them the stimulus and flexibility to respond to creative community action.

This is not to say that local government and public services can necessarily be regarded as adequately representing or meeting the needs and concerns of communities. Examples collected by the Local Government Association (2020) show that many cities and councils see themselves as leading local efforts to build 'inclusive economies', linking job creation, housing and skills, in partnership with other key local players such as housing associations, health authorities, universities and locally based private companies – a range of allies that communities cannot mobilise alone. Except for a few examples, however, it remains unclear from the literature how these partnerships actually relate to the voice of the communities within them.

Community support should be planned as an increase in the strength of the whole community sector of a place, both long-existing, new and potential groups. This has implications for the way community support is commissioned and planned, and for the skills and contributions of individual workers (Chanan and Fisher, 2018). A community support team must be big enough and have diverse-enough skills to cope with the whole range of social issues – the key ones being housing, employment, safety, education, environment, welfare, health, care, transport, leisure and amenities. If there are no community groups on the patch that are concerned with one or more of these issues, that does not mean they are not of concern to the community but that the concern has not yet found expression and that it should be found and nurtured.

This kind of approach cannot be widely achieved without a serious new national commitment. However unlikely that seems at present, it is futile to pretend otherwise. But a large part of the necessary investment could take the form of adjusting the remit and training of a proportion of existing frontline workers and their managers in other public services (Miller and Chanan, 2009). With globalisation somewhat in retreat, and a resurgence of mass unemployment and social problems, experiences under regeneration, both good and bad, are highly relevant to the question of what sort of society we want to build now.

Despite having been written off numerous times, the nation state is still the pre-eminent site of power, both downwards to localities and upwards to international negotiation (or its failure). When the 2020 COVID-19 pandemic struck, no one was in any doubt that it was nation states, irrespective of their current politics, that had to make and implement the instant new rules.

Community-based thinking can become a trap if we think of it as potentially an entire replacement for a national perspective and state action. The very extent of inequality is only known because we have a national overview. Some of the key measures to combat inequality, such as benefits and public services, demand redistribution from richer to poorer communities, and therefore must be centrally provided for in line with national standards, even if delivery is often best devolved to the local level. But state action must be understood as subject to all the necessary checks and balances of a vigorous democracy.

Inevitably, there are tensions between services and communities. They work through two very different cultures (as explored in Chapter 6). Public services have to be systematic. That requires rationalisation, planning, measurement and formal accountability. Communities work by feelings, friendships, mutuality and passion. You would not get community action through rationalisation and measurement. On the other hand, you would not want benefits or regeneration contracts distributed by feelings and friendships. We need a transformation strategy that makes use of all the instruments.

One reason why the relative success of regeneration is frequently overlooked is that it almost never achieves the 'catching up' rashly invoked by funders, let alone the total overcoming of inequality sought by community development utopians. The real choice is between being a society that ignores and exacerbates inequality and one that is committed to permanently working to ameliorate inequality even if it can never wholly eradicate it. Economic development produces contrasts of wealth and poverty under *any* type of political regime, so the need for regeneration is not only acute but also permanent, and would be achieved more effectively if this was admitted by all stakeholders.

The way forward

There is much we can learn from the extensive UK regeneration experience over the period 1980–2010. We should draw on the lessons regarding what worked and what did not, and apply them to the strengthening of communities' influence, capacity and quality of life from here on. I will conclude this chapter with four key recommendations:

- Building on regeneration experience, there should be a new national strategy for community involvement, providing ringfenced resources to local authorities to revive and improve their community support functions in dialogue with local communities.
- A standard level of community amenities and support should be available in each neighbourhood, especially the more disadvantaged

ones. The loss of community amenities during 'austerity' should be made good and surpassed.

- The planning system should restore and improve the power to councils to shape local development, in dialogue with resident forums and neighbourhood plans. The Community Infrastructure Levy (CIL) should be retained, expanded and changed from a 'penalty'-type ethos to positive partnership in building communities.
- The NHS should play a large part in new regeneration schemes and the community support strategy. The model for integrating environmental, building and community criteria – based on the Healthy New Towns scheme developed by NHS England (TCPA, 2016) – should become the norm for all development.

References

Bookchin, D. (2019) 'The future we deserve' in Barcelona en Comu, *Fearless Cities: A Guide to the Global Municipalist Movement*, Oxford: New Internationalist.

CDF (Community Development Foundation) (1999) *Regeneration and Sustainable Communities*, London: CDF.

Chanan, G (2019) *Barton Healthy New Town: Concluding Evaluation*, Oxford: Oxford City Council, https://irp-cdn.multiscreensite.com/9163ad55/files/uploaded/Barton%20Healthy%20New%20Town%20Evaluation%20final%20ACTUAL%2028iii19.pdf.

Chanan, G. and Fisher, B. (2018) *Commissioning Community Development for Health*, London: Coalition for Collaborative Health, https://irp-cdn.multiscreensite.com/9163ad55/files/uploaded/0%200%200%200%200%200%200%20Community%20Dev%20for%20Health%20screen%20FINAL%20PUBD%20Dec%2017.pdf.

Chanan, G. and Miller, C. (2013) *Rethinking Community Practice*, Bristol: Policy Press.

Cohen, S. and McDermot, M. (2016) 'When things fall apart', in O'Brien, D. and Matthews, P. (eds) *After Urban Regeneration: Communities, Policy and Place*, Bristol: Policy Press.

Collinge, C. and Hall, S. (1997) 'Hegemony and regime in urban governance', in Jewson, N. and MacGregor, S. (eds) *Transforming Cities: Contested Governance and New Spatial Divisions*, London: Routledge, pp 130–40.

Communities and Local Government (2006) *The Community Development Challenge: Together We Can*, London: Communities and Local Government Publications.

Corry, D. (2020) *Where are England's Charities?*, London: New Philanthropy Capital.

Geddes, M., with Davies, J. and Fuller, C. (2007) *Evaluating Local Strategic Partnerships: Theory and Practice of Change*, Warwick: Local Government Centre, University of Warwick. Also *Local Government Studies*, 33(1): 97–116.

Gregory, D. (2018) *Skittled Out? The Collapse and Revival of England's Social Infrastructure*, London: Locality.

Local Government Association (2020) *Building More Inclusive Economies*, London: Local Government Association.

MHCLG (Ministry of Housing, Communities and Local Government) (2020) *Planning for the Future*, London: MHCLG.

Miller, C. and Chanan, G. (2009) *Empowerment Skills for All*, Leeds: Homes and Communities Agency.

Nathan, M. (2016) 'Microsolutions for megaproblems', in O'Brien, D. and Matthews, P. (eds) *After Urban Regeneration*, Bristol: Policy Press, p 72.

NHS (National Health Service) (2019) *The NHS Long Term Plan*, London: NHS England, www.longtermplan.nhs.uk.

O'Brien, D. and Matthews, P. (eds) (2016) *After Urban Regeneration: Communities, Policy and Place*, Bristol: Policy Press.

Pearce, S. (2020) *Evaluation in Reinforcing and Resisting Hierarchical Relations between State and Civil Society*, Cardiff: Wales Centre for Social and Economic Research Data and Methods, Cardiff University.

Pogrund, G., Midolo, E. and Greenwood, G. (2020) 'Robert Jenrick overruled civil servants to push through Tory donor's £1bn housing plan', *The Sunday Times*, 28 June.

Robson, B. T., Bradford, M. G., Deas, I., Hall, E., Harrison, E., Parkinson, M., Evans, R., Harding, A., Garside, P. and Robinson (1994) *Assessing the Impact of Urban Policy*, London: HMSO.

Sendra, P. and Fitzpatrick, D. (2020) *Community-led Regeneration*, London: UCL Press.

TCPA (Town and Country Planning Association), The King's Fund, Young Foundation, PA Consulting, Public Health England and NHS England (2016) *Putting Health Into Place: Introducing NHS England's Healthy New Towns Programme*, London: TCPA, The King's Fund, Young Foundation, PA Consulting, Public Health England and NHS England.

5

Worker co-operatives and economic democracy

Pat Conaty and Philip Ross

Insecure jobs and weakened communities

The piecemeal 'gig economy' – no guaranteed work, hours or income – has become ubiquitous in Europe since the financial crisis in 2008. Casual work, temping, zero-hours contracts and diverse forms of self-employment are characteristic of an expanding marketplace of atypical, precarious and increasingly unprotected work, with a pervasive lack of legal rights. In the United Kingdom (UK), some seven million people in employment (one in five of the workforce) are in precarious forms of work – considerably more than the 5.4 million public sector jobs (Conaty et al, 2018). This has a devastating impact on many communities plagued by job insecurity and poor pay.

Under European Union regulations, temporary and agency staff are entitled as 'workers' to sickness and holiday pay, but this is not the case for self-employed freelancers. In the UK today, 4.8 million people are self-employed (15 per cent of the workforce) and they have generated two thirds of new jobs since 2008 (Conaty et al, 2018).

While a proportion of the self-employed do well financially, they are today the exception. Indeed, the stereotype of the self-employed as small businesses is less true now than ever before. Eighty-three per cent of self-employed people in the UK work alone and 70 per cent are living in poverty (Conaty et al, 2018). Their median annual income plummeted by a third from £15,000 in 2008 to about £10,000 in 2015 – below the level when income tax is payable (Conaty et al, 2016).

Low pay, however, is only part of the picture – an absence of worker rights and support services aggravates hardship and makes matters far worse. Without a regular salary, housing access is limited and rents are often extortionate.

Labour market expert, Ursula Huws (2014), estimates that up to five million people in the UK are currently being paid for work through online platforms. This is rapidly transforming the future of work. Intuit Management Consultancy forecast in 2018 that 43 per cent of the workforce in the United States (US) will be contingent on on-demand labour in a few years.[1] McKinsey forecasts that platform labour services will account for a global Gross Domestic Product (GDP) of $2.7 trillion by 2025 (Conaty et al, 2018).

Digital corporations operate to extract value at commission rates of 20 per cent or more via a 'black box' system that blocks any direct relationships between producers and consumers (Scholtz, 2017). Decision making in respect to pricing and policies is not co-determined and profits are exclusively generated for the platform owners. Command and control is the old name for this new money-making game.

Body sourcing, crowdsourced labour, liquid labour, micro-tasking and mini-jobs are all part of the new vocabulary of platform capitalism. All workers are required to be self-employed. This brave new world of 21st-century corporations is reviving the 18th-century 'putting-out system' comprehensively.

The trades impacted by the digitalisation and casualisation of labour are in both online and offline work sectors (Scholtz, 2017). In addition to Uber there is now a growing plethora of online labour-sourcing corporations, including:

- Deliveroo for takeaway food delivery;
- Taskrabbit for small jobs;
- Handy for residential cleaning;
- Clickworker for 'surveys, data management, etc';
- MyBuilder for household repairs and improvements;
- Helpling for domestic help on demand;
- Axiom for tech-assisted legal services;
- SuperCarer for social care;
- Teacherin for supply teachers; and
- Upwork for higher-skilled freelancers. (Conaty et al, 2018)

Most ambitiously, Amazon Mechanical Turk's mission is to process the sale of digital skills on a global industrial scale, like it does with books and consumer goods. The more than 500,000 workers, known as 'Turkers', operate from more than 190 countries (Scholtz, 2017). They

---

[1] See https://www.hireimage.com/wp-content/uploads/Intuit-Inc.-Intuit-Forecast_-7.pdf.

bid for jobs specified as 'human intelligence tasks' (HITs) by employers and the ruthless competition for work can drive prices down to below half the US minimum wage and, as Trebor Scholtz's research shows, there is no enforcement of any humane standard (Scholtz, 2017).

Technology is not neutral, as these examples and any cursory knowledge of history show. Who owns and most importantly controls the means of production and how this ownership and control is distributed and concentrated have a direct impact on levels of inequality. The Bank of England has shown that since 2010 the national share of income to capital has increased by 10 per cent and real wages have fallen to the lowest level since the 1860s (Haldane, 2015).

Worker empowerment

In the battle against digital economy injustice and its corrosive effects on community life, an increasing number of trade unions are adapting their thinking and their organising methods and, like the GMB in the UK and the New York Taxi Worker Alliance (NYTWA) in the US, taking class-action lawsuits in many cities and countries to secure worker and aligned social rights (Johnston and Land-Kazlauskas, 2018). The 2021 landmark victory by the App and Courier Drivers Union against Uber in the UK Supreme Court to secure Worker Rights and the national minimum wage comes after a five year battle through the courts. (Russon, 2021).

In addition to legal action campaigns, communities affected by precarious forms of work need to consider how the lopsided risks and heavy overhead costs can be collectively overcome, and replaced by fair trade terms and protective conditions. Worker co-operatives exist all over the world and, at times like these, attention is turning to the theory and practice of worker control. In New York City, both the NYTWA and the International Association of Machinists and Aerospace Workers (IAM) are organising Uber and Lyft drivers (Johnston and Land-Kazlauskas, 2018 and Sainato, 2019). The GMB is doing the same for taxi drivers in Cardiff and putting into action the proof of concept from Edinburgh where taxi co-ops working hand in glove with Unite on securing decent work have been successful for decades in protecting worker rights (Bird et al, 2020).

To consider the scope for these 'working together' strategies, it is helpful to revisit the social movements for economic democracy in the 1970s to find guidance. The recession in the wake of the OPEC oil crisis led to massive redundancies unseen since the 1930s. Trade union efforts to save jobs and find alternatives became widespread in many countries of the Organisation for Economic Co-operation and Development (OECD). The Mondragon co-operatives in Spain with roots back to the 1950s provided inspiration about the potential for federated forms of economic democracy and, in Northern Italy, worker co-ops had already been established in the building trade where they provided about 10 per cent of production (Birchall, 1997). The CMC federation of builders' co-ops of Ravenna had become the fifth largest construction federation in Italy with 2,700 worker members. Between 1975 and 1985, there were about 1,000 worker co-op rescues of firms facing closure.[2]

In the UK, the conversion of the chemical manufacturer, Scott Bader, into a co-operative commonwealth benefited from the active involvement of Fritz Schumacher, who worked on the commonwealth model in the conversion from 1951 to 1963 (Schumacher, 1973). The 'commons' building success of Scott Bader both inspired and seed-funded the emergence of the Industrial Common Ownership Movement (ICOM) in 1971 (Boyle, 1978). UK worker buy-outs during the 1970s had less longevity but the generative work by Lucas workers from many trade unions began as a defensive trade union strategy in 1971 to prevent 4,000 redundancies from a workforce of 18,000 and yielded a practical vision in 1975 when their alternative corporate plan was launched. The Lucas Shop Stewards Combine engaged their own members extensively on the idea of what non-military beneficial products they could design based on their own skills, the Lucas plant technology and the needs of their own communities (Smith, 2016). Within a year, the workers in groups designed 150 socially useful products, including kidney dialysis machines, renewable energy solutions (including heat pumps and wind turbines) and energy-saving transport innovations (including hybrid car engines and the road–rail bus) (King, 2016). They launched their Lucas Alternative Plan and advocacy for a 'human-centred technology' in 1976.

The negotiations with Lucas management rolled on and although never implemented, Shop Steward Combine's concept of 'socially useful production' aligned with the growing worker co-op, peace and environmental movements. Shop Stewards Combine built links with

---

[2] In 1985, successful joint advocacy by the Italian trade union and co-op movements secured the passage of the Marcora law – a unique law internationally that supports worker co-op buy-outs and provides enabling financing mechanisms (Conaty et al, 2018). See also https://www.ica.coop/en/media/news/marcora-law-supporting-worker-buyouts-thirty-years.

a number of polytechnics near to Lucas plants, which offered to help develop prototypes of the products and Lucas workers organised road-shows and teach-ins. Indeed, researchers and students worked with the Lucas workers to develop and test products for the Plan at North East London, Coventry and Lancashire Polytechnics and the University of Manchester Institute of Science and Technology (UMIST).

The Plan was nominated for the Nobel Prize in 1979 and attracted support and solidarity from trade unions in manufacturing and aerospace in the UK and internationally, including the Transport and General Workers' Union (TGWU), the IAM and United Auto Workers (UAW) in the US, and their counterparts in Australia, Germany and Sweden (Wainwright and Elliot, 1982). To promote the strategy to its 150 members in 70 countries, the International Metalworkers Federation produced and disseminated a report on the Lucas Plan in seven languages (Cooley, 1987). Meanwhile, the IAM produced a Workers' Technology Bill of Rights (IAM, 1984).

Work on the Plan coincided with support during the 1970s from the Labour government for the setting up of co-operative development agencies and industrial common ownership, with legislation in 1976 and 1979 to support worker co-operatives. Indeed, CECOP, the European confederation of co-operatives in industry and services, was launched in 1979 in Manchester and hosted by ICOM. This is the description of their culture-changing uniqueness by the International Co-operative Alliance (ICA): 'Worker co-operatives have the objective of creating and maintaining sustainable jobs and generating wealth, in order to improve the quality of life of worker-members, dignify human work, allow workers' democratic self-management and promote community and local development' (Smith, 2014).

CECOP has 26 member organisations across 15 European countries, which represent 50,000 enterprises employing 1.3 million workers across three main categories of industrial and service co-operatives (Whellens, 2019):

- 35,000 worker co-operatives;
- 12,000 social co-operatives in the fields of social, cultural, educational and environmental services; and
- 1,000 co-operatives of self-employed producers such as freelancers, taxi drivers, journalists, artists, artisans, graphic designers, IT workers and so on.

Since CECOP was founded in 1979, the pattern of development in European countries has been strongest in three countries with the largest clusters of labour-managed firms in 2019: Italy with 25,000, Spain with 20,000 and France with 2,000. Public policy recognition and infrastructure support (advice, education, access to finance and so on) were similarly strong in the UK for a dozen years from 1975 and by 1985 the number of worker co-operatives was more than 1,000, which had created 10,000 jobs, with a further 500 start-ups awaiting legal recognition (Osmond, 1986). The growth in the number of worker co-operatives continued over the next decade and peaked at about 2,000 and has since then fallen back to under 600 (Cockerton and Whyatt, 1986 and Co-operatives UK, 2012).

Social co-operatives were developing in the UK in the early 1990s but failed to secure infrastructure support as was won with new legislation in Italy, France and Quebec during the recession 30 years ago (Spear et al, 1994). However, advocacy for this change at the time from ICOM was strong (Conaty, 2014). Indeed, the Italian co-operative movement has pioneered the provision of social care through both worker and multi-stakeholder co-operatives (see Chapter 11). Decent work has been created for disabled people, ex-offenders and those recovering from addiction. Furthermore, 'economies of co-operation' and distributed scale have been secured through regional and national co-operative consortia that provide shared back-office services and joint negotiating teams to deliver long-term contracts.

The three main co-operative confederations in Italy have national collective bargaining agreements with the Italian trade unions who represent 60 per cent of all social and worker co-operative members (Bird et al, 2020). Legislation passed in 2003 and shaped by a social dialogue with trade unions defines the rights of a worker within a co-operative and sets out the protection afforded to employees of co-operatives and also the position of worker-owners in relation to worker co-operatives.

As we can see from this overview of worker co-operative development trends in Europe, the 'cousins of the labour movement' – trade unions and co-operatives – have the potential to unite their efforts to help communities develop decent work opportunities and enhance their economic capability (Conaty et al, 2018). Let us now look at the opportunities for the self-employed/freelance sector working hand in glove with trade unions.

New approach to self-employment

Trade union services for self-employed workers in Europe are both limited and patchy but there is a wide range of innovation seeking to meet the challenges and make the necessary breakthroughs that we will consider (Fulton, 2018). Organising has been most successful in areas of the digital economy and particularly in the media, the arts and creative industries (Conaty et al, 2016). This is the case in Denmark, Germany, the Netherlands and the UK. A typical package of trade union services for freelance workers includes advice, advocacy, legal guidance on contracts, insurance provision, help with debt collection and training.

The Federation of Entertainment Unions is the UK network of trade unions in media and covers journalists, film technicians, actors, musicians, writers and so on. A common union strategy is to secure 'worker status' for freelance members and then to negotiate worker rights.

A good example is the nine music teacher consortia co-operatives formed by the Musicians' Union across the country (Bird et al, 2020). The members of the co-operatives are all self-employed but work through the co-operative. They pay a small percentage of their hourly fee to cover admin costs and support services, which include invoicing, debt control, dispute mediation, timetabling and other services. The Musicians' Union has a good reputation among members for pursing late payments and resolving disputes with clients. As an example, the Swindon Music Co-operative has 50+ members who deliver 1,300 lessons a week to 74 schools and colleges.[3]

What can be done to help more community-minded, democratically owned and controlled enterprises to set up and grow? There will be those who, out of principle, choose a co-operative or democratic business model and are willing to persevere. We need to encourage and support this constituency of co-operatives, but we also need to reach out to others who may not be thinking about adopting a co-operative model out of conviction.

There are many co-operatives of farmers and taxi drivers in France, Italy and Spain. The workers tend to be individuals and small businesses who work for themselves but come together through a local co-operative to find markets, negotiate contracts and manage their administration – and much more besides.

---

[3] See information on the Swindon Music Teachers Co-op at https://swindonmusiccoop. co.uk. Actors' co-ops have expanded to 30 in England and Wales. Through their Co-operative Personal Management Association (CPMA), they work closely with Equity, the actor's union (Bird, 2020).

If being in the co-operative helps you find a market for your goods and services, reduces your costs and raises capital, it would make a lot of sense to join it. Crucially, the decision is not to form a co-op, but to form a business and for that business to join the co-op. Detractors would say that there is a big difference between growing and selling lemons in Andalucía and selling IT services in London, video editing in Manchester and making wallpaper in Wolverhampton. But they would be wrong. The principles of co-operation and collaboration remain both true and relevant. The workers may not be sharing lemon presses or tractors but there are other services to share and there is the opportunity to reuse infrastructure. This infrastructure can predominately be virtual. Today, technology is used to find work/get business, manage contracts, process payments and manage business in the long term. Co-ops work for the lemon pressers because they help find a market for their goods and help them to reduce their costs.

Technology for co-operation

In *Co-operation in the Age of Google*, Robin Murray (2012) indicated in 2012 that the smartphone revolution was massively changing the economic landscape locally and globally, and could open the opportunity to unleash co-operative economy and common ownership solutions. He cited the growing sharing and collaborative economy and noted the success of Linux, Wikipedia and other collaborative projects.

The world of work has continued to change since then. There has been a huge growth in the number of self-employed people in the UK, to more than five million workers, who contributed more than £305 billion (14.8 per cent) to the national economy in 2019 (IPSE, 2018). The self-employed are working in every economic sector (see Figure 5.1).

Many of the self-employed are supplying services for larger firms. These large firms tend to contract out projects and distinct services. Opportunities for commerce are likely to be in the provision of services and labour to larger clients, or to intermediate supply services to these larger clients.

The product that is being provided is often knowledge based and is in terms of services that can be offered. It can make sense for ten bakers to come together to form a workers' co-operative to bake and sell bread. But for ten software developers, with different levels of experience and expertise, they may be selling consultancy and they may or may not all be working, or may be all working for different clients. It would make sense for them to form a consortia co-operative (like the lemon farmers) to help them. If the developers all produced

Figure 5.1: Self-employment/one-person businesses by industry type

The solo self-employed are present in all major industry groups

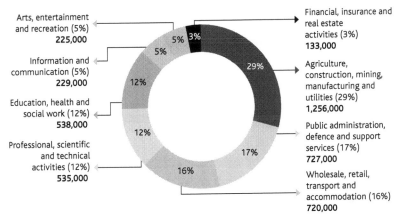

Arts, entertainment and recreation (5%)
225,000

Information and communication (5%)
229,000

Education, health and social work (12%)
538,000

Professional, scientific and technical activities (12%)
535,000

Financial, insurance and real estate activities (3%)
133,000

Agriculture, construction, mining, manufacturing and utilities (29%)
1,256,000

Public administration, defence and support services (17%)
727,000

Wholesale, retail, transport and accommodation (16%)
720,000

Note : Percentages do not sum to 100% due to rounding

Source: IPSE (2018)

a single product and sold it or could all work consistently on the same project, it would make sense too.

Smart and Green Taxis

In Belgium and France, integrated services for self-employed workers are provided through business and employment co-operatives. A fast-growing one is Smart in Belgium, which specialises in providing workspace, back-office services, insurance, debt collection and income liquidity for freelancers. Guidance and training are provided by a specialist advice and legal team. Smart members pay €25 a year plus 6.5 per cent for each invoice processed (Bird et al, 2020) and the co-op guarantees payment to members within seven days. The co-operative additionally provides access to finance, equipment and vehicles. It supports 97,000 freelance workers in cities and towns across Belgium, a further 22,000 in France and supports Smart co-ops in seven other countries in Europe with a further 20,000 freelancers.

Another good example from the US showing how trade unions can support co-ops to co-develop the technology is Green Taxis in Colorado. Since its launch as a co-op in Denver in 2012, it has expanded its membership in partnership with the Communication Workers of America. This union co-op strategy has led to the development of a super-efficient mobile app (Bird et al, 2020). Through the partnership,

Green Taxis has grown to 800 members, secured 37 per cent of the regulated cab market in Denver and has rapidly become the largest taxi co-op in the US.

It is the transformative share of the economic pie that highlights how re-purposing the technology can unleash economic democracy once the message gets out. For example, before Green Taxis was founded as a worker co-op, most drivers were working for private taxi corporations and paying leasing and other fees to the company of $800 to $1,200 a week (Conaty et al, 2017). With the help of the trade union, Green Taxi members have co-financed their mobile app and now pay just $80 a week for back-office and dispatch services. This represents a 90 per cent plus savings of economic rent otherwise payable to a private corporation. The success of Green Taxis highlights how worker-owned platforms can be replicated and has been taken up and supported by other unions from Madison, Wisconsin to New York and elsewhere (Conaty et al, 2018).

WorkerTech

The solution underpinning the services offered by Smart and Green Taxis is technology owned and controlled by co-op members who empower these organisations at scale to deliver top-class services to their members and in turn to their clients.

Technology needs to be reusable and cost effective. Many agile bespoke technology solutions have emerged over recent years. Indeed, the growth in the financial industry has been fuelled by curating the technical software products that are already there. It is called Fintech and is about technology-enabled financial innovation. It is building products using payment engines, banking products and wealth management software from different sources. What previously required millions of pounds of investment in software is no longer needed.[4]

There are positive lessons to be learnt here. Imagine if there was a movement within commerce that has in its DNA both the willingness to share and co-operate and a set of tangible shared values. With the growth in technology now the cornerstone of every business, it is there. It is the co-operative movement. It is Co-opTech or WorkerTech.

Increasingly, we need the ability to come together in a flash to collaborate, to bid for work and to deliver projects. Just as film companies

---

[4] As such, we have seen the emergence of challenger banks such as Metro and Revolut, and new regional co-op banks are under development in Wales and regions of England (see, for example, https://www.csba.co.uk).

create a time-limited company for the lifetime of a project, we need to be able to flash up a viable co-op with infrastructure, move forward and then wind it up when the project is completed.

The growth of internet platforms such as eBay and Amazon occurred because they addressed risk and trust. In those retail operations, market disruption was unleashed because consumers trusted Amazon with their credit card details and thus assured by both corporations involved (the credit card provider and Amazon) they did not need to worry about the reputation of any particular retailer.

For firms coming together, or workers coming together to form a co-op, there is a need to trust each other. Governance models are needed that can be trusted. The co-operative and other democratic models have an opportunity here. WorkerTech combined with a trusted governance model can help, but how?

Workplace democracy and union co-ops

There is not a one-size-fits-all solution. Worker co-ops will not fit into every solution, but variations of the ICA and CECOP co-op model will. *Don't mourn, organise*, is the solidarity spirit needed for the co-operative and trade union movements to come together to listen and learn from each other on appropriate ways forward (Bird et al, 2020).

If workplace democracy movements providing aligned services organise themselves into co-operatives (like the musicians' co-operative cited earlier), then the driving force in organising is not so much to give them a stake in the co-operative, but to give them bargaining power with their prospective and active clients. This, of course, represents a huge challenge to the trade union movement, which has been designed to represent workers to their employers. But in such a situation we need to rethink who the employers/workers are and what support is really needed.

Today's reality is that workers are often working as self-employed (maybe through a co-op or their own small business), possibly through an agency, to an end-client who may even be serving an ultimate end-client who could be in a tax haven. It is a complicated relationship.[5] For these workers, what matters most are their rights

---

[5] Ironically, for tax purposes, HM Revenue & Customs (HMRC) is trying to look through these complex relationships in order to suggest that a freelancer is effectively an employee of the ultimate end-client and that the final fee paid to the freelancer should be taxed at source as if they were an employee. Unfortunately, the same criteria are not being applied to employment rights, which could mean that workers are taxed as employees but have no employment rights.

to be paid on time, to a proper contract, to be treated fairly and to safely reject doing certain work without undue repercussions. One of the traditional goals of the trade union was to provide dignity at work. That goal remains true but needs to be applied on behalf of the self-employed and indeed claimed by 'knowing your rights'. Here is where joint trade union and worker co-operative organising and aligned worker education come into the picture.[6] Fundamentally, the self-employed need to survive and thrive as economic agents of their communities.

Smart, for example, brought together the physical infrastructure that is their office and factory buildings near the centre of Brussels alongside the invisible infrastructure of providing services to the freelancers who have joined it. The freelancers like those with the musicians' co-operatives are technically self-employed. Yet what they get is not just business services to members, such as invoicing and contract management, but also a scheme that interfaces with the benefits system, as well as longer-term support and education for their members' careers as independent workers. These are less like services offered to clients by a business and more like mutual-aid help offered to members of a trade union.

Twenty per cent of Smart members are actively billing all the time and 80 per cent come and go on contracts. But together they have a business turnover of more than €204 million in Belgium and France, with co-op services in seven other countries and 40 European cities as well (Bird, 2020).

But it goes beyond this. Smart empowers self-employed workers not just to work together or pass work between each other, but also to be able to form project teams and take on larger pieces of work. The structure of the social security system in Belgium has a mutuality history and this means that freelance workers can interface effectively with the welfare system and via Smart can claim benefits in between work. They can do this because the co-operative services transform self-employed workers into salaried workers.

Because Smart is large enough, organisations that build up a history of being late or poor invoice payers will effectively find themselves blacklisted as too bad a credit risk, until they pay and then are welcomed back if appropriate. Also with 32,000 self-employed full members and

---

[6] For an excellent account of the five categories of human rights and how they apply here and are not being adhered to or enforced by the UK government, see Hunt (2017).

300 worker members providing back-office services, it is regarded as a large co-operative employer and thus has a strong voice with government. Contrast that with the UK and five million isolated self-employed workers.

Thus, Smart is not just a collection of individuals using a platform, but a hub-and-spokes worker co-op commonweal, a cohesive force that helps to create a sense of place and bargaining power for the self-employed.

This is the key point. All the services being offered to an individual could be purchased individually or provided by an employment agency that engages and sells them on. The difference is that when these services are provided by an agency or similar, they are provided during a single transaction – or as a gig-based occurrence. While the worker is providing services via the agency (and in doing so is earning them revenue), these services are provided. When work ceases, the services tend to cease. Working via a co-op such as Smart, these services are there because you are a member and continue on.

Community wealth building, union co-ops and co-operative education

An international review of the evidence has demonstrated that worker co-ops grow at comparable rates to other conventional businesses, survive longer as start-ups, are larger by comparison to their counterparts in different categories, are more agile and are more resilient (Perotin, 2016). This analysis confirms CECOP data (Whellens, 2019) that in France, Italy and Spain, the policy recognition of the social and economic benefits of worker co-ops and the appropriate infrastructure support have been facilitating (CECOP, 2020). Internationally, social justice movements are recognising the joint organising potential.

The 'union co-ops' concept has been co-developed under a joint agreement between the United Steelworkers in the US and Mondragon International, which since 2015 has been advanced by the '1worker1vote' movement, which serves as the formal continuation of this collaboration. Today, union co-ops are being set up in a range of industries and cities in the US, from New York to Los Angeles, with a growing range of trade union sponsors. In Cincinnati, Ohio, five union co-ops, either established or under development, include a food hub (Our Harvest), an energy services co-op (SustainEnergy), a childcare co-op, an affordable housing agency, and a worker- and community-owned supermarket (Apple Street Market).[7]

It is early days, but informed by Green Taxis, union co-op apps for childminders are being jointly developed in Illinois by the ICA Group and Service Employees International Union (SEIU). The targeted savings for worker members are $800 to $1,200 annually through the union co-op (Bird et al, 2020). A new Nursing and Caregivers Co-operative has been registered in Oakland, California by SEIU and the ICA, which builds on the success of the SEIU-affiliated Co-operative Home Care Associates in Brooklyn, New York, with 2,000 workers – the largest worker co-op in the US.

To build on their success more widely, SEIU has developed draft legislation with worker co-operative specialists in California – the Cooperative Economy Bill – which creates and incentivises a new form of labour market intermediary, the co-operative labour contractor (CLC). Designed to employ workers, including those who were misclassified as independent contractors, CLCs create a new employment paradigm where workers not only receive employment protections, but also own and govern their workplaces and have access to collective bargaining through a labour union. To develop and support CLCs, the bill creates a Federation of Cooperative Labor Contractors (the 'Federation').[8] The Federation is a membership organisation for CLCs, organised as a non-profit mutual benefit corporation. Its purpose is to establish new CLCs, to oversee CLC compliance with democratic governance standards and to establish CLCs' labour policy.[9]

In the UK, an emerging Co-operative University Project and Federation will seek to address and negate a deficit in appropriate and relevant co-operative learning at all levels (Noble and Ross, 2019). It proposes instead a radical and co-operative focus on the capabilities and social activism needed for new co-operative times. With ideas rooted in alternative governance, ownership and control, and knowledge making, a future co-operative educational initiative of this kind, about association as well as entrepreneurship, will significantly strengthen the

---

[7] More examples in other US cities can be seen on the Union Co-ops Council's website at http://unioncoops.org and at www.1worker1vote.org.

[8] In addition to supporting workers, the legislation also creates clarity for companies that contract with CLCs, including companies that formerly used large workforces of independent contractors.

[9] See https://www.shareable.net/how-domestic-workers-built-americas-first-co-op-franchise.

co-operative ecosystem. Co-operation is consolidating internationally with the Mondragon University, the Co-operative University and work on the union co-op. As part of this international co-operation, the co-operative movement on both sides of the Atlantic could build its own standards around WorkerTech and the interoperability of technology. There is an opportunity, with good stewardship, as Robin Murray (2012) suggested, for the co-op movement to provide leadership in the development of democratically controlled technology and the interoperability of technology, which would be available to those using the co-operative model. Ultimately, it will mean that software developed by the co-operative movement can all be plugged together because it has all been built following an agreed set of standards and protocols. It creates a market for such software.

There is already a thriving community of Worker Co-operative Council members focusing strategically on harnessing open co-operative thinking and innovation. In the UK, there is an Open Co-op network and also Co-Tech. Co-Tech is a co-operative consortium that unites 45 worker co-operatives that provide technology, digital and creative services. Each co-op is owned and democratically run by its workers and in some cases also its service users.

The success of Green Taxis highlights how worker-owned platforms can be replicated in other cities and for other trades. Both online and offline economic democracy solutions offer potential for the reach and impact of joint organising. Bearing in mind the IAM coined the term 'workers' technology' in 1984 (IAM, 1984), the union co-op work in US cities that is making breakthroughs offline and online, could through 'common ownership and control' of the technology, unite a number of aligned social movements for decent work and fair trade.

Consider these breakthroughs, noted by the International Labour Organization (ILO), as a big piece of the jigsaw (Johnston and Land-Kazlauskas, 2018 and Monaco and Pastorelli, 2013). Using a guild organising strategy, the IAM has sponsored the Independent Drivers Guild (IDG), which through grassroots organisers gives voice and collective advocacy for 120,000 'gig economy' drivers in New York State. This joint organising methodology shows the potential to get a seat at the table with global corporations such as Uber and Lyft and has secured the first minimum pay rate protection for app-based drivers in New York City. With a 2018 report revealing that the median wage for Uber drivers after expenses and fees was $9.21 an hour, the IAM and IDG landmark win to secure $27.86 per hour has put more than $1 billion in drivers' pockets (Independent Drivers Guild, 2019).

Worker co-ops and economic democracy – back to the future?

Public policy makers and government at all levels need to learn to be far more supportive, particularly by recognising that worker co-operatives are culturally distinct from other businesses as they are both owned *and* controlled by their workforce (Yeo, 2001). Where this unique autonomous identity based on self-help and mutual aid is understood and respected, worker co-operatives can achieve the social, economic and community strengthening benefits that has been evidenced.[10] However, for worker co-operatives to succeed, an equitable system of support is vital, as the Perotin international review (Perotin, 2016), CECOP data for France, Italy and Spain highlight (CECOP, 2020 and Whellens, 2019).[11]

Going forward, the following four elements should feature in strategies to support worker co-operatives and advance economic democracy so that tomorrow's communities can have a better chance of attaining equitable, thriving and sustainable socioeconomic conditions (Conaty, 2019):

- Form a collaborative partnership with local authorities to establish an ecosystem of development support for worker co-operatives, including advice and legal and technical assistance provided by seasoned practitioners.
- Extend and adapt the successful examples and best practices of union co-op solutions highlighted in other sectors [such as supply teachers, creative industries, journalism, social care, construction and others in Figure 5.1], while harnessing and democratising technology in agile ways to support new modes of working, as innovation from the IAM and SEIU is demonstrating.
- Utilise Open Co-op organising methodologies to respond practically and strategically to the scale of precarious work challenges. Harness broad-based organising by aligning the common values of the co-operative movement, unions, community groups and

---

[10] The *Working Together* report (Conaty et al, 2018) sets out nine recommendations for supporting the growth of worker co-ops (see https://www.uk.coop/newsroom/working-together-push-back-co-ops-and-trade-unions-starts-here).

[11] For a helpful summary of the benefits of worker co-operatives with reference to a wide range of reviews, see Amanda Silver, Organizing Complexity, 2019

democracy campaigners to unleash the ethos and untapped potential of economic democracy.

- Carry out joint work with community development finance providers, credit unions and the co-operative movement to design appropriate co-operative development finance tools and draw on best practices internationally.

Acknowledgements

The authors would like to acknowledge the expert help for this chapter from members of the Union Co-ops UK collective and in particular the input and guidance from Cilla Ross at the Co-operative College, Mick McKeown at the Preston Co-op Development Network, Alex Bird at the Consultancy Co-op in Wales and Anita Mangan at the University of Bristol. We would further like to thank, for their specialist guidance and expertise, both Michael Peck at 1worker1vote and Ra Criscitiello of SEIU-UHWW in the US as well as Colm Massey at the Solidarity Economy Association in the UK.

References

Birchall, J. (1997) *The International Co-operative Movement*, Manchester: Manchester University Press.

Bird, A. (2020) 'Self-organising the self-employed', speech and presentation made on SmartB at the Labour Party conference, 21 September 2020.

Bird, A., Conaty, P., McKeown, M., Mangan, A., Ross, C. and Taylor, S. (2020) *Union Co-ops UK: A Manifesto for Decent Work*, London: Union Co-ops UK.

Boyle, G. (1978) *Community Technology: Control of Technology*, Milton Keynes: The Open University.

CECOP (2020) *All for One - Response of worker-owned cooperatives to non-standard employment*, Brussels, CECOP.

Cockerton, P. and Whyatt, A. (1986) *The Workers Co-operative Handbook*, London: ICOM.

Conaty, P. (2014) *Social Co-operatives: A Democratic Co-production Agenda for Care Services in the UK*, Manchester: Co-operatives UK.

Conaty, P. (2019) 'Developing public co-operative partnerships' in Tam, H. (ed) *Whose Government is it? The Renewal of State–Citizen Co-operation*, Bristol: Bristol University Press.

Conaty, P., Bird, A. and Ross, P. (2016) *Trade Union and Co-operative Solutions for Self-employed Workers*, Manchester: Co-operatives UK, Wales Co-operative Centre and Unity Trust Bank.

Conaty, P., Bird, A. and Ross, C. (2017) *Organising Precarious Workers*, London: Trades Union Congress.

Conaty, P., Bird, A. and Ross, C. (2018) *Working Together: Trade Union and Co-operative Innovations for Precarious Work*, Manchester: Co-operatives UK and the Co-operative College.

Co-operatives UK (2012) *The Worker Co-operative Code*, Manchester: Worker Co-operative Council.

Cooley, M. (1987) *Architect or Bee?: The Human Price of Technology*, New York: Vintage.

Fulton, L. (2018) *Trade Unions Protecting Self-employed Workers*, Brussels: European Trade Union Confederation.

Haldane, A. (2015) 'Labour's share', speech of the Bank of England chief economist to the TUC, 12 November.

Hunt, P. (2017) *Social Rights are Human Rights: But the UK System is Rigged*, Sheffield: The Centre for Welfare Reform.

Huws, U. (2014) *Labor in the Global Digital Economy: The Cybertariat Comes of Age*, New York: Monthly Review Press.

Independent Drivers Guild (2019) 'New York Uber, Lyft drivers call for right to bargain legislation at NY state assembly hearing today', press release, 5 December.

International Association of Machinists (1984) *Workers' Technology Bill of Rights*, Upper Marlboro: International Association of Machinists.

IPSE (2018) *Exploring the Rise of Self-employment in the Modern Economy*, London: IPSE, https://www.ipse.co.uk/resource/exploring-the-rise-of-self-employment-in-the-modern-economy-pdf.html.

Johnston, H. and Land-Kazlauskas, C. (2018) *Organising Gig Economy Workers*, Conditions of Work and Employment Series No. 94, Geneva: International Labour Organisation.

King, D. (2017) 'The Lucas Plan and the politics of technology', *People and Nature*, 26 October.

Monaco, M. and Pastorelli, L. (2013) 'Trade unions and worker co-operatives in Europe: a win–win relationship', *International Journal of Labour Research*, 5(2): 227–50.

Murray, R. (2012) *Co-operation in the Age of Google*, Manchester: Co-operatives UK.

Noble, M. and Ross, C. (2019) 'Now is the time for reforming co-operative higher education', in Noble, M. and Ross, C. (eds) *Reclaiming the University for the Public Good: Experiments and Futures in Co-operative Higher Education*, Basingstoke: Palgrave.

Osmond, J. (1986) *Work in the Future: Alternatives to Unemployment*, London: Thorsons Publishing.

Perotin, V. (2016) *What Do We Really Know about Worker Co-operatives?*, Manchester: Co-operatives UK.

Russon, M. A. (2021) 'Uber drivers are workers not self-employed, Supreme Court rules', *BBC News*, 19 February.

Sainato, M. (2019) '"I made $3.75 an hour": Lyft and Uber drivers push to unionise for better pay', *The Guardian*, 22 March.

Schumacher, E. F. (1973) *Small is Beautiful*, New York: Vintage.

Silver, A. (2019) 'Organizing Complexity: The Path to Ownership through Worker Cooperatives', The Startup Medium, 24 June 2019.

Smith, A. (2016) 'The Lucas Plan: what can it tell us about democratising technology today?', *The Guardian*, 22 January.

Smith, S. (2014) *Promoting Co-operatives: An Information Guide to ILO Recommendation No. 193*, Geneva: International Labour Organisation.

Spear, R., Leonetti, A. and Thomas, A. (1994) *Third Sector Care: Prospects for Co-operative and other small care providers,* Co-operative Research Unit, The Open University.

Wainwright, H. and Elliott, D. (1982) *The Lucas Plan: A New Trade Unionism in the Making?*, London: Allison and Busby.

Whellens, S. (2019) *Report to Worker Coop Solidarity Fund to CECOP-CICOPA Europe*, September 2019.

Yeo, S. (2001) 'The new mutualism and Labour's Third Way', in Birchall, J. (ed) *The New Mutualism in Public Policy*, Abingdon: Routledge.

PART B

Transforming collaborative behaviour with communities

6

Four factors for better community collaboration

Steve Wyler

Impediments to collaboration

Why is it so difficult for those who work in formal institutions (national, regional or local), and those who operate at the community level, to find common cause and to build effective alliances? The benefits of doing so seem obvious. Working in isolation only gets you so far. As the proverb says: 'If you want to go quickly, go alone. If you want to go far, go together.'

Cross-agency and cross-sector collaboration has long been promoted by government, policy makers and funding bodies, to overcome fragmentation or duplication of effort, to reduce costs, to achieve regeneration of deprived communities and, more recently, as a means to bring about the systems change needed to tackle complex problems, notably those associated with multiple disadvantage (Kail and Abercrombie, 2013; Kippin and Billiald, 2015; Helgerson and Price, 2017; Knight et al, 2017; Becker and Smith, 2018; Lowe and Plimmer, 2019).

But all forms of partnership are difficult. 'Don't do it unless you have to!' (Huxham and Vangen, 2005) is advice that will resonate with many. It is hard enough to build effective and lasting collaboration among public sector agencies, or even departments within a single institution (Miles and Trott, 2011). And collaborative efforts among charities and community groups are often equally fraught with difficulty, even when they operate in close proximity, and would seem, on the face of it, to have much in common (Baker and Cairns, 2011; Broomhead et al, 2016; Wyler and Adjaye, 2018).

Yet, perhaps most difficult of all, it seems, are the attempts to build collaboration between those who operate at the community level – at the grassroots, on the front line – working often informally and horizontally, and those who operate from above, often vertically, in formal institutions, notably in the public sector but also in universities, larger charities and housing associations, for example (Balloch and Taylor, 2001; Cairns and Harris, 2010; Rees et al, 2012).

And yet, it is this type of collaboration, the intersection of those operating from below and those operating from above, which may matter most of all if, as has been suggested, it is 'the diagonal fault line through which a new society can and must be born' (Lawson, 2019) (see Chapter 8). Collaborative efforts are usually prompted by the best intentions, but they often fail, whether initiated from above or below. Those led from above can be met with adversarial behaviours or unrealistic expectations from below, while those led from below can find themselves patronised and sidelined by those from above.

Trust, it seems, can be extraordinarily difficult to accomplish, even when, as is so often the case, many of the individuals involved themselves have multi-level roles (for example, the school teacher who is a member of a community association, the board member of a small charity who is also a ward councillor or the parent of a disabled child who is a manager in a local health service).

Various reasons have been advanced for these difficulties. Some commentators have pointed to lack of capacity, especially in the most deprived communities, citing the time, funding and material resources required to build relationships and maintain partnership activities. It is often suggested by those operating from above that failure to achieve successful collaboration is produced by a lack of skills below, and an overdependence on a few individuals, sometimes derided as 'the usual suspects' if they prove unamenable (University of Cambridge, 2019; Cairns and Harris, 2010). Those working from above will experience frustration at what they see (sometimes correctly) as the disorganised and unconstructive behaviour of community activists. On the other hand, those working at the community level will resent what they perceive (also sometimes correctly) as the arrogance of professionals who believe they know best.

However, these types of difficulties, while certainly significant to those who experience them, can be regarded as of a secondary order. The underlying and primary difficulties can be identified as the following: incompatibility of purpose, imbalance in power, exclusionary practice and weak infrastructure.[1]

---

[1] A similar analysis has been proposed by the Lankelly Chase Foundation, which has examined how systems support or fail people facing severe and multiple disadvantage. It has concluded that behaviours that share perspectives, share power and encourage

Incompatibility of purpose

Purpose for communities (especially those characterised as deprived) can look very different when seen from above and from below:

- From above, the tendency is to see the primary goals as tackling defined problems (such as crime, low productivity, poor health or low educational attainment) and achieving standardisation (reducing deviation from a regional or national norm).
- From below, a different set of desired outcomes is likely to emerge. These are usually driven in the first instance by first-hand local knowledge, of antisocial behaviour or the plight of isolated older people, for example. But over time, a different type of outcome can emerge, for example building resilience, solidarity and self-sufficiency – in short, 'building community'. These are more likely to be based on an appreciation of strengths within a particular community, of its complexity and diversity, and of its difference and distinctiveness compared with other communities.

These differences in purpose generate profound underlying tensions and often prove incompatible. As a result, many attempts to build local collaboration are built on the shakiest of foundations.

Imbalance of power

The problem is exacerbated by an imbalance of power. It is true that power to bring about change is not confined to one section of society, and that even those who are regarded as powerless can in certain conditions discover their own latent power, organise with others like themselves and challenge the status quo. However, in almost all places, funding, policy decisions, systems design and public amenities are overwhelmingly in the hands of those operating from above, whether that is central government, local government, health services and other statutory agencies, large companies, universities and colleges, housing associations, larger charities, religious institutions and so on.

As a result of this imbalance of power, the identification of purpose as established from above becomes a driving force, corralling all into a direction already decided on. Various mechanisms are deployed to

---

participation are more likely to produce positive results, and need to be present and continually promoted in every part of the system (Lankelly Chase Foundation, 2018).

reinforce this dominance, not least the apparatus of commissioning and procurement, whereby the deployment of funding is used to ensure that on-the-ground community efforts are brought into line with the goals of institutional funders.

No wonder, then, that so many exercises in engagement, consultation and (in the more recent terminology) co-design and co-production are experienced by so many as fraudulent.

Exclusionary practice

There may be an assumption, explicit or implicit, that the benefits of the collaborative enterprise will be for all those in a community, across boundaries of class, gender, age, ethnicity, sexuality and so on. But, in practice, if embedded structures of inequality are not recognised and addressed, that will not be the case. Collaborative efforts too often degenerate into a chaotic and divisive scramble for money, resources and influence, pushing others aside in the process.

Most forms of collaboration take the form of programmatic interventions, led by professional elites. When the tendency of those operating from above to standardise services and categorise people becomes the dominant pattern in the design and delivery of local programmes, they fail to deal with the endless variety and complexity of people and of communities. Typically, the response to such failure is to designate the people themselves as the problem, or as 'hard to reach', and this might include, for example, young people, older people, people from Black, Asian and minority ethnic communities, migrants and refugees. And so programmes that are intended to benefit people across a community, and which are presented as collaborative efforts, may end up perpetuating divisions within the community, reducing participation, reinforcing a prevailing sense of 'them and us' and drawing a line even more firmly between those who 'do' and those who are 'done to'.

Weak infrastructure

Considerable effort is frequently devoted to the 'governance' of local partnerships, and attempts are made to achieve a spread of representation on partnership boards, to allocate decision-making powers, to avoid conflicts of interest, to establish risk management registers and so forth. These can give the appearance of a well-managed partnership and even a semblance of balance between 'above' and 'below'.

But all too often, the appearance belies the reality. This is usually because too little attention is paid to establishing effective and lasting forms of local infrastructure capable of building community capacity and of addressing the tensions produced by differences in purpose, imbalances in power, and exclusionary and divisive practices.

Examples of place-based collaboration

Over the past two decades, there have been numerous attempts in the United Kingdom (UK) to foster place-based collaboration, bringing together those operating above and below in a common cause (see Chapter 4). In some cases, funding from central government or elsewhere has been deployed to stimulate activity across the country. So, what can we learn from that experience?

Who gets to set the purpose? Examples

Where large-scale resources were deployed, programme design was predominantly from above. For example, the Single Regeneration Budget (SRB) programme, which was launched in 1994, allocated £5.7 billion over six funding rounds, to 1,028 schemes.[2] The headline purpose was established by national government, and this was to meet a variety of goals, for example 'to enhance the employment prospects, education and skills of local people, particularly the young and those at a disadvantage, and promote equality of opportunity' (Rhodes et al, 2007). The New Deal for Communities (NDC) programme was launched in 1998 and operated in 39 neighbourhoods, each with a population of about 10,000 people, and in each case around £50 million of national funding was deployed over a period of ten years. Again the purpose was set by national government, to 'close the gaps' between these 39 areas and the rest of the country in respect of crime, community, housing and the physical environment (HPE), education, health and worklessness (Batty et al, 2010).

In contrast, where programmes allowed purpose to be defined largely from below, by local residents and those operating at the front line of neighbourhood activity, the level of funding was much lower, and

---

[2] In addition to central government's allocation, the scheme brought in funding from other sources such as local authorities, European funds, and voluntary and private sectors. The overall spend was around £26 billion.

often only available for a short duration. For example, the Our Place programme, launched in 2014, was intended to allow local people to 'design and deliver local services that focus on local priorities and reduce costs' (MHCLG, 2014). Purpose was to be established locally and (in theory at least) this was to be a shared task among a mix of local actors. But the resources available to local areas were modest in the extreme: grants of between £13,000 and £33,000. Furthermore, the duration of support was very short: one year only, with no follow-through funding or support. Despite this, enthusiasm to join this programme was high, and there were 280 applications in the first round (Hayden et al, 2016).

Big Local was one of the very few national programmes to allocate significant funding, over a long period, and allow community-led design. Between 2010 and 2012, the National Lottery Community Fund identified 150 areas that had historically missed out on Lottery and other funding. Each of those areas was allocated £1 million of Big Local funding to be spent over ten to 15 years. A new national charity, Local Trust, was set up to manage the programme.

In this case, purpose was not set by the National Lottery Community Fund nor by Local Trust, other than some very broad-based outcomes (for example, 'The community will make a difference to the needs it prioritises'). Rather, purpose would be determined locally by residents in each neighbourhood, who would organise themselves into a Big Local partnership to agree themes to be addressed, draw up a local Plan and decide projects to be funded. In practice, a very wide variety of goals have been set, for example: reducing poverty, working better with local agencies, increasing employment rates, increasing confidence, providing community spaces, engaging more residents, improving health and wellbeing, increasing skills, improving the physical environment and engaging young people. Often the goals are revised substantially over time, in the light of experience (Street, 2020).

How is power shared? Examples

In most cases, such as the NDC programme, the local authority was nearly always firmly in the driving seat. Claims were often made that the community was 'at the heart of' the initiative, but community involvement in design and decision making was usually restricted to a few 'community representatives' appointed to partnership boards or committees. In the case of the SRB programme, only 31 (3 per cent) of the partnerships were led by community organisations. The prevailing view was that 'local people did not always possess the knowledge, skills and administrative resources to be effective partners and/or lead on regeneration'. However, it was also noted that budgets for capacity building were small and 'in any event lead partners/accountable bodies tended to retain this element of the funding' (Rhodes et al, 2007).

A very different picture was presented by the Our Place programme, where, of the 141 local areas that were approved to join the first wave, 79 were led by voluntary or community sector agencies, 38 by local authorities, 18 by parish or town councils and six by others. Local areas had considerable freedom to define their own goals, and the only requirement was that in doing so they should find ways to engage local residents as much as possible. Various techniques were used for this, including door-knocking by community organisers, local surveys, community discussion events and focus groups with residents (Hayden et al, 2016).

Local Trust requires that more than half of the members of each Big Local partnership must be local residents who do not represent any other organisation. So the local authority or other local institutions can participate in decisions made by the partnership but they cannot dominate them. In order to administer the funds, a locally trusted organisation is selected by the partnership but this has no role in decision making.

However, those initiatives that are predominantly led from below have often struggled to achieve wider policy or systems change. Furthermore, the evidence suggests that the Big Local partnerships have found it difficult to influence local institutions such as the local council, and where they have had some success in that, it is often at the operational level and dependent on personal relationships (Terry, 2020).

How effective is the involvement? Examples

The experience of partnership in the traditional top-down large-scale regeneration programmes was often poor. The SRB evaluation (Rhodes et al, 2007) noted that 'it is better to avoid "arranged marriages" in partnership formation' but this was often the case. In the worst instances, partnerships were little more than 'the temporary suppression of mutual loathing in the interests of mutual greed' (Headlam and Rowe, 2014). Organisational self-interest predominated over social goals, and the 'gaming' of targets to produce the appearance of success and to draw down the money was widespread (Hood, 2006).

Despite the gaming, the published outcomes were often disappointing, even when the investment was considerable. At the end of the NDC programme, its supporters were able to claim that it broadly achieved its 'closing the gap' goals: the gap between the NDC areas and the national average was reduced in 18 of the 24 indicators where comparisons were possible. However, when the NDC areas were compared with comparatively deprived areas that did not receive the large-scale investment, the results were disappointing. In that comparison, while there were some health and crime benefits, there was no positive change in relation to worklessness, and the gap worsened rather than improved in terms of educational attainment (Batty et al, 2010).

Moreover, the wider community benefits were limited. In the NDC programme, those few individuals who were appointed as community representatives may have derived some benefits, but the number of people who felt they could influence local decisions actually fell compared with the national average, as did the number of people who felt that they were living in a place where neighbours look out for each other. Evaluation of the programme also noted 'intra-community strife, perhaps fuelled by a sense that some parts of NDC areas receive more than others' (Batty et al, 2010).

Where programmes had a greater degree of community leadership, there is evidence of more inclusive practice, engaging more people across the whole community. Even in those cases, there were shortcomings. For example, while Big Local is resident-led as we have seen, the residents acting as partnership members tend to be those who are older and better educated (Terry, 2020). Moreover, only 27 per cent of workers employed on the Big Local programme are also residents in the area that they work in (Terry and Fisher, 2020).

In some cases, certain groups of residents may be consciously or unconsciously excluded by those in community leadership roles, with transient communities seen as 'hard to engage', and migrants demonised as 'other', in contrast to a settled community that sees itself as under threat (Fancourt and Usher, 2019). However, the evidence from Big Local also suggests that there are many cases of creative, interesting ways in which partnerships are drawing in the wider community (Terry, 2020).

Where is the supportive infrastructure? Examples

It has long been obvious that some form of local infrastructure is necessary to achieve effective and sustained above-and-below collaboration. For example, in 2001, the government launched the Neighbourhood Management Pathfinder Programme to 'enable deprived communities and local services to improve local outcomes, by improving and joining up local services, and making them more responsive to local needs' (SEU, 2000), This operated in 35 places, with a combined budget of £100 million. In each case, a small professional team was led by a neighbourhood manager, usually employed by the local authority, with oversight from a multi-agency board, including local residents (SQW Consulting, 2008). A review in 2018 of neighbourhood management in 36 local authority areas found that there had been a move beyond the original 'crime and grime' focus to address additional themes, such as mental health, play and youth work, employability and jobs. However, the review also noted that neighbourhood management was rarely seen as a tool to empower local citizens through decision making or spending power (Houghton, 2018).

Where specialist technical assistance was needed, it was often difficult to access this, especially by those working at the community level. For example, the network of community technical aid centres, which had been established in the 1970s to improve community participation in planning and the design of the built environment, had largely vanished by the early 2000s, although some support continued to be provided by national bodies such as Planning Aid England.

Indeed, the weakness of local infrastructure meant that national agencies often attempted to fill the gap. In the case of the Big Local programme, for example, 'reps' appointed by Local Trust provide advice on establishing a Big Local partnership and helping with addressing any conflicts, as well as providing support in creating, submitting and reviewing the Big Local plans. The reps are expected not to impose their own views, but rather to provide assistance and constructive challenge where needed. Local Trust also convenes a national network of the Big Local areas, to help them exchange skills and ideas and learn from each other. A similar (but lighter-touch) system of support had been developed for the Our Place programme, with training and specialist advice as well as nationwide networking opportunities delivered through a coalition of national community development agencies, led by Locality.

As these examples indicate, it is never an easy task to reconcile the different views of purpose as seen from above and from below, to overcome the deeply embedded imbalances of power (control over funding, amenities, systems design and so on) at the local level, to develop effective and inclusive practices, and to establish the sustained infrastructure necessary for good collaboration.

As Big Local is demonstrating, and others such as Locality have long argued, the capabilities of local residents, including those living in adverse circumstances, are far greater than has sometimes been appreciated by those who plan solutions from above (Locality, 2020; Street, 2020). Furthermore, the case has been growing in recent years for a profound shift in favour of what Danny Kruger has called 'community power' (Kruger, 2020). But, at the same time, it is clear from the evidence of collaborative practice across the past two decades that neither efforts designed and led wholly from above, nor those designed and led wholly from below, are likely to achieve the full benefits that can come at the intersection of the two.

What might achieve better collaboration?

The COVID-19 pandemic has demonstrated that, at least in the face of an urgent crisis, there can be a willingness to 'leave the lanyards on the floor' and, indeed, in many cases during the pandemic, people appear to have set aside formal roles or rank in order to do what was needed together (A Better Way, 2020b). At the same time, it seems that those working from above have developed greater respect for those working from below, as the latter were often much quicker to respond to the crisis, and in some cases more able to connect to sections of the community most at risk in the pandemic (A Better Way, 2020a; Wyler, 2020). There has, it seems, been a widespread shift from doubt to trust (Robinson, 2020). However, it is by no means clear that this more collaborative and relational way of operating will persist, as the initial sense of crisis recedes.

Above all, the lesson of the past two decades is that collaboration in a place cannot be taken for granted. For it to flourish and to be sustained, especially between those working in formal institutions and those operating at the grassroots community level, it needs to be actively and systematically pursued. It requires a reframing of purpose in a way that can capture the imagination and ignite the energies of all concerned, and a shift in power in favour of those operating at the front line of community activity. And these changes need to be accompanied by the growth of practices that are adaptive and inclusive, and by investment in connective infrastructure.

A reframing of purpose

A reframing of purpose is necessary because, as we have seen, purpose as seen from above and below is often so different that it is extraordinarily difficult to reconcile the two. And as indicated earlier in this chapter, when purpose is defined in terms of narrow policy-driven outcomes, it tends to focus on problems and deficits and reinforce us-and-them practices, further marginalising sections of society.

Just how purpose can be reframed has been explored by A Better Way, which was established in 2016, and is a cross-sector network of leaders who want to improve services and build strong communities. It has called for a radical shift to liberate the power of connection and community. The framing of purpose in this way allows the possibility of combining bottom-up and top-down work to improve the lives of individuals, to build solidarity and inclusion across a community, and to create the societal structures and systems that can support such efforts (A Better Way, 2019), so that:

- Everyone is heard and believed in, given a fair opportunity to thrive and has the ability to influence the things that matter to them.
- Every community comes together, looks out for each other, respects difference and enables everyone to belong.
- Society as a whole values and invests in everyone and in every community.

Critically, when purpose is conceived in terms such as these, it can encourage institutions to prioritise individual, community and systems benefits over organisational goals. As has been pointed out, this means something beyond being 'citizen-centred'. It requires a willingness 'to set aside the boundaries of organisations and even directorates within organisations, and focus on the outcomes for the place, people and systems above and beyond what it means for your organisation' (Kippin and Billiald, 2015).

A shift in power

It can sometimes seem that everything is against those who want to work collaboratively: 'too often policies and systems divide and disempower and politicians and organisations hoard rather than share power' (A Better Way, 2019). The building of grassroots community action by itself is not enough, and there is a need for radical systems reform in order for the power dynamic to 'shift permanently' (Terry, 2020).

To bring this about, fundamentally different approaches to control are required by public authorities, 'shifting decision-making power out of public service institutions into communities with consequent changes to governance arrangements' (Lent and Studdert, 2019). The case for the transfer of assets (land and buildings) into community ownership has long been made, and as the government review on this topic declared, 'fundamentally, it's about giving local people a bigger stake in the future of their area' (DCLG, 2007). However, with more than 4,000 publicly owned buildings and spaces sold off for private use each year between 2012 and 2017, this opportunity to shift power and strengthen communities has been slipping away (Locality, 2018).

A shift in power is not only the responsibility of the public sector. An independent inquiry into the future of civil society concluded that a key role is to bring about a 'radical and creative shift that puts power in the hands of people and communities, preventing an "us and them" future, connecting us better and humanising the way we do things', and that to fulfil this role, civil society organisations themselves need to change (Civil Society Futures, 2018).

Perhaps most importantly, and this applies to all sectors, power needs to be continually devolved to the front line, so that 'those people closest to a complex situation are free to engage with its uniqueness and context and to use their initiative to respond to it' (Lankelly Chase Foundation, 2018).

Adaptive and inclusive practices

As A Better Way has recognised, 'changing ourselves is better than demanding change from others' (A Better Way, 2019). Those involved in local action, including grassroots community activists, as well as larger well-established charities, public sector bodies and private sector companies, can take a first step by reconsidering their own practices, sometimes at a fundamental level.

A Better Way has described, for example, the practice of 'radical listening', in which residents in a community are heard and their agency is built, and those in leadership roles avoid the temptation to problem solve, but rather make time to listen, often on a one-to-one basis or in small groups. This can lead to profound internal organisational change, reducing 'us and them' barriers, and engaging successfully with many people who had previously been excluded (Woodley, 2019).

Perhaps most difficult of all, a reframed purpose and a shift in power require all concerned to abandon the apparent certainties conferred by centralised command-and-control methods: it is clear that we have to become much more comfortable in embracing uncertainty, doubt and ambiguity (Lawson, 2019). This is especially important in a community context, where it is always a mistake to see community as something fixed, stable and homogenous, and important to recognise that in modern times, communities are made up of many shifting elements, and 'must be constructed, symbolically and socially' (Coates, 2010).

The necessary change in practice could therefore be summarised as follows: make time to listen, accept uncertainty and respond accordingly.

Connective infrastructure

To achieve a reframing of purpose and a shifting of power requires local actors dedicated to this task, able to encourage and support sustained efforts over time. Good leadership from above and from below clearly has a big role to play in this. But there is also a need for those who can operate at intermediate levels, building bridges and common cause, sounding a warning when some people are left out and treated unfairly, and constantly promoting more inclusive practices.

Often this function can be carried out by independent community anchor organisations, rooted in the local community, but also able to engage tactically and strategically with public and private sector agencies, and to play a long game (Locality, 2020).

Similarly, there are important roles for 'community connectors' – individuals who work with local residents to help them come together and support each other and discover their own agency, but also to help them to engage more effectively with those in positions of formal power, challenging where needed. This can take several forms, including for example community organising (Community Organisers, 2020) and local area coordination (LACN, 2020).

There is also a need for 'systems stewards' – people who can operate across agencies and across sectors, who understand that faced with complexity, outcomes are produced by systems, not by single projects, programmes or organisations, and who take responsibility for the health of the system, creating the conditions in which others can work effectively (Lowe and Plimmer, 2019). Generalist intermediary agencies such as councils for voluntary service, or specialists such as young people's foundations, can often achieve most when they work in this way.

Finally, there is a need to enhance the regional and national infrastructure that helps those working in one place to make contact more easily with those working elsewhere, to exchange knowledge and skills, and to connect dispersed efforts to bring about wider systems change. In a digitally connected world, the opportunities for this increase (Lawson, 2019), but that does not mean it happens of its own accord, and change driven from local areas will require high levels of organisation to counter the inevitable resistance and inertia from those at the centre who are content with the status quo.

Without some combination of these elements of connective infrastructure, available in every community, and extending beyond individual communities, and which are also capable of persisting over time, it is likely that efforts to reframe purpose and shift power in communities will fail, and that collaborative efforts at the intersection of above and below will continue to achieve less than we need them to.

Acting urgently and building on the best

The need to build a better practice in our communities, which can unite local grassroots action with wider systems change, feels urgent, at a time when the COVID-19 pandemic has exposed so starkly the correlations between poverty, poor housing, existing health inequalities and the COVID-19 death rate, and not least the impact on Black, Asian and minority ethnic communities (Charity So White, 2020; Robinson, 2020).

Raising the game for collaborative practice will take time, but that does not mean that some immediate steps could not start quickly, beginning with local and national investment in the types of connective infrastructure described in this chapter, always building on the best of what already exists.

References

A Better Way (2019) *A Call to Action for a Better Way*, London: Civil Exchange and Carnegie UK Trust.

A Better Way (2020a) Note of a first Better Way cell on 'Collaborative leadership in place', 3 June, https://www.betterway.network/collaborative-leadership-in-place-cell-first-meeting-june-2020.

A Better Way (2020b) Note of a third online roundtable on the coronavirus crisis and the power of connection and community, 18 June, https://www.betterway.network/coronavirus-connection-and-community-18-june-2020.

Baker, L. and Cairns, B. (2011) *Supporting Collaboration and Partnerships in a Changing Context: A Study for the Big Lottery Fund*, London: Institute of Voluntary Action Research.

Balloch, S. and Taylor, M. (2001) *Partnership Working: Policy and Practice*, Bristol: Policy Press.

Batty, E., Beatty, C., Foden, M., Lawless, P., Pearson, S. and Wilson, I. (2010) *The New Deal for Communities Experience: A Final Assessment*, (Volume 7 of the The New Deal for Communities Evaluation), Sheffield: Centre for Regional Economic and Social Research, Sheffield Hallam University.

Becker, J. and Smith, D. B. (2018) *The Need for Cross-sector Collaboration*, Stanford: Stanford Social Innovation Review.

Broomhead, P., Walters, S. and Lam, O. (2016) *Collaboration: More Than the Sum of the Parts*, London: FSI.

Cairns, B. and Harris, M. (2010) *Local Cross-sector Partnerships: Tackling the Challenges Collaboratively*, London: Institute for Voluntary Action Research.

Charity So White (2020) 'Racial injustice in the COVID-19 response', https://charitysowhite.org/introduction.

Civil Society Futures (2018) 'The story of our times: shifting power, bridging divides, transforming society', https://civilsocietyfutures. org/wp-content/uploads/sites/6/2018/11/Civil-Society-Futures_ _The-Story-of-Our-Future.pdf.

Coates, T. (2010) 'Conscious community: belonging, identities and networks in local communities' response to flooding', PhD thesis, Middlesex University.

Community Organisers (2020) 'Introduction to community organising', https://www.corganisers.org.uk/what-is-community-organising/intro-about-community-organising/.

DCLG (Department for Communities and Local Government) (2007) *Making Assets Work: The Quirk Review of Community Management and Ownership of Public Assets*, London: HMSO.

Fancourt, G. and Usher, R. (2019) *Rethinking Home: Engaging Transient and New Communities in Big Local*, London: Local Trust.

Hayden, C., Houghton, J., Lee, B. and Wilkinson, J. (2016) *Evaluation of the Our Place Programme: 2014–15*, London: Shared Intelligence.

Headlam, N. and Rowe, M. (2014) 'The end of the affair: abusive partnerships in austerity', *Journal of Urban Regeneration and Renewal*, 7(2): 111–21.

Helgerson, J. and Price, J. (2017) *Cross-sector Collaboration is a Game Changer for Social Change*, London: NHS Confederation.

Hood, C. (2006) 'Gaming in Targetworld: the targets approach to managing British public services', *Public Administration Review*, 66(4): 515–21.

Houghton, J. P. (2018) *Doing the Right Thing: How a New Model of Strategic Locality Working is Transforming Public Services at the Very Local Level*, London: National Association of Neighbourhood Management, http://localneighbourhood.org/wp-content/uploads/2018/07/Doing-the-right-thing-2018-040718.pdf.

Huxham, C. and Vangen, S. (2005) *Managing to Collaborate: The Theory and Practice of Collaborative Advantage*, Abingdon: Routledge.

Kail, A. and Abercrombie, R. (2013) *Collaborating for Impact: Working in Partnership to Boost Growth and Improve Outcomes*, London: New Philanthropy Capital and Impetus Trust.

Kippin, H. and Billiald, S. (2015) *Collaboration Readiness: Why it Matters, How to Build It, Where to Start*, London: Collaborate CIC.

Knight, A. D., Lowe, T., Brossard, M. and Wilson, J. (2017) *A Whole New World: Funding and Commissioning in Complexity*, London: Collaborate CIC.

Kruger, D. (2020) 'Levelling up our communities: proposals for a new social covenant', https://www.dannykruger.org.uk/sites/www.dannykruger.org.uk/files/2020-09/Levelling%20Up%20Our%20Communities-Danny%20Kruger.pdf.

LACN (Local Area Co-ordination Network) (2020) 'Local area coordination in a nutshell', https://lacnetwork.org/local-area-coordination/.

Lankelly Chase Foundation (2018) 'Our approach to change', https://lankellychase.org.uk/wp-content/uploads/2018/04/Our-Approach-To-Change-1.pdf.

Lawson, N. (2019) *45 Degree Change: Transforming Society From Below and Above*, London: Compass.

Lent, A. and Studdert, J. (2019) *The Community Paradigm: Why Public Services Need Radical Change and How It Can Be Achieved*, London: New Local Government Network.

Locality (2018) *The Great British Sell Off: How We're Losing our Vital Publicly Owned Buildings and Spaces, Forever*, London: Locality.

Locality (2020) *We Were Built for This: How community Organisations Helped Us Through the Coronavirus Crisis – and How We Can Build a Better Future*, London: Locality.

Lowe, T. and Plimmer, D. (2019) *Exploring the New World: Practical Insights for Funding, Commissioning and Managing in Complexity*, London: Collaborate CIC.

MHCLG (Ministry of Housing, Communities and Local Government) (2014) '123 communities to take control of neighbourhood schemes', press release, 14 April, https://www.gov.uk/government/news/123-communities-to-take-control-of-neighbourhood-schemes.

Miles, E. and Trott, W. (2011) *Collaborative Workin,* InsideOUT series number 5, London: Institute for Government.

Rees, J., Mullins, D. and Bovaird, T. (2012) *Partnership Working,* Research Report 88, Birmingham: Third Sector Research Centre.

Rhodes, J., Tyler., P. and Brennan, A. (2007) *The Single Regeneration Budget: Final Evaluation,* Cambridge: Department of Land Economy, University of Cambridge.

Robinson, D. (2020) *The Moment We Noticed: The Relationships Observatory and our Learning from 100 Days of Lockdown,* London: Relationships Project.

SEU (Social Exclusion Unit) (2000) *National Strategy for Neighbourhood Renewal: Policy Action Team report summaries: a compendium,* https://www.artshealthresources.org.uk/docs/policy-action-team-report-summaries-a-compendium/

SQW Consulting (2008) *People, Places, Public Services: Making the Connections. Neighbourhood Management Pathfinders: Final Evaluation Report,* London: HMSO.

Street, L. (2020) *Power in Our Hands: An Inquiry into Positive and Lasting Change in the Big Local Programme,* London: Local Trust.

Terry, L. (2020) *Power in Our Hands: An Inquiry into Resident-led Decision Making in the Big Local Programme,* London: Local Trust.

Terry, L. and Fisher, L. (2020) *Power in Our Hands: An Inquiry into Place-based Funding in the Big Local Programme,* London: Local Trust.

University of Cambridge (2019) *Achieving Local Economic Change: What Works?,* London: Local Trust.

Woodley, K. (2019) 'Radical listening', https://www.betterway.network/karin-woodley-radical-listening.

Wyler, S. (2020) *Community Responses in Times of Crisis,* London: Local Trust.

Wyler, S. and Adjaye, M. (2018) *Community Business and Collaboration,* London: Power to Change.

7

The importance of community-based learning

Marjorie Mayo

This chapter starts by examining definitions of community-based learning, focusing on the theoretical case for popular education, building proactive support for alternative futures from the bottom up and working towards shared agendas for solidarity and social justice. Community-based learning can enable communities to develop shared understandings of the underlying causes of their problems. This can provide the basis for developing strategies for collaborating across differences and divisions, tackling discriminatory attitudes and behaviours rather than blaming 'the other', building democratic alliances and movements for social change, and responding to climate-change challenges.

Such understandings have particular relevance in the current context, with increasing pressures from austerity policies along with divisive messages from Far Right populists, exacerbated by the effects of the COVID-19 pandemic. These pressures have been having the most severe impact on those who have been among the most disadvantaged already, particularly people from Black and minority ethnic communities, exacerbating tensions and prejudices, and posing major challenges for the future. Community-based learning can contribute to the development of more hopeful alternatives, it will be suggested in this chapter, without in any way implying that deep-rooted inequalities can be resolved by communities on their own, without wider structural changes. This is absolutely not about promoting 'resilience' as a backward-looking strategy for communities to turn inwards, as they attempt to pull themselves up by their own bootstraps – rather the reverse. This is about enabling communities to support each other inclusively rather than exclusively, as part of wider strategies for social justice.

Having outlined the potential contributions of community-based learning approaches as well as recognising their inherent limitations, the chapter moves on to explore these approaches in practice. How can the approaches be provided and resourced in disadvantaged areas *in partnership with local communities*, rather than being parachuted in from the outside? How can civil society organisations and public services work together without the former becoming substitutes for the underfunding of the latter? How can they manage the power imbalances within such partnerships? And what might local organisations learn about ways of addressing issues with wider ramifications, beyond the local?

Recent research has been exploring a range of initiatives that engage with these questions via informal as well as more formal approaches to community-based learning. Drawing on international case studies as well as British examples, the chapter focuses on projects that have brought communities together across their differences to deal with their shared anxieties, finding ways forward for the future. There are lessons here about ways of raising critical understandings about the underlying causes of structural inequalities – while meeting immediate community needs. And there are potential lessons about the tensions between developing mutual aid and solidarity within and between communities at the local level and the need to build wider movements for social justice, challenging neoliberal agendas for the longer term.

Community-based learning and popular education in the current context

'Community-based learning' refers to learning within communities, whether these are geographical communities, such as neighbourhoods, or whether they are communities of interest, based around shared identities and common concerns. 'Community' is a slippery concept, in any case, covering a range of meanings, which shift over time (Stacey, 1969; Williams, 1988; Bauman, 2001; Popple, 2015). And 'learning' covers a range of approaches in addition, from formal schooling through to adult education and informal learning, learning by doing as volunteers and community activists in different spaces, over time. Rather than trying to address such a range of activities and approaches, this chapter focuses on 'popular education' more specifically, exploring its potential relevance for communities in the contemporary context.

Popular education has been defined as being rooted in the real interests and struggles of ordinary people, overtly critical of the status quo and committed to progressive social change (Crowther et al, 2005). Far from being neutral, 'popular education is aligned with wider efforts to promote a more socially just social order through democratic change processes based on a clear understanding of the underlying causes of social inequality, exploitation and oppression, and the power relationships that underpin them' (Mayo, 2020, p 19). More specifically, the curriculum comes from communities' own issues and concerns, learning together so as to gain shared understandings of the underlying causes of their problems, in order to take collective action to address them more effectively.

Popular education has a long history, both in Britain and internationally. The Chartist movement in 19th-century Britain provides a case in point, demonstrating the links between popular education and movements for social justice. The Chartists had links with corresponding societies and co-operative societies, which were promoting 'really useful knowledge', for example, knowledge to enable people to campaign for democratic social change (including campaigns for the right to vote). More recent influences include the contributions of educationalists who have focused on the potential for learning for social transformation more specifically (Brookfield, 1987; Bell et al, 1990; Mezirow, 1991). The most widely quoted source of contemporary thinking about popular education, however, and perhaps the most misquoted, has been the Brazilian educationalist, Paulo Freire.

Paulo Freire – his theoretical roots, and his critics

Paulo Freire developed his ideas through teaching literacy to farmers living in poverty in north-east Brazil – until he was forced into exile following the military coup of 1964. He spent many years in exile, including a number of years as special education adviser to the World Council of Churches in Geneva, before finally returning to Brazil in 1980, developing literacy programmes for the Workers Party in São Paulo. Through these experiences he refined his approach to learning for human liberation (Freire, 1972, 1996). Coming from a Catholic background, heavily influenced by liberation theology, Freire was concerned that the oppressed should learn how to recover their lost humanity.

This learning needed to start from their own experiences, engaging in critical dialogues with their teachers/educators in order to develop critical understanding of the causes of their problems and so to develop strategies for democratic social change. Part of the problems lay in the ways in which oppressive social relationships could be internalised within the heads of the oppressed themselves, leading them to accept unjust situations as inevitable, unchangeable, even justifiable, the 'common sense' of the existing social order. People needed to be able to develop their own understandings in order to move on. But they needed to do this for themselves, on the basis of active learning through problem-posing processes of dialogue. Educators needed to work *with* people rather than *for* them, in other words, if people were to become active agents of social change within their communities and beyond.

Paulo Freire's work has been widely misinterpreted and misapplied as well as criticised from a number of perspectives. These have included criticisms from feminists, arguing that he paid too little attention to issues of gender, or indeed to issues of race, ethnicity and culture, as these intersect with divisions of social class (Tett, 2018). These were criticisms that Freire himself acknowledged and took on board, in his later writings, just as he recognised and took on board the relevance of Marxist approaches to cultural phenomena and the battle of ideas, drawing on the writings of the Italian Marxist, Antonio Gramsci (de Figeiredo-Cowen and Gastaldo, 1995). Freire was also clear that educators and communities *could* work in partnership with governments and other agencies (Bell et al, 1990) – but only where there was scope for doing so in genuinely collaborative ways, based on mutual respect and shared democratic values.

In summary, then, Paulo Freire's writings have relevance far beyond their Brazilian origins. Popular education, based on Freirian approaches, offers communities ways to unpack the underlying causes of the problems that concern them most, supported by educators to enable them to engage in cycles of action and reflection, forming the basis for more effective strategies for social change. As it has already been emphasised, however, popular education is far from representing any kind of silver bullet, let alone offering any kind of magical formula for community-based social change.

How, then, can governments, universities and other partner organisations and agencies provide support for popular education in the current context? This is especially problematic after a decade of austerity, leaving communities to cope as best they can – was learning for active citizenship to be about learning to compensate for the yawning gaps in public service provision? This is not what Freire and others thought that popular education should be aiming to achieve.

While poplar education needs to start from communities' *own* agendas, then, this alternative, bottom-up approach raises further questions in its turn. Who exactly are the ordinary people, the communities who are to be popular educators' targets? Do they share real interests in common, or are there differences within as well as between communities and social movements (Kane, 2005)?

Communities can be mutually supportive and co-operative. But this is not necessarily the case. Communities can also be exclusive and inward looking, stereotyping outsiders and blaming them for their problems (Kenny et al, 2015). These questions have particular relevance in the current context, given the processes of polarisation that have been taking place within as well as between communities in recent years, exacerbating and exacerbated by the growth of Far Right populism. Popular educators need to be able to challenge racist stereotypes, along with Islamophobic anxieties and fears, Far Right blame games that target 'the other', typically the most vulnerable members of society including migrants and refugees, polarising the country in potentially damaging ways for the future.

Ali Smith's prize-winning novel, *Autumn* describes the situation in Britain following the Brexit referendum as follows:

> All across the country, people felt it was the wrong thing. All across the country, people felt it was the right thing ... All across the country people felt like they counted for nothing ... All across the country, racist bile was general ... All across the country, money money money money. All across the country, no money no money no money no money. (Smith, 2016, pp 60–1)

And then there was COVID-19

There were plenty of challenges and dilemmas already, at the beginning of 2020, even before the COVID-19 pandemic. Albert Camus' (2013) novel, *The Plague*, has been much read and much quoted since then, drawing out potential parallels with a (fictional) outbreak of plague in Algeria during the Second World War (with people's responses to this fictional plague providing a metaphor for people's uneven responses to the Nazi occupation of France). The pestilence was at once blight and revelation, Camus reflected, bringing the hidden truth of a corrupt world to the surface.

Similar arguments are being made about COVID-19. This has already led to some half a million deaths worldwide, with Britain among the worst-performing countries, in both relative and absolute terms. It may be years before the total effects emerge, as people die from heart disease and cancers that could have been successfully diagnosed and treated earlier, had it not been for the impact of COVID-19. The long-term effects of lockdown can be expected to be wider still, from the impacts on people's mental health through to the impacts on children's education, not to forget the effects in terms of job losses, and increasing poverty and homelessness, as people fall behind with the rent and mortgage repayments. It is the most disadvantaged who have been experiencing the worst effects across the globe, just as they have been the most seriously affected in Britain, re-enforcing existing inequalities of race, ethnicity, faith and social class. Poverty and inequality have been powerfully evident as both causes and effects of the pandemic, exacerbated by discrimination by race, ethnicity, gender, age and disability. These are factors that emerge within Britain as well as internationally.

The pandemic has also been exacerbating divisions within and between communities. At first there were incidents of hate speech directed at those who looked Chinese, who were blamed for the spread of the virus from China. Since then, there have been disturbing incidences of hate crimes against other groups too, including Africans, with the tragic death of a woman of African heritage who was deliberately infected by being spat on. There is not the space to go into the effects of the pandemic in further detail in the context of this chapter, whether generally or more specifically in relation to the spread of hate speech and hate crimes. The point is simply to emphasise the importance of working with communities to facilitate the development of mutually supportive responses, challenging the spread of divisive stereotypes based on people's (all too understandable) anxieties and fears. How, then, could popular education contribute to more hopeful rather than more hateful futures?

Evidence from popular education in practice

There is plenty of evidence to illustrate the contributions that popular education can make, enabling communities to address their needs, including their health needs, more effectively. And there is plenty of evidence to illustrate ways in which popular education initiatives can contribute to addressing racism, along with other forms of discrimination and conflict. These examples include initiatives based on Freirian approaches, starting from people's own priorities and concerns, building more equal forms of partnerships between communities and service providers in particular contexts, both in Britain and beyond.

The UK government's 'Together We Can' and 'Take Part' programmes (2003–10) have provided illustrations of ways to promote Active Learning for Active Citizenship (ALAC), bringing voluntary and community organisations together with university and college partners, setting up hubs to promote learning for active citizenship.

These were to start from people's own experiences and interests, critically reflecting on these as the basis for developing effective strategies for change, initiatives that were to be monitored and evaluated in participatory ways, as well. As one of those who had been directly involved in developing ALAC reflected subsequently, 'the emphasis on grass roots control and attempts to alter power relationships in favour of the less powerful' (Woodward, 2010, p 105) were inherently likely to prove challenging.

There were also initiatives to challenge racism and discrimination head on, in a climate of insecurity and fear. Rapid change due to privatisation and the continuing loss of manufacturing jobs was being compounded by increasing flows of migration in the areas in question at that time, in the first decade of the 21st century, with migrants and asylum seekers being demonised as 'the root of all social ills' – stereotypes that were being exacerbated by the growth of Far Right political parties (Grayson, 2010, p 157). More recent parallels are only too striking.

The responses included the development of courses to build solidarity and alliances around issues of common concern – across ethnic divides. This was described as aiming at 'developing critical consciousness and providing "really useful knowledge", linked to political action in a traditional popular education way' (Grayson, 2010, p 162). There were teach-ins, residential courses and a range of other learning activities and events as a result, including sessions on 'Challenging Racism for Community Trainers' and 'Resolving Conflict in Communities'.

These were potentially controversial issues, as I personally witnessed when I participated in an evaluation session, along with representatives from projects based elsewhere. There were instances when community activists did find some of these discussions challenging. But, as one of those who had been directly involved concluded, issues do not disappear if you do not talk about them. On the contrary, what was needed was 'a safe space where people can get together, with a skilled tutor, to discuss the difficult issues of the day' (Hartley, 2010, p 153). After the change of government in 2010, subsequent programmes reflected increasing pressures to focus on volunteering and engagement in formal structures of governance in the context of austerity, emphasising government objectives for civil society, with rather less emphasis on advocacy and campaigning – although there were still spaces for these wider aspects too. But much was achieved all the same, including innovative approaches to community-based learning, focusing on health and how to improve access to health services for Black and minority ethnic women, migrants and refugees.

Similar approaches (drawing on Take Part's Learning Framework) have been developed elsewhere, in Colombia and other parts of the Americas. Following the election of Donald Trump as President of the United States in 2016, the Community-Library Inter-Action (CLIA) group, a network of libraries. came together to respond to the rise of Far Right populism by providing safe spaces for community debates.

The Community-Library Inter-Action (CLIA) group set out to work *with* rather than *for* communities, to facilitate participatory dialogues and community action, contributing to advancing peaceful and sustainable communities. In addition to its work in the US, CLIA has been supporting workshops with around 100 librarians and community leaders in different localities in Colombia, Costa Rica and Peru.

Libraries can provide neutral spaces within communities (although they have also suffered serious cutbacks as a result of a decade of austerity in Britain). They can feel safe, as they clearly felt to the communities that were participating in library-based activities in Colombia as part of the CLIA programme. I was able to visit both urban and rural libraries that were engaging in these initiatives, including initiatives that were engaging young people through their participation in the performing arts. These were part of wider peace-building initiatives, working against the grain, given the massive (and continuing) challenges of conflict resolution in contemporary Colombia. Here too, popular education initiatives have had significant contributions to make, but only within the context of wider strategies for social justice and democratic forms of social change.

Popular education's strengths – and limitations – emerge from more recent initiatives in the UK. Community–university partnerships can support communities, enabling them to analyse their own histories in innovative ways. This can provide the basis for challenging negative stereotypes of themselves and their neighbourhoods, negative stereotypes that people have been internalising over the years.

The Economic and Social Research Council's 'Imagine – Connecting Communities through Research' programme provides evidence of the potential achievements as well as the potential limitations of just such approaches. Over a five-year period, researchers on this programme worked with community partners to explore the changing nature of their communities, understanding the implications of their pasts as the basis for identifying alternative ways forward for the future (Banks et al, 2019). The community–university partnerships included partnerships in areas that had experienced community development programmes in the past, such as areas of multiple deprivation in the North East and the West Midlands. The approach was to start from people's own experiences and needs, developing collective strategies to tackle unequal power relationships, promoting social justice and social inclusion from the bottom up.

These initiatives engaged local communities in creative ways, including through the use of graffiti art, as well as through oral histories and archival research. There was plenty of evidence of learning as a result, as participants developed new skills, engaging young people alongside others, exploring their neighbourhoods' pasts and expressing their hopes for the future. One of the most significant themes to emerge from these initiatives was the concern to challenge processes of neighbourhood stigmatisation. These areas had been selected for government community development programmes from the 1960s because of their concentrations of social deprivation. Decades later, in the 21st century, territorial stigmatisation continued to cause blight in these communities. People spoke of the effects of coming from a neighbourhood with such a negative reputation – not exactly a recommendation to potential employers, for a start.

But negative stereotypes could also be challenged. In one area, an intergenerational history project demonstrated just how an area could be put on the map in more positive ways, 'as a place of interest for reasons of culture and heritage rather than for its history of poverty, disadvantage and social unrest' (Banks et al, 2019, p 36). There was a clear emphasis on the positive – challenging negative stereotypes and potentially 'replacing alienation and hopelessness with more hopeful feelings of pride in past achievements and solidarity in the pursuit of alternative futures' (Mayo, 2020, p 150).

So far, so good, then. But major challenges in these areas remained, blighted as they had been by decades of industrial decline. However creative such initiatives might be – and they clearly did provide innovative learning experiences for all those involved – there were fundamental limits to what could be achieved, without addressing the underlying causes of poverty and deprivation in areas of long-term economic decline.

Hope Not Hate, Kick it Out and Show Racism the Red Card

The North East provides further examples of strategies to tackle negative stereotyping – in these cases negative stereotyping of 'the other' – although the North East is far from having been the only region to develop such strategies. Hope Not Hate was founded in 2004 to provide positive antidotes to the politics of hate that were being promoted by the Far Right in different locations across the country, in fact. Community-based educational activities were developed to form peaceful resistance to Far Right attempts to divide communities, playing on people's anxieties and fears for their futures. Hope Not Hate has organised a range of initiatives, including popular education workshops setting out to explore the bases for racist, xenophobic, anti-Semitic and Islamophobic attitudes and behaviours, exploring ways in which participants could respond more positively, building solidarity in the process.

Hope Not Hate education events start from the realities of where people are actually at, their previous experiences and their feelings, including their fears about sensitive issues such as migration and racism. The emphasis is on enabling people to have the confidence to engage with people in potentially constructive dialogues rather than simply confronting them – let alone simply telling them that they are in the wrong. Shared understandings and trust have to be developed, though, if people are to be engaged in such processes of dialogue. People's feelings need to be taken into account, especially when addressing highly emotive issues, such as people's (however unjustifiable) fears of 'the other'.

'Kick it Out' and 'Show Racism the Red Card' have drawn on similar approaches in order to challenge racism within football, including the development of popular education initiatives. Young football supporters have been targeted by the Far Right, as exemplified by Tommy Robinson's 'Democratic Football Lads Alliance', emerging in 2017 to attempt to mobilise young football supporters for the Far Right. Building on previous campaigns to tackle racism in football initiatives, the 'Show Racism the Red Card' project in the North East targeted young people who had been identified as being at risk of being drawn into the politics of the Far Right. Although the interventions themselves took place through schools and formal settings, the principles were those of popular education in the Freirian tradition. Young people's concerns were to be addressed in a safe, non-judgemental space. Rather than telling young people what to think, the aim was to engage them in developing critical thinking, thereby 'increasing their resilience to (resist) racist and far-right rhetoric' (Rodgerson, 2018, p 5). Their needs for safety and respect needed to be ensured first, however, thereby providing the basis for trust and confidence to address the emotive issues that were being put forward by the Far Right. Feedback from the young people and from the education providers both concluded that the project was being valued and that the objectives were being met (Rodgerson, 2018).

To summarise the learning from these examples, it seems that there is evidence that popular education initiatives can indeed make a difference. But they have needed to start from communities' immediate concerns as well as taking account of people's anxieties and fears, along with people's feelings of humiliation and shame when they have been treated without respect, as too often they have been treated in this way and stigmatised, especially in areas with a history of poverty and deprivation.

Mutual aid: communities doing it for themselves?

So far, the discussion has focused on popular education initiatives that have been sponsored and/or supported by governmental organisations, universities, voluntary sector organisations and social movement campaigns. But communities can and do organise – and learn – for themselves. The following examples from mutual-aid groups provide illustrations of what communities can do, and how they can learn together through their involvement in meeting immediate needs in the context of the COVID-19 pandemic. This type of learning may seem very different from the Freirian type of learning that has been identified so far. The learning may be far more incidental, for example, following its own patterns. But communities can and do learn from becoming involved as active citizens, whatever the starting point. And once involved as active citizens, people can – and frequently do – move on to become involved in other ways, including becoming involved in advocacy and campaigning for social changes beyond the community level. Not all do make such choices, of course. But as one of the tutors reflected in relation to their experiences within the Take Part programme, 'learners should set their own priorities in terms of how they choose to engage as active citizens' (Recknagel with Holland, 2013, p 31). This is inherent in the learner-centred approach.

Mutual-aid groups can provide opportunities for community-based learning, then, as the following illustrations suggest. There are numerous examples of mutual support and solidarity in the face of the COVID-19 pandemic, including examples from Greece, Italy and Portugal in Europe, through to examples from the Americas, Asia, the Middle East and Southern Africa (Sitrim and Sembrar, 2020). From food delivery to legal help, from women's autonomous collectives to the provision of educational support, solidarity networks in Turkey have been described as building 'a paradise in hell' (Ozdemir, 2020, p 19). As one of those interviewed for a review of the group's experiences reflected: 'In this process [of organising mutual aid] we see how precious solidarity networks are and how fast people can organise. People feel better when they come and think together, learn together, decide collectively. We are in a learning process' (Ozdemir, 2020, p 32).

Learning emerged as a major theme in Lisbon, Portugal too. A collective formed by anti-racist educators came together with other networks to provide practical and emotional support during the pandemic, including support for immigrant families. They concluded that the worst was still to come so 'mutual-aid networks and mental health support will continue to be essential to the survival of all' (Gomes Duarte and Lima, 2020, p 131). As another network (this time in Porto, Portugal) added, these were networks of mutual support, not charity. This initiative was 'generated from the ground up, rooted in horizontality and self-management' (Gomes Duarte and Lima, 2020, pp 135–6) and the development of intersectional solidarity through processes of engagement as active citizens.

How, then, have mutual-aid initiatives been developing in Britain? Groups seem to vary considerably in terms of the ways in which they organise themselves and the ways in which they define their respective remits. Systematic research will be needed to compile a comprehensive picture. There are extremely encouraging signs, though. From my own – very limited – experience, groups can be experienced as genuinely inspiring. Local people can come together as communities in such positive ways, organising collectively to provide mutual support. Volunteers can and do receive support themselves as well as providing assistance to others. This is mutual support and solidarity in action, and democratically organised and effective forms of active citizenship in practice.

As with the Freirian approaches that have been outlined in this chapter, mutual-aid activists start from the identification of immediate needs in their communities, developing collective strategies in response. This can lead activists on to engage in further forms of involvement, sharing learning about the underlying causes of so much unmet need. Why are some of their neighbours' food cupboards regularly empty? Why are people reliant on mutual aid's support in order to feed their children? How should we understand the inadequacies of the benefits system, along with the problems associated with low pay, job insecurity and zero-hours contracts? And what about the problems of being without recourse to public funds, as the result of Britain's approach to limiting immigration, fuelling suspicions about refugees and asylum seekers? These are the types of questions that can lead to community-based learning for social justice agendas, from the bottom up.

This is not to suggest that mutual-aid groups necessarily develop in such ways. Unsurprisingly, they have been facing their own challenges in the current context, given the extent of the problems that communities have been facing after so many years of austerity, compounded by the effects of the COVID-19 pandemic. There is so much to learn from getting involved in mutual aid, though, not least about the extent of unmet need within communities. Locally based initiatives need to be complemented by major shifts in public policies to tackle the underlying inequalities that have been exacerbated by the pandemic. There are major implications for health and social welfare, along with housing, employment and training, the arts and environmental sustainability, to list the most obvious, both in Britain and internationally.

There are inherent dilemmas for community organisers and activists here, dilemmas inherent in the processes of becoming involved as active citizens:

- where to draw the boundaries between mutual-aid provision, on the one hand, and public service provision, on the other;
- how to avoid substituting for public services as they struggle to meet increasing demands with diminishing resources as the result of the austerity policies of the past decade;
- when to move into advocacy and campaigning; and
- how to sustain the support networks that have been developing within communities, for the future.

Community action needs resourcing in its own right, too. These are questions that are being debated right now, as the situation develops.

What next?

With the prospect of economic recession and a consequent rise in unemployment, social needs can be expected to increase. But those who are going back into paid work may have less time for community activism, thereby increasing the pressures on those who remain active in mutual-aid groups. So how will communities respond to such challenges?

There is historic evidence that points to the ways in which crises can and do elicit negative as well as positive responses. Beneath the myths surrounding the 'community spirit' that Britain was supposed to have demonstrated during the Second World War, for instance, there were darker experiences too. Both then and now, there have been examples of seriously antisocial behaviour, whether hoarding or profiteering, commandeering toilet rolls or selling 'test kits' at inflated prices. Criminals have also been taking advantage of people's vulnerabilities and anxieties with scams and cybercrimes.

The scope for racist Far Right populists to arouse people's resentments and anxieties would seem considerable in such contexts. As Hoggett has so clearly pointed out, politicians do not create such feelings out of thin air (Hoggett, 2016). But feelings of envy and fear can be manipulated by politicians and amplified by the media, including the social media, leading to more hateful futures as a result. These are challenges that need to be confronted as a matter of urgency, as current mobilisations to tackle racist violence so clearly demonstrate. Black lives matter.

Meanwhile, there is growing evidence of increasing interest in understanding the underlying causes of contemporary problems, rather than blaming 'the other', along with a desire to share lessons about how to develop alternative strategies in response. Resources for community-based learning have been shrinking in the context of austerity, along with the resources for community and youth work more generally. But popular political education initiatives have been mushrooming all the same. Lockdown has resulted in rapid developments in electronic forms of provision, reaching new audiences more extensively in the process. Hundreds of participants have been logging on to webinars in which I have participated myself, exploring the possibilities of developing alternative approaches to contemporary challenges and examining the scope for promoting a Green Industrial Revolution to revive Britain's economy by creating socially useful employment

This is not to claim too much for such popular educational initiatives per se. On the contrary, popular education initiatives can have potentially important contributions to make, as part of wider strategies to build more hopeful communities for the future.

References

Banks, S., Armstrong, A., Bonner, A., Hall, Y., Harman, P., Johnston, L., Levi, C., Smith, K. and Taylor, R. (2019) *Co-producing Research*, Bristol: Policy Press.

Bauman, Z. (2001) *Community*, Cambridge: Polity Press.

Bell, B., Gaventa, J. and Peters, J. (eds) (1990) *We Make the Road by Walking: Conversations on Education and Social Change: Myles Horton and Paulo Freire*, Philadelphia: Temple University Press.

Brookfield, S. (1987) *Developing Critical Thinkers*, Milton Keynes: Open University Press.

Camus, A. (2013) *The Plague*, London: Penguin Classics.

Crowther, J., Galloway, V. and Martin, I. (2005) *Popular Education: Engaging the Academy*, Leicester: NIACE.

Figueredo-Cowen, M. and Gastaldo, D. (1995) *Paulo Freire at the Institute*, London: Institute of Education.

Freire, P. (1972) *Pedagogy of the Oppressed*, Harmondsworth: Penguin.

Freire, P. (1996) *Pedagogy of Hope*, London: Bloomsbury.

Gomes Duarte, L. and Lima, R. (2020) 'On intersectional solidarity in Portugal', in Sitrim M. and Sembrar, C. (eds) *Pandemic Solidarity*, London: Pluto, pp 123–37.

Grayson, J. (2010) 'Borders, glass floors and anti-racist popular adult education,' in Mayo, M. and Annette, J. (eds) *Taking Part?*, Leicester: NIACE, pp 156–68.

Hartley, T. (2010) 'Proving a point; effective social, political and citizenship education in South Yorkshire' in Mayo, M. and Annette, J. (eds) *Taking Part?*, Leicester: NIACE, pp 141–55.

Hoggett, P. (2016) *Politics, Identity and Emotion*, London: Routledge.

Kane, L. (2005) 'Ideology matters' in Crowther, J., Galloway, V. and Martin, I. (eds) *Popular Education: Engaging the Academy*, Leicester: NIACE, pp 32–42.

Kenny, S., Taylor, M., Onyx, J. and Mayo, M. (2015) *Challenging the Third Sector*, Bristol: Policy Press.

Mayo, M. (2020) *Community-based Learning and Social Movements: Popular Education in a Populist Age*, Bristol: Policy Press.

Mezirow, J. (1991) *Transformative Dimensions of Adult Learning*, San Francisco: Jossey Bass.

Ozdemir, S. (2020) 'Capitalism kills, solidarity gives life: a glimpse of solidarity networks in Turkey', in Sitrim, M. and Sembrar, C. (eds) *Pandemic Solidarity*, London: Pluto, pp 18–34.

Popple. K. (2015) *Analysing Community Work*, Maidenhead: Open University Press.

Recknagel, G. with Holland, D. (2013) 'How inclusive and how empowering? Two case studies researching the impact of active citizenship learning initiatives in a social policy context', in Mayo, M., Mendiwelso-Bendek, Z. and Packham, C. (eds) *Community Research for Community Development*, Basingstoke: Palgrave, pp 19–39.

Rodgerson, C. (2018) *Routes, Executive Summary and Local Context*, North Shields: Show Racism the Red Card.

Sitrim, M. and Sembrar, C. (eds) (2020) *Pandemic Solidarity*, London: Pluto.

Smith, A. (2016) *Autumn*, London: Penguin.

Stacey, M. (1969) 'The myth of community studies', *British Journal of Sociology*, 20: 134–47.

Tett, L. (2018) 'What Freire means to me', *CONCEPT*, 9 (3): 43–8.

Williams, R. (1988) *Keywords*, London: Fontana.

Woodward, V. (2010) 'Active learning for active citizenship (ALAC): origins and approaches', in Mayo, M. and Annette, J. (eds) *Taking Part?*, Leicester: NIACE, pp 101–22.

8

The 45° Change model for remaking power relations

Colin Miller and Neal Lawson

Introduction

Why, despite the rhetoric and long-term investment, have strategies directed at communities often failed to turn them around in the ways hoped for, and why have they failed to 'empower communities'? We argue that this is because of three fundamental errors of approach. First, a tendency to view community empowerment as having a utilitarian and managerialist purpose, rather than as an essential political and human right. Thus community engagement tends to only be valued for creating more effective and efficient services. Second, the failure to realise that the way in which local government and public services are structured has effectively prevented the state (nationally and locally) and communities from working together to transform communities. Third, the tendency to oversimplify our understanding of how radical change in communities can be achieved, through unhelpful slogans such as '*top down* doesn't work, only a *bottom-up* approach can work'.

If past governments had come to grips with these issues of empowering communities structurally and politically, they could have played a significant role not only in supporting community-based transformation, but also in addressing the long-developing crises of confidence in our political and democratic systems that many communities have (see Figure 8.1).

The development of the '45° Change' model (Lawson, 2019) and the follow-up pamphlet 'Participation at 45°' (Miller et al, 2020) confront these issues and argue that a key reason for the failure of 'top-down' government programmes and the weakness of the 'bottom-up' change model is because transformative change requires *both*. We need to bring together the vertical power of government with the horizontal power of civil society to create a deeper democracy based on shared and distributed forms of power (Lawson, 2019).

Figure 8.1: Political disillusionment

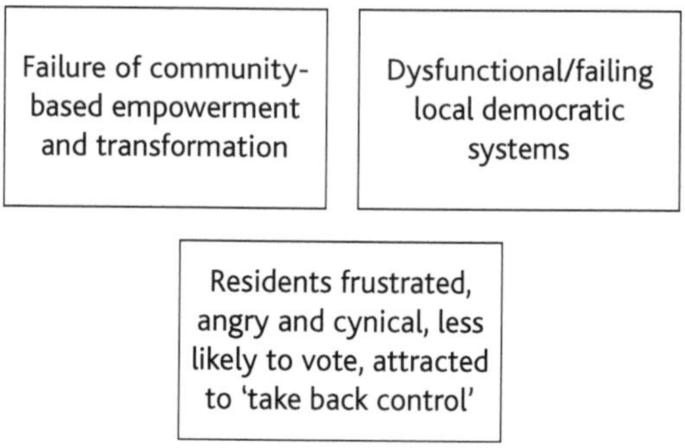

Failure of community-based empowerment and transformation	Dysfunctional/failing local democratic systems

Residents frustrated, angry and cynical, less likely to vote, attracted to 'take back control'

Crises in democracy: voting, alienation and taking back control

> 'Take back control' caught the mood like no other slogan in my lifetime. For too long, people felt decision-making to be remote and unaccountable, imposing change that is unwelcome, stripping them of meaningful choices and denying them urgency over their lives and communities. (Lisa Nandy MP, quoted in Lawson, 2019, p 4)

Government motivation for focusing on communities is usually based on concern with apparently intractable issues of poverty and deprivation but also, particularly during the Labour period (1997–2010), an underlying concern with the 'growing sense of citizens feeling inadequately empowered to influence local decisions and conditions' (DCLG, 2008, p 6). This latter concern was well placed: in the nine years between 1992 and 2001 (during which Labour was in power from 1997 onwards), the turnout at general elections crashed from 77.7 per cent to just 59.4 per cent.[1]

There were also, and still are, considerable differences in turnout between geographical areas. In the 2019 general election, the highest turnout in a constituency was 78 per cent and the lowest 56.8 per cent (see Figure 8.2). Over the past four out of five general elections, there has been a difference of between 26 and 32 points between the highest and lowest turnouts (see Table 8.1).

---

[1] It is worth noting that the claim that the European Union referendum in 2016 had, at 72 per cent, the biggest turnout in election history is a myth, but it was exceptionally high in comparison with recent general elections since 1997.

Figure 8.2: General election turnouts, 1983–2019 (UK)

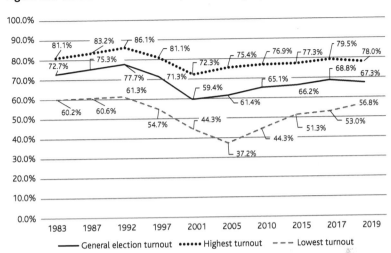

Table 8.1: Turnout in general elections (UK)

	General election turnout	Highest constituency turnout	Lowest constituency turnout	Points difference
1983	72.7%	81.1%	60.2%	20.9
1987	75.3%	83.2%	60.6%	22.6
1992	77.7%	86.1%	61.3%	24.8
1997	71.3%	81.1%	54.7%	26.5
2001	59.4%	72.3%	44.3%	28.0
2005	61.4%	75.4%	37.2%	32.6
2010	65.1%	76.9%	44.3%	32.6
2015	66.2%	77.3%	51.3%	26.0
2017	68.8%	79.5%	53.0%	26.5
2019	67.3%	78.0%	56.8%	21.2

Except when they coincide with general elections, turnout for local elections has always been low and appears to be getting lower (see Figure 8.3).[2] From a peak of 44 per cent in 1990, local election turnout

---

[2] Because the timing of local elections is so varied, they have been plotted to the nearest year preceding or succeeding a general election. County council elections are not included because they tend to take place outside this two-year 'rule'.

Figure 8.3: General and local election turnouts compared, 1983–2019 (UK)

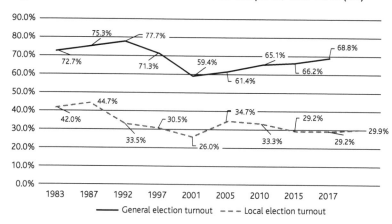

collapsed to just 26 per cent in 2001; since then it has improved a little, but remains stuck at around 30 per cent (Uberoi, 2019).[3]

As with general elections, there are distinct differences in turnout for local elections between areas. For example, the following are some figures from the 2018 local elections:

England
- 47.6%: South Lakeland
- 24.5%: Hartlepool

London
- 51.4%: Richmond Upon Thames
- 29.5%: Barking and Dagenham

By ward
- 61%: Hexham West, Northumberland
- 15.3%: Swadlincote North, South Derbyshire (Uberoi, 2019)

This apparent lack of motivation to vote in many areas is corroborated by the Hansard Society's 'Annual Audit of Political Engagement'. Since 2004, the audit has tracked a growing dissatisfaction with our political systems:

- 2004: just 36 per cent of those surveyed thought our political systems works well and that 'getting involved works'.

---

[3] Unless otherwise stated, local election turnout figures refer to the local authority, for example the district council or metropolitan council.

- 2009: the report found that 'voters were deeply disgruntled and disengaged'.
- 2013: just 30 per cent thought the government 'worked'.
- 2016: the audit estimated that approximately 60 per cent of Leave voters did not vote in the 2015 general election and 70 per cent said they did not believe they had any political influence.
- 2019: 72 per cent said that our system of governance needs a lot or a 'great deal' of improvement:
  - o 50 per cent said that the main parties did not care about them;
  - o 47 per cent said that they had no influence on national decision making;
  - o 54 per cent agreed that we need a 'strong leader who is willing to break the rules'.

Overall, dissatisfaction has increased, from 60 per cent in 2004 to 72 per cent in 2019 (Hansard Society, 2019).

Government, communities and empowerment

To overcome the participatory gap between citizens and their government, as indicated by the degrees of voter disengagement, it is thought that the public needs to be empowered to have a greater sense of real influence over their communities and public services. Since 1966, there has been a succession of programmes aimed at transforming communities by involving local people. These reached an apotheosis during the 1997–2010 Labour government – a period that witnessed 'the most concerted effort by government ... to turn community involvement aspirations into concrete reality' (DCLG, 2010, p 87) through the New Deal for Communities (NDC) and the National Strategy for Neighbourhood Renewal (NSNR) (DCLG, 2010). These programmes are discussed elsewhere in this volume (see Chapters 4 and 6) so here we will focus on the issues of impact and working with communities and questions of empowerment.

Given government rhetoric on the importance of community engagement in these programmes, there seemed to be remarkably little thought about what it would mean in practice. Consequently, a number of problems emerged in the NDC, the NSNR and other programmes that could have been avoided:

- a failure to define 'engagement';
- a failure to define 'community'; and
- a lack of clarity in structural functioning.

Defining engagement

From the outset, the lack of clarity on what was meant by community engagement resulted in conflicts as residents mistakenly thought they had the freedom to decide how programme money was to be prioritised and spent (Fordham, 2010). The confusion was compounded by declarations that 'communities are to be at the heart of the programme', while in fact community wishes were being quietly demoted by the imposition of targets set by government ministers and civil servants (Chanan and Miller, 2013).

Defining community

Fordham and others argue that the NDC programme was developed around a naïve view about what a community is and what a community could change; it tended to treat communities as single entities rather than complex networks of elements such as ethnic groups, differing age ranges and smaller neighbourhoods (Fordham, 2010; Chanan and Miller, 2013).

Tensions arose between smaller neighbourhoods and between ethnic groups, which a more sophisticated approach might have been prevented: '[T]here was a quite overt view amongst the community that it was a competition to grab resources for one ethnic community or another' (Batty et al, 2010, p 38). Such tensions led to a crisis in Birmingham Aston, where the programme had to be reconstituted because of a paralysis caused by voting patterns driven by ethnic differences (Batty et al, 2010, p 38).

Finally, while individual communities could have an impact on reducing antisocial behaviour and improving public health, significant improvements to employment and education required solutions to be developed in more than one area (Fordham, 2010).[4]

Structural functioning

Developing effective working relationships in the NDC partnerships was not easy as they had to deal with complex and contentious issues. Community members sometimes found the demands made on their time and emotional energy very challenging. In some areas,

---

[4] For example, it was found that in an average NDC area, around ten secondary and ten primary schools served the NDC area and a number of other areas.

relationships within the community could be damaged by rumours circulating that the community representatives were favouring their friends or 'on the take'.

The ability of community representatives to understand and make a contribution on issues and plans was not helped when some boards simply replicated the way local authorities work and make decisions, through committee meetings and policy papers. Community representatives also had to deal with tensions between services: 'we moaned about the council silos but, boy did we create our own' (Fordham, 2010, p 60). Although 61 per cent of community participants said they had a positive experience of being involved, 29 per cent said they felt out of their depth (Batty et al, 2010).

45° Change: remaking power relations

It has been argued that managerialist approaches to community empowerment actually leave people even more disempowered because they 'often have the effect of reinforcing the power base of the controlling institutions with only marginal gains at a local level' (Bailey and Pill, 2015, p 289), as the interaction between citizens and the wider powers is framed within a neoliberal paradigm that fragments power and benefits the most powerful.

The popular argument about how communities can be 'turned around' frequently follows the line that 'top down' tends to fail and what is needed is change 'from the bottom up'. The 45° Change model rejects the idea that radical change can be exclusively achieved from the bottom up *or* from the top down, and maintains that deep change can only come about when the 'vertical' power from top down government institutions and works with the 'horizontal' bottom up power of civil society (Lawson, 2019).

Horizontal power

Horizontal power underpins how civil society functions. It is a form of power generated by people joining together to demand and effect change. But while this type of power can pose profound challenges to government institutions, it has its limitations. Many civil society groups form in reaction to adversity, but lack resources and often work in isolation. These circumstances can lead to both an extreme resilience in groups, but also a tendency towards inward-looking defensiveness.

Vertical power

Progressive political parties have tended to focus on the idea of taking control of the machinery of the state and using the vertical power it provides to enable change. It is an approach that has achieved some important breakthroughs, such as the creation of the National Health Service (NHS) and the shortening of the working week. But as an approach it is increasingly limited.

The traditional way of doing things, of 'delivering policy ideas conjured up by some think tank', no longer suffices because the old 20th-century 'Fordist' command-and-control model of government is incapable of dealing with the complex and constantly evolving challenges and opportunities we face in the early 21st century. Nowadays, our future is increasingly negotiated, not imposed, and the modern state needs to reflect this reality. We need a system structured around a collaborative state apparatus founded upon a shared-power interrelationship between civil society and government institutions.

The 45° Change faultline

The space where government institutions and civil society meet can be envisaged as a 45° line forming the nexus where the interrelationship of shared power takes place (see Figure 8.4). To some extent, the model also describes existing processes. The model is not a blueprint, but rather provides an indication of how a co-operative model of progressive change can be developed into a force for radical transformation.

But to work, shared power requires a redistribution of power that will support emerging forces within civil society and counteract overbearing forms of vertical power and capitalism.

Participatory practice: refining the model

What does the 45° Change model have to say about community empowerment and transformation? The Deeper Democracy Group[5] argue that it is useful because it helps map relationships between the local state, communities and the work of participatory practice. The

---

[5] Founded by Colin Miller, the Deeper Democracy Group is an informal group interested in examining the contribution that participatory practice, such as community development, community organising and deliberative approaches to decision making, can make in creating a more deliberative and participatory democratic system in the UK (see www.deeperdemocracy.org.uk).

Figure 8.4: The 45° Change faultline

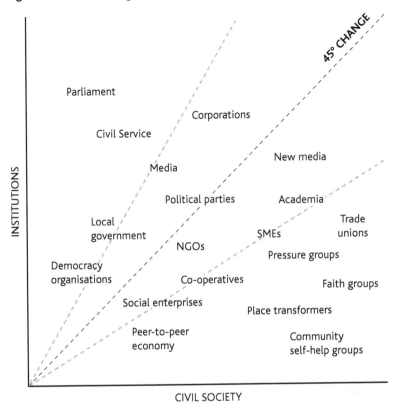

Note: NGOs = non-governmental organisations, SMEs = small and medium-sized enterprises.

model also offers an indication of how communities can be more effectively empowered.

The 45° line in Figure 8.4 could be deceptive, because it is not so much a hard border as a *space or zone* of interactions. This is the space where communities, local government and services argue, negotiate, invent and collaborate. It is also the space where participatory practice works to support citizens and residents in these interactions (see Figure 8.5).[6] It is the zone where power can and must be shared and

---

[6] Charities and voluntary organisations play a critically important role in civil society and in promoting change. It is a rarely discussed fact that a significant percentage of organisations within the 'community and voluntary' or the 'third sector', consist of very small, community based and led groups. The NCVO reported that in 2017/18 there were approximately 166,592 voluntary organisations in the UK, the majority being micro or small. About 47% (77,601 groups) have an income of less than £10,000

Figure 8.5: Institutions and civil society

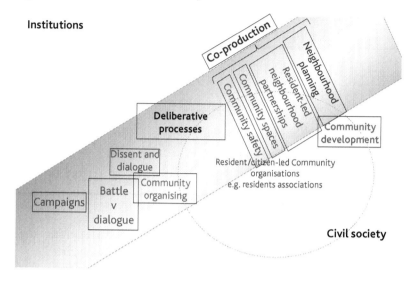

ultimately grown by and for the community. The predominant role of the state is to ensure this happens.

However, if communities are not properly supported and government institutions are not responsive to structural change, then we will, at best, remain stuck and fragmented within the 45° space, with an endless series of clashes and experiments that achieve little in terms of social or structural change. New municipalism may well be the vehicle that will help achieve the empowerment of communities through a practical 45° approach.

Rethinking local government

The growth of the new municipalist/co-operative council movement, as well as the independent council movement in Frome in Somerset in the UK, 'is a recognition that the traditional command-and-control, closed-loop systems of local government no longer work and new political and structural relationships between the local state, citizens and

---

and a further 35% (57,956) have an income of between £10,000 to £100,000. These micro and small organisations play an enormously important but largely unrecognised and invisible role in civil society within neighbourhoods and communities. These are the kinds of organisations supported by the likes of community development workers and community organisers (where they exist) (NCVO, 2020).

communities need to be developed' (Barcelona En Comu, Bookchin and Colau, 2019, p 16).

'New municipalism' is a self-proclaimed worldwide political movement with strong roots in Spain. In the UK, the co-operative council movement emerged out of a 'coalition of discontent' of community activists, local government officers and local and national politicians (Macfadyen, 2016), and over the 'democratic deficit', particularly in relation to local government (RSA, 2014). It is not as overtly political as the movement in Spain, but arose for similar reasons, especially in reaction against the imposition of austerity by governments following the financial crisis in 2008 and the growth of right-wing populism.

The rise of new municipalism in Spain is characterised by an ideology of 'radical localism' that emerged from the mass radical citizens' movements such as 15-M, which arose in response to the financial criss of 2010/11 in Spain (Errejon and Mouffe, 2016). Two important political groups emerged from these struggles: the 'left populist' party Podemos, and citizen platforms (CPs), which played a central role in developing many of the core ideas in new municipalism.

The CPs emphasised local action – *building power from the bottom up, both within and without formal institutions*. In the 2015 elections, the CPs took control of Spain's leading cities: Barcelona, Madrid, Valencia and Zaragoza (Roth, 2020). In 2017, new municipalism became an organised global movement through the Fearless Cities Network and has more than 50 city administrations and organisational members across the globe (Cumbers and Paul, 2020). New municipalism 'is not about implementing progressive policies, but about returning power to ordinary people' (Thompson, 2020, section II.I, para 4).

In its founding document, *Fearless Cities* (Barcelona En Comu, Bookchin and Colau, 2019), the authors say that new municipalism is informed by five guiding principles:

- Cities must seek to empower citizens.
- Competencies and resources must be transferred to local areas.
- Community-level decision making must be made via participative approaches.
- Digital platforms should be developed for easy access to decision making.
- Politics should be 'feminised' through:
  - ◦ ensuring gender parity in all spaces;
  - ◦ 'horizontalising' decision making;
  - ◦ discouraging confrontational approaches; and
  - ◦ embracing diversity.

It is commonly thought that local government is the lowest step of state administration, but *Fearless Cities* argues that the space for self-government must be around decisions that are taken that will directly affect those people and communities (Roth, 2020, para 4). Municipalism as a project is about contesting not only the functions of local government (and beyond), but also the forms through which we make collective decisions about ourselves and our territories.

Co-operative councils

The co-operative council approach was pioneered by the Labour administration of the London Borough of Lambeth in 2012/13 (London Borough of Lambeth, 2013). To date, the Co-operative Council Innovation Network has more than 20 members, including cities as wide-ranging as Birmingham, Edinburgh and London boroughs such as Barking and Dagenham, as well as smaller towns such as Kirklees and Rochdale.[7]

The key aims of co-operative councils echo those of *Fearless Cities*. They seek to create a 'new model for local government built on civil leadership, with councils working in equal partnership with local people to shape and strengthen communities' (RSA, 2014, para 1). At the same time, the so-called 'flat pack democracy movement',[8] pioneered in the small town of Frome in Somerset, has led to the emergence of a loose network of about 20 smaller towns (Harris, 2019).[9]

The key challenge for the long-term viability of the new municipalism movement's continuation is its overt 'leftist' political profile. For example, in the 2019 Spanish elections, the CPs had mixed results while retaining control in Barcelona, and a centre-right/far-right coalition took control of Madrid and appears to be in the process of dismantling participatory structures that had been developed over the previous five years (Cumbers and Paul, 2020). These elections generate uncertainty about the strength and potential for new municipalism and are a reminder that, despite being rooted in the local with proximity to ordinary people, new municipalism is not exempt from electoral logic (Agustín, 2020).

---

[7] See https://www.councils.coop.

[8] See https://flatpack2021.co.uk/home.

[9] Interestingly, Frome is a member of Fearless Cities rather than the Co-operative Council Network.

Three case studies

Two of the following case studies (Barking and Dagenham, and Frome) have been chosen because they have often been reported as exemplars that could shape local government strategies in the future (see Reed, 2019, for example). We also use the example of Madrid because it describes how the *Fearless Cities* new municipalist model has been put into practice. The question is to what extent do these councils reflect the ideas in the 45° Change model? Do they bring together the top with the bottom to work towards a system of shared power?

London Borough of Barking and Dagenham

The London Borough of Barking and Dagenham has a population of 210,711 and is the poorest borough in London. In 2006, the neo-fascist British National Party (BNP) came close to capturing control of the council but was electorally wiped out in 2010. In the years since, the borough has had its budget slashed, to half of what it was.

In response to these challenges, the council decided to rethink its role so that all policy must, at its core, seek to improve civic engagement and democratic participation in the widest sense, enabling citizens to challenge and grapple with the local instruments of power (Cruddas and Rodwell, 2019). The new model is built on 'three pillars':

- a new local inclusive economy;
- empowering public services; and
- citizenship and participation.

The new local inclusive economy dimension includes:

- founding a new, council-owned regeneration company;
- creating a new form of council-owned affordable housing offering private-rented properties at rates based on the income of the renter; and
- developing a council-owned green energy company so that new developments have access to affordable, sustainable energy.

By integrating traditional council departments and introducing forms of co-production and consultation processes with services users and providers, the council aims to transform itself from a paternalistic top-down bureaucratic system to one that is more open and better able to develop services that meet the needs of local people.

A core feature of the transformation is the 'Every One Every Day' (EOED) programme, which aims to develop a shared understanding of 'citizenship and participation', combining a focus on rights, responsibilities and cultural inclusion. The aim of the programme is to build social bridges and bonds in the community and forge a new politics of identity and belonging (London Borough of Barking and Dagenham, 2020).

EOED employs a team of participatory practitioners who work with residents to develop community initiatives and businesses. These include new arrivals programmes, community cooking, environmental improvement, after-school clubs, play centres and learning centres. The strategy is underpinned by a commitment to increase community engagement: '[A]ll policy must at its core seek to improve civic engagement and democratic participation in the widest sense, enabling citizens to challenge and grapple with the local instruments of power' (Cruddas and Rodwell, 2019, para 4).

A question of interest to us is: To what extent is the strategy aimed at embedding participatory and deliberative decision making into the way the *council* plans and makes decisions? And what has been the role of participatory practice in helping take forward the strategy? Is the council seeking to go about systemic change by democratising its functions or is it mostly concerned with what takes place within the lower part of the 45° line, that is, communities and civil society?

The Barking and Dagenham programme is ambitious, but the deliberative and participative systems in the heart of decision making within the council need to be developed. The development of the Citizens Alliance Network over the first national COVID-19 lockdown period from March 2020 saw the council and civil society share decision making about the way vital services such as food distribution were enacted. The challenge is how this power sharing and co-production can be embedded, sustained and accelerated beyond the crisis.

Madrid

Spain's capital city has a population of 3.3 million. The city had been a stronghold of the right-of-centre People's Party but in 2015 a coalition between Ahora Madrid (AM) and the Spanish Socialist Workers' Party (PSOE) took control of the council and Manuela Carmena (from AM) became the mayor. However, in 2019, a right-wing coalition between the People's Party and the neo-fascist Vox party regained control.

The left coalition developed a radical reshaping of how the council functioned by creating a system of devolved decision making through direct democracy and deliberation – a strategy based on the concept of 'disintermediation', that is, 'removing intermediaries from representative politics' (DeJohn, 2017, p 4) to enable citizens to make their own decisions. The system is founded on a dual-track approach: digital decision making and face-to-face deliberation.

Digital decision making

The strategy sought to integrate council decision making with traditional face-to-face forms of local decision making, such as neighbourhood meetings and deliberative processes, with an ambitious digital platform called Decide Madrid,[10] which is based on a new generation of 'open source civic technologies that can be used to engage the public in decision making'. The aim is to facilitate bottom-up, direct democracy where decisions that ultimately gain mass approval are binding. For example, on urban planning issues, a €100 million participatory budgeting scheme enables the money to be allocated according to proposals suggested by citizens, which are listed on the platform. If the proposal is supported by 1 per cent of citizens, it progresses to a final voting stage.

Face-to-face deliberation

In parallel with the digital processes, the council set up face-to-face deliberation spaces, with the aim of encouraging proposals 'from below' and promoting collective decision making. Citizens involved in the deliberative groups are selected through sortition. The council's strategy is based on the concept of 'distributed democracy', where decision making takes place via a series of decentralised nodes, ultimately verified and endorsed by the elected city council (CrowdLaw, 2018). This is an extremely ambitious programme that seeks to marry digitally based decision making with more traditional participatory and deliberative processes.

In 2019, a coalition between the Popular Party and the far-right Vox party took over the council. It appears that Madrid's exciting experiment in creating a radical participatory democracy could be swiftly dismantled, which begs the question of the staying power of a self-proclaimed new municipalist approach as a political movement.

---

[10] See https://www.involve.org.uk/resources/case-studies/decide-madrid.

Frome

Frome in Somerset, UK has a population of about 22,000 and is governed by a town/parish council. Parish councils are the lowest layer of directly elected government and do not run mainstream services. One of the advantages of this lowly status is that they are pretty free to do whatever they want within the law. Being small, they can also be close to local communities.

In 2017, a group called Independence for Frome (IfF) completely replaced the Conservative and Liberal Democrat councillors. The group argued that party politics is a form of 'gatekeeping' that discourages public participation in local politics; that political parties are more concerned with point-scoring and party tribalism than listening to what residents have to say and this prevents open listening and collaboration.

A core concept of IfF is that the council and residents of Frome share responsibility for resolving issues and taking things forward. Its ethos can be summed up as: 'You can't come to a meeting and demand "what are you going to do about some problem or other", but rather "what can we do together about the problem"' (Macfadyen, 2018, 4 minutes into video).

The council organises regular deliberative public meetings on issues, bringing together residents, experts and councillors. There is a commitment that whenever possible the council will implement the recommendations made at these meetings. The council also employs a participatory budgeting approach, 'which means that councillors encourage and enable other local people to decide what ... to spend money on. We make no apology to those who believe that councillors are elected to make decisions and don't need to work with the rest of the community' (Hellard, 2017, para 6).

Conclusion

The creation of a local form of 45° deep democracy is challenging and complex. To coin an aphorism, the more complex a society, the more complex is the democracy needed to run it. As the case studies in this chapter have shown, it takes sustained effort to involve communities in a meaningful way in steering public policies and practices.

The commitment and enthusiasm behind new municipalism, the co-operative council movement and the IfF to sharing and devolving power to citizens and communities are to be welcomed. But not enough has been done so far as to ascertain whether the citizens and communities involved feel more 'empowered' with the new structures than previously. So those of us engaged in working with and thinking about community empowerment and participatory practice need to exercise a degree of caution and to act as critical friends. We need to ask the questions that are not currently being asked.[11] This is particularly important because some of the initiatives discussed in this chapter are increasingly being promoted as exemplars and potential future national government models for local government (for example, see Cruddas and Rodwell, 2019).

One thing is certain: the kinds of devolution of power to communities envisaged in new municipalism, or the shared power described in *45° Change* (Lawson, 2019), cannot happen unless those communities have the resources and support to enable them to develop their own, independent voices. Without this they will always be an adjunct where the unwanted and questioning voices can be silenced or ignored, and where people will be unable to develop their own ideas.

Community resilience is a vital component of community empowerment and the ability of communities to fully participate in the new forms of governing relationships described in *45° Change* (Lawson, 2019). However, during the past ten years of austerity there has been a devastating loss of amenities and support for communities. This has both hampered communities, but it has also spurred creativity and innovation.[12]

For a new form of local and national governance based on shared or distributed power to work, we need the restoration of conditions for communities to thrive, as well as an opening up of dialogue with the grassroots of civil society, where local people can develop, share and implement ideas that can transform their communities and society for the better.

National political parties must deal with the complexities of the 21st century and make the cultural leap to see their role as essentially supporting people and communities, and making changes with them. But communities need to step up too, to get out of their silos and see a bigger, more strategic and political (small 'p') role. They have to help drive the change needed to change the system, not just the immediate services they are focused on.

---

[11] For more on the techniques for facilitating dialogues, see Miller et al (2020).

[12] See the 2020 Deeper Democracy Group's call for a National Community Support Plan at https://www.compassonline.org.uk/a-national-community-support-plan.

References

Agustín, Ó. G. (2020) 'New municipalism as space for solidarity', *Soundings*, 74: 54–67.

Bailey, N. and Pill, M. (2015) 'Can the state empower communities through localism? An evaluation of recent approaches to neighbourhood governance in England', *Environment and Planning C: Government and Policy*, 3(2): 289–304.

Barcelona En Comu, Bookchin, D. and Colau, A. (2019) *Fearless Cities: A Guide to the Global Municipalist Movement*, Oxford: New Internationalist.

Batty, E., Beatty, C., Foden, M., Lawless, P., Pearson, S. and Wilson, A. (2010) *Involving Local People in Regeneration: Evidence from the New Deal for Communities Programme: The New Deal for Communities Final Report: Volume 2*, London: Department for Communities and Local Government.

Chanan, G. and Miller, C. (2013) *Rethinking Community Practice: Developing Transformative Neighbourhoods*, Bristol: Policy Press.

CrowdLaw (2018) 'Decide Madrid', https://www.involve.org.uk/resources/case-studies/decide-madrid.

Cruddas, J. and Rodwell, D. (2019) 'Civic socialism in East London: a radical approach to local government', *Labour List*, 21 February, https://labourlist.org/2019/02/civic-socialism-in-east-london-a-radical-approach-to-local-government.

Cumbers, A. and Paul, F. (2020) 'Adapting to the political moment and diverse terrain of "actually existing municipalisms"', *Soundings*, 74: 54–67.

DCLG (Department for Communities and Local Government) (2008) *Communities in Control White Paper: Impact Assessments*, London: DCLG, https://www.legislation.gov.uk/ukia/2008/173/pdfs/ukia_20080173_en.pdf.

DCLG (2010) *Evaluation of the National Strategy for Neighbourhood Renewal: Final Report*, London: DCLG, https://extra.shu.ac.uk/ndc/downloads/general/Neighbourhood%20Renewal%20Final%20report.pdf.

DeJohn, S. (2017) 'Beyond protest: examining the Decide Madrid platform for public engagement', The Governance Lab (New York University), 13 November, http://thegovlab.org/beyond-protest-examining-the-decide-madrid-platform-for-public-engagement/. [accessed 13 January 2021]

Errejon, E. and Mouffe, C. (2016) *Podemos: In the Name of the People*, London: Lawrence and Wishart.

Fordham, G. (2010) *The New Deal for Communities Programme: Achieving a Neighbourhood Focus for Regeneration Vol 1*, London: DCLG.

Hansard Society (2019) *Audit of Political Engagement 16: The 2019 Report*, London: Hansard Society.

Harris, J. (2019) 'How to take over your town: the inside story of a local revolution', *The Guardian*, 12 June, https://www.theguardian.com/society/2019/jun/12/how-to-take-over-your-town-the-inside-story-of-a-local-revolution.

Hellard, K. (2017) 'Let the people decide', *Frome Times*, March.

Lawless, P. (2011) 'Big Society and community: lessons from the 1998–2011 New Deal for Communities programme in England', *People Place and Policy Online*, 5(2): 55–64, https://extra.shu.ac.uk/ppp-online/issue_2_060711/article_2.html.

Lawson, N. (2019) *45° Change: Transforming Society from Below and Above*, London: Compass, https://www.compassonline.org.uk/wp-content/uploads/2019/02/Compass_45-degree-change-1.pdf.

London Borough of Barking and Dagenham (2020) 'We are everyone', London: London: Borough of Barking and Dagenham, https://www.weareeveryone.org.

London Borough of Lambeth (2013) *London Borough of Lambeth Cooperative Council Constitution*, London: London Borough of Lambeth.

Macfadyen, P. (2016) *Flatpack Democracy: A DIY Guide to Creating Independent Politics*, Frome: eco-logic books.

Macfadyen, P. (2018) 'Peter Macfadyen – flat pack democracy', *The Tree Conference Online*, https://thetreeconference.com/speakers2018/peter-macfadyen.

Miller, C., Beddow, N., Chanan, G., Fisher, B., Gardham, N., Foot, J., Hall, J., Kettleborough, H., Miller, C., Rhodes, B., Scott, M., Tam, H., Warburton, D., and Wilcox, D. (2020) *Participation at 45° techniques for Citizen-led Change*, London: Compass, http://deeperdemocracy.org.uk/library.

NCVO (National Council Voluntary Organisations) (2020) *UK Civil Society Almanac 2020*, London, https://data.ncvo.org.uk/profile/size-and-scope/.

Reed, S. (2019) 'From paternalism to participation: putting civil society at the heart of national renewal', https://acevoblogs.wordpress.com/2019/06/11/from-paternalism-to-participation-labours-new-civil-society-strategy.

Roth, L. (2020) 'Which municipalism? Let's be choosy', https://www.opendemocracy.net/en/can-europe-make-it/which-municipalism-lets-be-choosy.

RSA (2014) 'Cooperative Council Network – about', https://www. councils.coop.

Thompson, M. (2020) 'What's so new about new municipalism?', *Progress in Human Geography*, https://journals.sagepub.com/doi/abs/ 10.1177/0309132520909480.

Uberoi, E. (2019) *Turnout at Elections 1918–2017*, London: House of Commons Library.

9

Connecting at the edges for collective change

Alison Gilchrist

Introduction

Tomorrow's communities need to be resilient and optimistic. Yet many of today's most challenged communities are operating 'at the edge': socially, economically and geographically. In many ways, this puts them at a disadvantage – vulnerable and fragmented, as described in Chapter 1. Tomorrow's communities must find ways to overcome these fringe 'dis-benefits', using internal resourcefulness and cross-cutting connections to become resilient and more integrated despite a manifestly uneven distribution of wealth, power and life chances. A decade of austerity cuts in public spending, coupled with the impact of the COVID-19 pandemic and subsequent recession, has further exposed inequalities, leaving many feeling 'left behind' compared with others; just about surviving but certainly not thriving (Baldwin et al, 2020). Left-behind areas are characterised by Oxford Consultants for Social Inclusion as having 'high levels of need, multiple deprivation and socio-economic challenges', along with 'poor community and civic infrastructure, relative isolation and low levels of participation' (OCSI, 2019).

Recent research discovered that areas of particular 'community need' tend to be located around the coast, on the peripheries of more prosperous cities and out-of-town estates (OCSI, 2019). While the study distinguishes between deprivation and lack of collective assets, there is clearly an issue arising from poor connectivity and reduced access to public services or fast broadband, causing poor health and shrunken life opportunities, especially for urban dwellers without secure jobs or living in rented accommodation. Many are also vulnerable to energy poverty, unpredictable weather conditions and severe flooding. The precarity of this existence has been exacerbated by the pandemic and in the long term it will affect many people's mental health, educational attainment and general self-esteem. These are the challenges facing tomorrow's communities, and younger generations in particular. This chapter looks at how improving and extending connections within and between communities contributes to how they function as complex systems, especially through nurturing inclusive networks of relations based on trust and mutual understanding.

During the COVID-19 pandemic, many communities have demonstrated remarkable capacity for self-organising, using local knowledge and connections to ensure that services are tailored to hyper-local conditions and without excessive coordination by infrastructure bodies in either the voluntary or statutory sectors. But there have also been gaps, resentments and mutual suspicion, so it would be misguided to suggest that all communities are inherently resilient or resourceful, capable of withstanding any amount of catastrophe or long-term deprivation (MacKinnon and Derickson, 2013). For some at the margins of society, specific support and investment are needed to build capacity, increase citizen participation and develop resident-led proposals for recovery and resistance.

Responsive and open networking underpins effective collaboration and alliance-based campaigning on issues prioritised by communities themselves through continuous engagement and debate. While good relationships are vital for survival and wellbeing, dysfunctional or hostile links can be damaging to individuals as well as reducing the ability of communities to provide mutual aid and develop strategies for social change. Despite common, but mistaken, assumptions about unity and sense of belonging, local tensions and disagreements are inevitable and must be honestly acknowledged and negotiated. As the poet, Audre Lorde (1979), wrote: 'Without community there is no liberation ... but community must not mean a shedding of our differences, nor the pathetic pretence that these differences do not exist.' Indeed, a diversity of opinion, interests, backgrounds and identities enriches the experience of community, encouraging enterprise and the kind of creative assembly that arises from adjacent but contrasting or incompatible ideas (Sarasathy, 2008). These juxtapositions, often located at system edges, are vibrant and ripe with potential, as well as being fraught with possible spark-generating frictions. Extensive and diverse informal networks are valuable because they enable people to explore controversial issues. These off-stage 'muted debates among known allies ... allow them to reveal risky thoughts and rehearse arguments' (Gilchrist, 2019, p 94) that could, through inclusive and self-empowering deliberation, generate alternative visions of how things could be different or better – a necessary condition for social transformation. Such conversations allow new ideas and awareness to emerge, in processes similar to Freire's (1972) concept of 'critical dialogue and conscientisation'.

The overlapping networks of diverse actors and assets characterise complex systems, such as communities and natural ecologies. The links that reach across boundaries are perhaps most significant, enabling community-based intermediaries or 'bricoleurs' to pull together ideas, resources and influence, in ways that can make things happen while building long-term capacity and restoring cohesion. The Social Integration Commission (2018) describes community strengths as 'the extent to which people positively interact and connect with others who are different to themselves ... determined by the level of equality between people, the nature of their relationships, and their degree of participation in the communities in which they live'. Recent research indicates that communities that are better connected and accustomed to diversity tend to be more open, hopeful and capable of evolving in response to disruption; in other words, they are more resilient (Clarke et al, 2020).

Policy context

The idea of 'community' has long figured in government thinking about tackling society's 'wicked and squishy problems', those that seem most intractable and complicated (Strauch, 1975; Grint, 2008; Taylor, 2011). Grint argues that 'wicked problems' require 'clumsy solutions' and that these can best be arrived at through a pragmatic acknowledgement of uncertainties. Drawing on the 'community capital' of local connections and social infrastructure harnesses the collective and diverse 'wisdom of experience' located in the wider community (Parsfield et al, 2015). For many policy makers and funders, 'community' represents a flexible and willing resource that can be mobilised to devise and deliver 'solutions' that are tailored to particular localities or populations.

It would be a mistake, however, for politicians to assume that the recent resurgence of 'community spirit' will be maintained without various forms of support or the means to coordinate its efforts. Valuable collective intelligence is generated through shared observations and reflection, and stored in the web of relationships, but it is often not sufficiently respected by outside agencies and professional experts. Effective community networks comprise a kaleidoscopic array of diverse links, clusters and patterns of connection. Their extent and configuration are shaped by a variety of factors: the local social and organisational environment, the nature of interpersonal relationships, power dynamics and myriad, intersecting social identities. Together they constitute an unbounded, but communal system in which ideas are exchanged and initiatives are trialled, evolve or expire, according to prevailing conditions and 'rules' of interaction.

External support and other forms of investment for community-level programmes usually aim to address specific problems, arriving with targets and success criteria (see Chapters 4 and 6). Sometimes these are established through prior consultation between community representatives and public agencies, articulated as specific objectives to be achieved over a fixed (often unrealistically short) timescale. Theories of change tend to reflect linear models of progress, with so-called 'logic frameworks' setting out the interrelationships of aims, inputs, outputs and outcomes. It is assumed that improvement will come about through strategic, but 'top-down', interventions that result in predictable increments, eventually leading to the desired transformation. In recent years there has been a welcome, if slightly apolitical, emphasis on community assets rather than deficits, epitomised most clearly in the asset-based community development model (Green and Haines, 2015) and appreciative enquiry methods (Cooperrider and Whitney, 2001). Both these approaches reflect a long tradition in community development in that they reinforce and mobilise local aspirations, collective strengths and individual talents to achieve change, sometimes through the active and skilled support of paid community workers. The focus is generally on projects, campaigns, group facilitation and organisation development, in the hope that these will accomplish agreed goals and become self-sustaining.

While problem solving is not the same as social transformation, nonetheless there are common processes that can be discerned, notably an emphasis on outcomes and non-linear change. There seems to be a growing willingness among policy makers to adopt broader ambitions for community development, using terms such as 'empowerment', 'resilience' and 'collective efficacy'. In this respect, community-level interventions and funding programmes aim to improve capacity generally by removing obstacles to self-help and collective action rather than being focused on particular ends or issues (Ramalingam and Jones, 2008). Communities and intermediary voluntary agencies have demonstrated that they can be trusted to handle complex multi-agency arrangements and plan strategic responses to escalating challenges. Funders and policy makers should be more willing to allocate financial support directly into the hands of the community organisations, rather than via overly bureaucratic organisations and government agencies.

This would allow community life to flourish and people to maintain their connections, as well as consolidating links across local partnerships.

Using complexity-informed approaches for community-driven transformation

In the past, community development was commonly claimed to be non-directive, while asserting core principles of social justice, equality and participation. In practice, such interventions have often been funded, and therefore influenced, by the priorities of foundations or government programmes. This approach has resulted in only superficial improvements or long-term failure, mainly due to poor community engagement, bureaucratic procedures and widespread disillusionment among the intended 'beneficiaries' (Hills, 2019). Regeneration programmes and public health strategies have been particularly prone to this kind of model, although as other chapters in this book indicate, this is changing and there is growing interest in models of community-led development (see Chapters 4 and 10).

Some more enlightened approaches enable communities themselves to establish a vision and strategy that build on strengths and address locally identified needs. The key to this appears to be creating a foundation of strong connections and informal ways of working that favour both flexibility and social innovation, unconstrained by statutory infrastructure and government 'red tape' (Gilchrist, 2016; Wyler, 2020). However, this is not to say that infrastructure should be regarded as a hindrance to effective collective action, but it is a question of finding a balance between excessive control versus random activity, ensuring that the social ecosystem of neighbours, friends, volunteers and allies can function co-operatively, with only light-touch coordination and support (see Chapter 6).

Complexity science suggests that communities that are well connected resemble systems at the 'edge of chaos', an optimal state of dynamic equilibrium that facilitates adaptation to changing circumstances and provides plentiful opportunities for solutions to emerge and evolve (Gilchrist, 2019). Clusters of activity may become formally organised, but are often initiated and coordinated through informal networks and micro-organisations operating 'below the radar' of most local authority and voluntary sector infrastructure bodies (Soteri-Proctor, 2011). This layer of grassroots activity has proved vital during the COVID-19 pandemic and other forms of crises such as environmental degradation (see Chapter 13), but is often underestimated and misunderstood by policy makers and funders (Hornung et al, 2020). Successful communities of the future will need to be agile and responsive, with a collective sense of mutual commitment and efficacy. 'Low-cost' relationships that are rooted in familiarity, everyday proximity, informal interactions and shared identity form the essential groundwork for self-organisation, cross-cutting alliances and empowered action (Reagans, 2011).

Complexity thinking has been used to understand society, organisations, cities and programmes for social development (Mitleton-Kelly, 2003; Pflaeging, 2014; Byrne, 2015; Batty, 2019). It explains the unpredictability of collective action, user empowerment and citizen participation (Gilchrist, 2019). Consequently, new models for funding, accountability and evaluation have been devised that allow maximum flexibility and prioritise the value of co-operation and relationships. Some major funders are applying ideas from complexity science and systems thinking to the implementation and evaluation of community-led transformation. So instead of an array of imposed targets and monitoring procedures, these social investment programmes favour non-directive support and long-term investment so that communities can grow their internal capacity for leadership and self-organisation to be sustained long after the funding has ended. In England, the Big Local[1] and Community Organisers[2] programmes are current exemplars of this, with notable success both during the pandemic and in pursuing long-term goals (Wilson and Taylor, 2020).

The Lankelly Chase Foundation has adopted a systems approach for its funding and learning programme. It supports associates and frontline workers to become 'system changers' working with communities to promote place-based development. As independent actors, their role is not to facilitate pre-designed solutions, but to support and shape the messy and emotional web of community connections. This encourages people to draw on a range of perspectives, to reveal local system dynamics and drive change through a coalition of local actors. It has been used successfully in the Midlands to promote collaborative co-production (Billiald and McAllister-Jones, 2015; Bashir et al, 2019).

Evaluation processes are fundamental to developing community confidence, understanding and shared commitment. New trends in evaluation favour using multi-pronged web-based methods to measure the effects of complex interventions, for example in public health, education and community safety (Komro et al, 2016; Lowe, 2017).

---

[1] https://localtrust.org.uk/big-local/about-big-local/
[2] https://www.corganisers.org.uk/

The performance management models developed by the Lankelly Chase Foundation and by the FSG consulting firm in the United States advocate partnerships based on trust and respect, with an emphasis on evaluations that are open, flexible and oriented towards collective learning. Evaluation is seen as an important dimension of mutual accountability and serves to develop a shared interpretation of change processes 'on the ground' and in real time.

The 'collective impact' model (Kania et al, 2018; Cabaj and Weaver, 2016) and 'human learning systems' approach (see https://www.humanlearning.systems/) both emphasise continuous reflection and discussion. Complexity-friendly models of evaluation value learning from direct experience for understanding current and unexpected changes in the system, and how impact can be demonstrated (or not). This involves continuous data gathering, analysis and dialogue in order to examine causal relationships and so adapt the nature of practice interventions (Bamberger et al, 2015). Patton's (2006) model for complexity-based developmental evaluation recognises the value of emergent and innovative processes that may result in transformative system-wide change. His recommendations assert that evaluation should be ongoing and integral to the project's work, using iterative feedback loops to allow flexibility and adaptation to change. The data gathered will 'capture system dynamics, interdependencies and emergent inter-connections', revealing the contributions of community members, as well as funders working in partnership with practitioners and other agencies. It should also foster a 'hunger for learning' (Patton, 2006, p 30).

Lessons from practice

These ideas are being put into practice in a coastal resort in the West of England. The National Lottery Community Fund has provided grant-aid to a five-year project on the southern outskirts of the town. In three adjacent neighbourhoods, local people are being encouraged to connect with one another using a variety of methods – at local hubs, community-led groups and a regular forum and through social media. The project is loosely based on asset-based development and inspired by the principles and ethics of permaculture, taking a regenerative, whole ecosystems approach to project design and delivery (Holmgren, 2011). Permaculturists are particularly interested in 'edge effects' at the interface between different ecosystems, creating a region of heightened interaction and creativity. This thinking is similar to the 'well- connected community' model of community development (Gilchrist, 2019) in that it is informed by complexity science and prioritises boundary-spanning networks that nurture the social environment for activities and groups to emerge and flourish. Those that suit the prevailing conditions survive, evolving through cycles of support and challenge by the workers and fellow residents. This emphasis on networking is embedded in the project's title, 'Our Neighbourhood Network', its aim being to nourish webs of interpersonal relations, but also to enhance links with organisations working in and with the local communities.

The team working on the 'Our Neighbourhood Network' project in the West of England supports existing projects but just as importantly actively canvasses for new ideas and people with a passion or skill to share. They use a strengths-based engagement strategy, seeking out talents and creativity, and encouraging local people to experiment with taster sessions or trial events. Wherever possible, ways are found to overcome practical and psychological barriers so that individuals can pursue chosen aspirations, for themselves and the wider community. There is a thriving horticultural society with its own allotments, a lantern-making group and an arts club. The project has adopted an inclusive approach, acknowledging that these communities face challenges around ingrained poverty, due to worklessness, disability and minimal wage rates, alongside other forms of deprivation such as poor health.

The majority of community members are from working-class backgrounds, in low-paid, insecure jobs, unemployed or retired on low pensions. Cutting across this economic disadvantage are inequalities arising from gender, disability, age and ethnicity. Regrettably, these shape individual life chances and identities, and are sometimes associated with intra-communal tensions and barriers that prevent people from achieving their ambitions or participating fully in community activities.

It is entirely possible that without positive action strategies, the desired outcomes might be differentially spread. Improved connectivity will probably not be uniform across neighbourhoods, with networks containing exclusive clusters forming patterns of in-groups and outsiders. The team is especially focused on addressing unconscious biases and favouritism; working to boost skills and confidence, thereby tackling sometimes hidden power dynamics and social isolation. These need to be examined openly, as well as being dealt with in practice through role modelling, holding difficult conversations and generally adopting a whole-systems approach to oppressive attitudes and behaviours.

Connections are regarded as the basis for people's sense of community and the foundation for collective action, so progress is achieved through growing inclusive local networks and building links with agencies that can bring public resources into the neighbourhood or enable people to access services beyond their immediate area. Community hubs provide informal meeting places (dubbed 'bumping spaces') that foster casual encounters and impromptu conversations. The team of paid workers primarily sees its role as encouraging participation, mentoring individuals and nurturing a sense of local leadership. The individuals involved in proposing and developing ideas have described how their confidence has grown, reporting improved mental health and sense of belonging.

Some training is provided to develop the knowledge and self-reliance of local people to run projects independently, thus establishing a foundation of sustainable and endogenous collective capacity. Various initiatives are up and running that encourage groups to 'explore the rich seam of human experience that underpins our community' through storytelling, and this offers an additional means of capturing the project's successes and what has been learnt along the way. The neighbourhood's green places, such as the parks and communal allotments, are largely shaped by the interests and skills of the particular individuals who are caring for them and have become vital outdoor spaces for interaction and play. In addition, they have enabled 'socially distanced' meetings to continue during the pandemic, thereby maintaining some semblance of community life while the planned hubs have been out of action.

As has been amply demonstrated during the COVID-19 crisis, communities have always demonstrated an independent ability to self-organise for mutual aid, solidarity and social change. There are numerous examples across the country (Wyler, 2020; Taylor and Wilson, 2020), illustrated here by one story from the neighbourhoods that are the focus of this chapter.

Normally, a food bank had operated from the local Healthy Living Centre but this became impossible under COVID restrictions. Mo, an enterprising and compassionate local woman, took responsibility for redelivering the surplus food from Fair Share and making sure it would find its way to those who needed it most, mainly more isolated older people, too worried to go to shopping and not connected enough to know about the help that was available through other means. She used her local knowledge, and trusted reputation, along with existing good relations through the 'grapevine', to ensure that those on the community edge remained connected to other services, to listen to their needs and provide some social comfort.

The overarching purpose of Our Neighbourhood Network is to support individuals and strengthen connections within and between communities. This requires deep-rooted community participation to ensure adjustments can be made and new avenues for collective action explored. The current range of activities has evolved in response to the suggestions, energy and interests of community members. These individuals became key nodes in the wider neighbourhood network and often contribute as much as the paid workers towards cultivating beneficial relationships within the community, using their enthusiasm to mobilise and benefit others.

Personal development is central to the project's ethos and the networks increase opportunities for this to happen, bringing about the positive changes that people want. For example, the setting up of an outdoor gym is happening because David, the key activist, had the original idea and has developed his self-belief, sense of empowerment and communication skills. He has been assisted through others in related fitness networks responding positively to his passion and helping him with advice on fundraising and organising sponsored events. Similarly, the colouring club and Crafty Chats sessions have been fuelled by the energy and commitment of Emma and Debi, who bring their own visions, gifts and creative ideas to the sessions. A small team of paid workers engages with individuals and groups, helping them to organise whatever people are interested in, using existing assets, while acquiring new skills and resources to sustain activities and create the conditions for new initiatives to evolve. Their role has largely been to promote good group facilitation and coach emergent leaders, mostly through informal conversations and networking. Collective deliberation takes place via forums where community members aim to gather three times a year to celebrate their achievements and generate ideas for future development.

In the original plan, broad outcomes are mentioned but delivery of specific projects is not predetermined and there are no set targets. An early community mapping exercise identified local assets and aspirations that would drive forward resident-initiated activities. Community ownership has been a core value, with key participants referred to as 'contributors' rather than activists, volunteers or leaders. The project's paid staff offer basic support such as seed-funding and training, which provides some infrastructure to act as trellising or 'scaffolding' to support collective action. This means that their input remains flexible, unconstrained by a *linear* theory of change or predicted results (Abercrombie et al, 2018).

The author is working with the team to devise an evaluation strategy based on the complexity-informed rationale of the project and incorporating its values. Five core themes have been agreed for the evaluation framework, namely: connectivity, collaboration, resilience, collective efficacy and community capability. Evidence will be collected to track and understand change through a variety of means, including storytelling, social network mapping, surveys and participation records. By recognising the complex nature of communities, the project is pioneering new methods of neighbourhood evaluation that endeavour to identify optimal levels of interaction and inclusion that allow 'order' to emerge from 'chaos'.

There are a number of issues and limitations associated with this approach, mainly because complex systems are inherently unpredictable, so the likelihood of unforeseen events, such as recurrent 'lockdowns' or the closure of local amenities due to a lack of funds, has to be acknowledged. Uncertainty about cause and effects means that it is difficult to definitively attribute developments to particular episodes or actions, let alone pursue specific goals. Nevertheless, it will be important to reflect on data collected on an ongoing basis to explore, and possibly explain, the dynamic relationship between different inputs (whether by the team or resident-initiated) and local change.

The neighbourhoods and their various components are seen as part of a multi-tiered social and organisational system and this raises additional issues around scale or levels of intervention. The project operates through multiple practices, for example, individual support, group maintenance and neighbourhood events, community projects and area-wide networking. In reality, the boundaries between the designated neighbourhoods are porous, with notional borders blurred by connections between families and friends living in adjoining areas, so that people attend community hubs and participate in activities outside of their immediate locality. This makes it even more complicated to trace and evaluate the causal links between specific happenings and overall outcomes.

Conclusions

Patton (2006, p 30) recommends 'continuous progress, ongoing adaptation and rapid responsiveness', with broad, transparent and honest communication leading to shared responsibility. Nevertheless, despite strong commitments to community-led evaluation, transformation projects are likely to encounter resistance to change as well as locally experienced forms of discrimination and social exclusion. Those with a vested interest in maintaining the status quo may stifle ambition through subversive tactics that undermine or distort progress. Dissent or sabotage can become a fruitful stimulus to learning but it can also be hugely destructive if not sensitively handled. Evaluation methods must take this into account and an emphasis on learning rather than measuring is likely to be more useful if changes are to be owned by the community and sustained beyond the end of funding (see Chapter 7).

Complexity-informed paradigms for development and evaluation can be summarised as a series of principles or propositions (Preskill et al, 2014; Patton, 2017). The main lessons boil down to the following practical advice:

- Be realistic about costs and timescales.
- Prioritise 'mission-critical' outcomes.
- Adopt a holistic, systems-based approach.
- Use an iterative process providing continuous feedback loops.
- Promote collective learning and understanding.
- Be flexible and adapt to changing circumstances.
- Be aware of emerging patterns of interaction and collaboration.
- Focus on points of synergy and influence.
- Explore connections and interdependencies.
- Embrace happenstance and serendipity.

In particular, make time to notice liminal incidents or trends occurring at the edges of the system because this is often where warning signs and the most innovative developments first appear (Johnson and Boulton, 2014).

As a general rule and in keeping with the strengths-based approach, community evaluations should include positive feedback loops that encourage creativity and constant development. Evidence should be considered at regular intervals or at crucial junctures that capture step-changes (non-linear transformations), and account for all contributions to progress, not just external inputs (funds and worker time). The complexity approach is interested in examining connections and dynamics within the community 'system', by tracing patterns of influence, flows of energy and power relations. There will be both planned and unanticipated change emerging at different levels, with consequential alterations to the project's environment and internal processes. While all evaluation is concerned with accountability, complexity-friendly models adopt a horizontal, peer-led approach, using a 'positive error culture' (Gigerenzer, 2014), with apparent failure seen as an opportunity for learning, rather than blame or recrimination.

Treating communities as complex and dynamic systems means seeing community activities not as control mechanisms or 'outputs' but as a critical catalyst for transformation. Chance encounters or tweaks to the normal course of procedures sometimes set off ripples of change and interaction that reconfigure local networks and expectations. In community development terms, it is the quality and the extent of the web of connections that matter, transmitting and exchanging energy, assets and ideas so that groups coalesce around shared aspirations and individual passions, some of which survive and become formal organisations.

The concept of 'order emerging from chaos' has led to this zone of community connectivity becoming known as 'chaordic', poised at the rather off-putting term: 'edge of chaos' (Block, 2009). But this kind of edge is a good place to be. It represents the point at which a self-organising equilibrium is achieved, such that communities are able to adjust to changing circumstances and generate novel forms of collective agency to replace moribund or dysfunctional bodies. It is a state where complex living systems can adapt to deliberate or accidental disruption through adaptive innovations that set seed, grow and co-evolve.

Most communities are full of tensions and contradictions in how people and organisations behave compared to the values they espouse, so conflicts of interest and opinion are often drivers for change, however difficult and unwelcome. Tomorrow's communities will be no different, especially given the impact of Brexit and the economic consequences of COVID-19 for the foreseeable future.

Ultimately, holistic, complexity-friendly development and evaluation seeks to generate intelligence rather than just data. Broadly, whatever methods and metrics are selected, community members should be involved actively in designing a vision outlining priority outcomes and accumulating evidence to assess progress towards these. Strengthening and enriching the web of connections at local levels means that communities are better able to co-operate around shared goals through self-organised groups and campaigns. They are also in a stronger position to collaborate with potential partners and to influence decision making through participation in neighbourhood planning and similar cross-sectoral co-production exercises (Durose and Richardson, 2015). While not necessarily leading to transformation, this relatively weak form of empowerment makes it more likely that the users of services can shape how they are delivered, thus achieving better policy outcomes or highlighting specific injustices or gaps. Whole-system transformation requires more time and more resources, alongside different kinds of expertise and connectivity. Network weavers and 'smart' intermediaries are adept at brokering across perceived or traditional boundaries to foster enterprise and innovation (Krebs and Holley, 2004), thereby creating locally tailored interdisciplinary strategies for tackling long-standing problems, by assembling assets, energies and local knowledge in ways that are often unimagined by public or private agencies (Durose et al, 2020; Anderson et al, 2012).

For tomorrow's communities to function well in providing services and opportunities for collective action and personal growth, as well as securing democratically agreed policy outcomes, the prominence given to integrating connections in this chapter cannot ignore dimensions of power, discrimination and social division. These will inevitably shape the success or otherwise of community-level transformation. Treating communities as adaptive living systems will promote collaborative behaviour, mutual aid and self-help, all of which will be essential for communities 'at the edge' to thrive in whatever future we face.

Acknowledgements

Thanks to Mary Morgan, Kate Eastment, David Parry and Helen Wheelock, of Alliance Homes, for their comments on an earlier version of this chapter.

References

Abercrombie, R., Boswell, K. and Thomasoo, R. (2018) *Thinking Big: How to Use Theory of Change for Systems Change*, London: Lankelly Chase with New Philanthropy Capital.

Anderson, B., Kearnes, M., McFarlane, C. and Swanton, D. (2012) 'On assemblages and geography', *Dialogues in Human Geography*, 2(2): 171–89.

Batty, M. (2019) *Inventing Future Cities*, Cambridge: MIT Press.

Baldwin, C., Vincent, P., Anderson, J. and Rawstorne, P. (2020) 'Measuring well-being: trial of the neighbourhood thriving scale for social well-being among pro-social individuals', *International Journal of Community Well-Being* (published online).

Bamberger, M., Vaessen, J. and Raimondo, E. (eds) (2015) *Dealing with Complexity in Development Evaluation: A Practical Approach*, Thousand Oaks: Sage.

Bashir, N., Ameyaw, N., Sahota, S., Bajwa, M. and Dayson, C. (2019) *Culture, Connection and Belonging: A Study of Addiction and Recovery in Nottingham's BAME community*, London: Lankelly Chase.

Billiald, S. and McAllister-Jones, L. (2015) *Behaving Like a System: The Preconditions for Place-based Systems Change*, London: Collaborate/ Lankelly Chase.

Block, P. (2009) *Community – the Structure of Belonging*, San Francisco: Berrett-Koehler.

Byrne, D. (2015) *Complexity Theory and the Social Sciences*, London: Routledge.

Cabaj, M. and Weaver, L. (2016) *Collective Impact 3.0: An Evolving Framework for Community Change*, Waterloo, Ontario: The Tamarack Institute.

Clarke, C., Carter, R. and Fairly, D. (2020) *Understanding Community Resilience in our Towns*, London: Hope not Hate Charitable Trust.

Cooperrider, D.L. and Whitney, D. (2001) 'A positive revolution in change: appreciative inquiry', *Public Administration and Public Policy*, 87: 611–30.

Durose, C. and Richardson, L. (2015) *Designing Public Policy for Co-production*, Bristol: Policy Press.

Durose, C., van Ostaijen, M., van Hulst, M., Escobar, O. and Agger, A. (2020) 'Transforming urban neighborhoods: everyday practices in four European cities', Political Studies Association Annual Conference.

Freire, P. (1972) *Pedagogy of the Oppressed*, Harmondsworth: Penguin.

Gigerenzer, G. (2014) *Risk Savvy: How to Make Good Decisions*, London: Allen Lane.

Gilchrist, A. (2016) *Blending, Braiding, Balancing: Strategies for Managing the Interplay between Formal and Informal Ways of Working with Communities*, working paper 136, Birmingham University: Third Sector Research Centre.

Gilchrist, A. (2019) *The Well-connected Community: A Networking Approach to Community Development*, Bristol: Policy Press

Green, G. and Haines, A. (2015) *Asset Building and Community Development*, London: Sage.

Grint, K. (2008) 'Wicked problems and clumsy solutions: the role of leadership', *Clinical Leader*, 1(2).

Hills, D. (2019) *Evaluation Failures: 22 Tales of Mistakes Made and Lessons Learned*, London: SAGE Publications.

Holmgren, D. (2011) *Permaculture: Principles and Pathways beyond Sustainability*, East Meon: Permanent Publications.

Hornung, L., Kane, D. and Jochum, V. (2020) *Below The Radar: Exploring Grants Data for Grassroots Organisations*, London: Local Trust/NCVO.

Johnson, S. and Boulton, J. (2014) *Impact Assessment of Financial Market Development through the Lens of Complexity Theory*, Bath: University of Bath, https://researchportal.bath.ac.uk/en/publications/impact-assessment-of-financial-market-development-through-the-len.

Kania, J., Kramer, M. and Senge, P. (2018) 'The water of systems change', https://www.fsg.org/search-results?sq=waters%20of%20system%20change.

Komro, K.A., Flay, B.R., Biglan, A. and Wagenaar, A.C. (2016) 'Research design issues for evaluating complex multicomponent interventions in neighbourhoods and communities', *Translational Behavioural Medicine*, 6(1): 153–9.

Krebs, V. and Holley, J. (2004) *Building Smart Communities through Network Weaving*, Athens: Appalachian Center for Economic Networks.

Lorde, A. (1979) *The Master's Tool Will Never Dismantle the Master's House*, London: Penguin Modern.

Lowe T. (2017) 'Performance management in the voluntary sector – responding to complexity', *Voluntary Sector Review*, 8(3): 319–31.

MacKinnon, D. and Derickson, K. (2013) 'From resilience to resourcefulness: a critique of resilience policy and activism', Progress in *Human Geography*, 37(2): 253–70.

Mitleton-Kelly, E. (ed) (2003) *Complex Systems and Evolutionary Perspectives on Organisations: The Application of Complexity Theory to Organisations*, London: Pergamon.

OCSI (Oxford Consultants for Social Inclusion) (2019) 'Left behind? Understanding communities on the edge', https://ocsi.uk/2019/09/05/left-behind-understanding-communities-on-the-edge/.

Parsfield, M., Morris, D., Bola, M., Knapp, M., Yoshioka, M. and Marcus, G. (2015) *Community Capital: The Value of Connected Communities*, London: RSA.

Patton, M.Q. (2006) 'Evaluation for the way we work', *Nonprofit Quarterly*, Spring, 28–33.

Patton, M.Q. (2017) *Principles-focused Evaluation: The Guide*, New York: Guilford Press.

Pflaeging, N. (2014) *Organize for Complexity: How to Get Life Back Into Work to Build the High-Performance Organization*, New York: Betacodex Publishing.

Preskill, H., Gopal, S., Mack, K. and Cook, J. (2014) 'Evaluating complexity: propositions for practice', https://www.fsg.org/publications/evaluating-complexity.

Ramalingam, B. and Jones, H. (eds) (2008) *Exploring the Science of Complexity: Ideas and Implications for Development and Humanitarian Efforts*, London: Overseas Development Institute.

Reagans, R. (2011) 'Close encounters: analyzing how social similarity and propinquity contribute to strong network connections', *Organization Science*, 22: 835–49.

Sarasvathy, S.D. (2008) *Effectuation: Elements of Entrepreneurial Expertise*, Cheltenham: Edward Elgar.

Social Integration Commission (2018) *Integrated Communities Strategy Green Paper*, London: Ministry of Housing, Communities and Local Government, pp 10–11.

Soteri-Proctor, A. (2011) *Little Big Societies: Micro-mapping of Organisations Operating Below the Radar*, working paper 71, Birmingham: University of Birmingham, Third Sector Research Centre.

Strauch, R.E. (1975) '"Squishy problems" and quantitative methods', *Policy Sciences*, 6: 174–84.

Taylor, M. (2011) *Public Policy in the Community*, Basingstoke: Palgrave Macmillan.

Wilson, M. and Taylor, M (2020) *Locally Rooted: The Place of Community Organising in Times of Crisis*. Warminster: Community Organisers

Wyler, S. (2020) *Community Responses in Times of Crisis*, London: Local Trust.

PART C

Transforming policy outcomes by communities

10

Co-production and the role of preventive infrastructure

David Boyle

Come with me for a moment to the Alvanley Family Practice, a small GP surgery in Stockport, where the Manchester mayor is opening a set of new allotments. David and Julie Ashton are 'practice health champions' at the practice and came up with the allotment idea. Stockport Council donated the land and a local builder provided apprentices to clear the site. The council's investment fund also provided £10,000 towards the allotment's hut.

This sounds like the kind of arrangement that used to be known as 'partnership' working. What is unusual is for GP practices to preside over the creation of new allotments – although, since the famous Peckham Experiment in the 1930s, not unprecedented. But there is also something about the informal style of Dr Mark Gallagher and his practice partner, Dr Jaweeda Idoo – without pomposity – calling their patients 'friends', as he did in his speech, that might raise a few eyebrows in professional circles.

Even so, in a period when general practice is struggling with dwindling general practitioners (GPs) and rising demand, Alvanley has bucked the trend. It has managed to reduce demand and at the same time to begin to nibble away at some of the causes of ill-health. It was not just a technocratic business of tackling rising demand either. The changes in the way their surgery works was partly a response to the exhaustion of the professional partners. "I remember, we had our heads in our hands," Dr Idoo says now. "We had 200 letters to reply to and piles of test results. We were thinking of giving up. Then a few things happened."

The problem was that the practice was faced with an increasing number of people coming for appointments who were struggling with life, or had needs that a GP cannot meet – primarily the social determinants of health – and it was looking for a new way of collaborating with the community to support it.

The doctors describe the events as a "perfect storm", which led to the radical shift in the way things are done. The first of these was Dr Idoo becoming chair of the local GP federation and beginning to think practically about the long-term sustainability of general practice – not just theirs. The second was the arrival of a new business manager, Kay Keane, who was keen and ready to try out new ideas. Third, the local people who were already trying to do something about supporting people struggling with their lives locally, like Nicola Wallace-Dean at Star Point Café, and her mum, Ann, at the local fish and chip shop, were using their profits from a credit union to invest in the local community by training young people.

The last part of the jigsaw was the arrival of Altogether Better, the Yorkshire-based innovators behind the idea of 'health champions'. They were part of a pilot funded by public health director, Donna Sagar, and she appealed for practices in Stockport to take part. Dr Idoo and Dr Gallagher applied successfully, and soon they were writing to their patients, sending them individual invitations to help. There was a huge response and, while Altogether Better has moved on elsewhere, the effects are still rippling out and there is now a long list of activities that the champions run, from singing and walking through to the new allotments.

On average – it is certainly the case in Alvanley – at least one in five GP consultations have no strictly medical purpose (Malby et al, 2019). So the GPs at Alvanley direct patients in this category towards a patient who can help. If there is no relevant activity that suits, they might even encourage these patients to become a health champion and set up their own activities. Apart from allotments, one can take part in coffee and conversation, new mums' social events, pram pushers, Knit and Natter, IT training, phone support, Veg on Prescription, exercise sessions, Feed the Birds, arts and wellbeing, and training in community organising and listening – all organised by the collaboration between the practice, the health champions and the local community.

Whatever their specific formula, it seems to work. This is genuine co-production in practice – *but it also provides a clue about what a democracy looks like, where everyone does not just vote every few years, but also plays an active role in society.* Except that it operates no triage system (the receptionist offers a range of appointments, from a GP to a health and wellbeing appointment and, in effect, the patients triage themselves), Alvanley looks much like other surgeries. The GPs probably only reach for their social prescribing pads about five times a week. Yet they believe this intense mutual support in the community diverts patients enough to cover the workload of one GP.

Alvanley is instructive, also because it shows what might be possible when services are delivered alongside local people. It may not work everywhere like that – Alvanley has an older population – but parallel approaches have also worked among Black, Asian and minority ethnic communities in Washington in the United States (US), south London in the UK (United Kingdom) and impoverished communities across the UK.

There is, of course, professional opposition to this kind of idea. Alvanley shares its new health centre with three other practices. It is very popular and, although the health champion and volunteer activities are open to anyone local, some aspects require patients to be on the practice list. This may affect the other practices, of course, who see the per-capita payments affected, because surgeries are paid per member. Dr Idoo recalled a conversation she had with a doctor in one of the other practices as she headed out to support their weekly singing event. "Going singing?" he asked, adding, rather rudely: "I'm staying here to do proper medicine."

Why this is important

Let us look first at public services, which are now in crisis, thanks partly to the COVID-19 pandemic and partly to the austerity years. The Beveridge Report, published in 1942 – the only government report ever to have been a bestseller – set out the blueprint for the future, caring world.

The problem was that Beveridge assumed that a national health service would cost less to run over time, because need would be reduced. That was the assumption on which the new welfare state rested, and it was wrong – in fact it has been wrong everywhere, not just in Britain.

Beveridge set out to slay what he called the 'five giants': ignorance, want, squalor, disease and idleness. The problem is not that he failed to vanquish them – he killed them stone dead. But something he never expected happened. They come back to life again every generation and have to be slain all over again and, every time, it gets more expensive.

Through 75 years of peace and plenty, Beveridge's legacy has not managed to narrow inequalities of income or health significantly or to strengthen mutual support. Neither, in general, has the welfare state successfully tackled the underlying reasons why problems emerge in the first place.

What went wrong? This is such an important question that we hardly dare ask it, in case it is taken as a political excuse to wind up the Beveridge experiment altogether, and because the failure of the welfare state to create a sustainable improvement in social welfare threatens to overwhelm the public finances.

It is true that Beveridge was in some ways a victim of his own success – the welfare settlement led to longer lives, which sometimes (although not always) led to higher costs. It led to different diseases and to disabled children surviving into adulthood. These are partial explanations, but they do not really cover everything. Why has health spending risen so fast for all generations, not just the old (Hawksworth, 2006)? Why is 70 per cent of National Health Service (NHS) time spent dealing with chronic health problems?[1] Why has crime risen so much in the same period?[2] It is not just that people are living longer.

But Beveridge himself was more aware of this conundrum than his reputation suggests. He was aware that the NHS, for example, was being rolled out by the Attlee government on lines very different from those he had suggested. His overlooked third report, *Voluntary Action*, crystallised his thinking and his warnings about what might happen if the welfare state became too paternalist, and if people's instincts for self-help, and their ability to find solutions, were allowed to atrophy (Beveridge, 1948).

He wrote that the state had an important role but equally important were what he called: 'Room, opportunity and encouragement for voluntary action in seeking new ways of social advance … services of a kind which often money cannot buy.'[3] He was afraid that his reforms were encouraging people to focus passively on their needs. To emphasise his fears, he never used the term 'welfare state', preferring the phrase 'social services state', which he used to highlight our duties or services.

We need to take the decline in voluntary action seriously, especially as rationed public services increasingly use 'need' as their currency of access. The only assets people have, then, are their own needs, which must be maximised if they are to access help. It is hardly surprising that needs seem to grow.

But there is another problem as well, as the needs increase: the over-professionalisation that Beveridge warned against seems to have widened the basic divide in all public services – between an exhausted,

---

[1] https://fullfact.org/factchecks/nhs_budget_chronic_care_long_term_conditions-2731

[2] https://www.gov.uk/government/publications/historical-crime-data

[3] Quoted in Participle (2008).

remote professional class and their clients, who are expected to remain passive and easy to process. This is not just disempowering, it can also be corrosive.

The co-production critique follows Beveridge's third report. It suggests that the reason our current services are so badly equipped to respond to a changing society is that they have largely overlooked the underlying operating system they depend on: the social economy of family and neighbourhood, also known as the 'core economy' (see Chapter 3).

We can no longer rely on continuing economic growth to provide enough finance for public services, and we find that our services have also become constrained by the New Public Management of centralised targets, deliverables, standards and customer relationship management software, which has narrowed the focus of many services and often undermined the relationships between professionals and patients, or between teachers and pupils (Boyle, 2020).

The difficulty is that, although one can point to highly successful small examples of co-production in action in almost every service, very little has been written that sets out what taking these ideas to scale might mean.

The origins of co-production theory

The clue that potentially modernised the idea of voluntary action, since its pre-Beveridge days, emerged in Chicago. It was there that Elinor Ostrom, the 2009 Nobel prize winner for economics, was asked by the Chicago police to tackle a particularly confusing question for them: why was it that, when they took their police off the beat and into patrol cars – and gave them a whole range of hi-tech equipment that can help them cover a larger area more effectively – did the crime rate go up (Ostrom and Baugh, 1973)?

This remains a problem and not one that is confined to the police. It lies at the heart of why public services become less effective on the ground as they become less personal and more centralised. Elinor Ostrom's team decided that the reason was because that all-important link with the public was broken. When the police were in their cars, the public seemed to feel that their intelligence, support and help were no longer needed.

She called this joint endeavour that lies at the heart of all professional work 'co-production' (Parks et al, 1981). It explained why doctors also need patients, why teachers need pupils, and why politicians need the co-operation of the public, if they are going to succeed.

Chicago was also the city that Robert Sampson studied in the mid-1990s with his team from the Harvard School of Public Heath, trying to get to grips with the social factors behind violent crime. They split the city up into more than 900 different neighbourhoods and found, to their surprise, that none of the factors that are traditionally supposed to make a difference to crime – poverty for example – really seemed to be a key factor (Sampson et al, 1997).

What did make a difference was what you might call a latent sense of co-production among local people. It was whether they were prepared to intervene if they saw youngsters hanging about. Sampson called it 'collective efficacy'. He described it as a 'shared willingness of residents to intervene and social trust, a sense of engagement and ownership of public space' (Sampson et al, 1997).

Here is the potential link between services and communities. The implications are that professionals need their clients as much as the other way round, and that service users – who are supposed to be such a deadweight on an exhausted public service system – are also assets, miserably wasted by the current system. This is one of the key contributions of the social innovators Edgar Cahn and his wife, Chris Gray (Cahn, 2001).

The proposition here is not that service users are in the same category as public service professionals. It is that they are a potential resource for providing the kind of human skills and support that service systems find quite hard to provide, but which are enormously important for their effectiveness – befriending people, listening to them, coaching them perhaps, or just being there. These are emphatically untrained, human skills that are needed.

The third implication is around the concept of a *core economy*, a phrase coined by the economist, Neva Goodwin (Goodwin et al, 2003). This is the notion that all local activity – bringing up children, looking after older people or making neighbourhoods work – is not some magically inexhaustible resource outside the economic system. It is what makes the rest of the economy possible (see Chapter 3).

Those are the basic assumptions of the set of ideas called 'co-production', and emerging on both sides of the Atlantic. It is a slippery phrase, taken on and rendered meaningless by senior managers in the NHS and a number of Whitehall departments, but it can broadly be defined as follows: 'Co-production means *delivering* public services in an equal and reciprocal relationship between professionals, people using services, their families and their neighbours. Where activities are co-produced in this way, both services and neighbourhoods become far more effective agents of *change*' (Boyle and Harris, 2009, p 11, emphasis added).

What co-production is not

Like all buzzwords, 'co-production' tends to be hollowed out by those who wield it. The two words in the definition that are critical to making this idea transformative as public policy are italicised. It is about *delivering* services. It is also about *doing*, and the purpose is a shift in the power relationships around services, philanthropy and charity.

There is no doubt that both user management and consultation are co-production in a sense, and they are hugely important for other reasons – although consultation itself has become the object of cynicism on both sides these days. But co-production emphasises people using their *human* skills, not their advice or their instructions to managers. People do not become mini-bosses in co-production. They are recognised for their potential to broaden and deepen services because of what they *do*, not because of what they think. It is the *doing* that is important.

Politicians are hugely bad at seeing this because most have devoted their lives to being around tables, taking decisions, and they fail to see how this excludes people whose skills are less verbal. That is not to downplay the importance of consultation, just to suggest that other forms of involvement are important too.

Nor does co-production mean personalisation or personal budgets, important as they are too. The danger of personal budgets is that those who receive them can get flung into an atomised world, where everything has to have a price and where – as the story in the *Daily Mail* (2008) said – recipients might have to pay people to come to the pub with them. Where personal budgets are relevant is when people can use them to produce the kind of support networks that mean they do not have to pay for friends. Personal budgets may be necessary for that, but they are not sufficient.

Finally, co-production is not 'trolley management'. The Australian post office says that, when people put their postcodes on their envelopes correctly, they are co-producing postal services. Some supermarkets claim that people are co-producing when they stack their trolleys obediently and neatly, and get their £1 coin back.

But the whole purpose of co-production as Ostrom and Cahn understood it is to change the power relationships, to give people an equal stake in their services, to give them a means by which they can provide themselves with the kind of support they need – to help services tackle problems much earlier.

It will not work if it is just about saving money for managers. Without that objective of change – that promise of transformation for both sides – then co-production is just nudging or manipulation, and it will not have the staying power to work sustainably. Co-production has to be about change, personal change and a change in the power relationships involved in the delivery of services.

Co-production is sometimes described in terms of six examples, where services are designed to (Slay et al, 2010):

- **build on people's existing capabilities**, to seek out what they can do, as they do in the time-bank network – among the poorest people – not just define people by what they *cannot* do;[4]
- **provide services that depend on reciprocal relationships** between professionals and clients, or services and communities, like the co-operative nurseries of London, Scandinavia and North America;[5]
- **encourage mutual support networks among users**, especially to take over from professionals at the inevitable moment when professional help moves on;[6]
- **blur the distinctions between professionals and users**, by forming community justice panels, for example;[7]
- **be catalysts for broader services**, such as some aspects of extended schools; and[8]
- **recognise users as assets to the service**, like expert patient schemes and the Alvanley Family Practice do.[9]

Services that use their clients, and their clients' friends and families, in this way are able to build a much broader range of activities. They also suggest an answer to the welfare conundrum, that delivering services to people who are supposed to accept them gratefully and passively, which undermines their ability to resist life's difficulties, also fundamentally

---

[4] See, for example, www.rgtb.org.uk

[5] http://www.nurseryworld.co.uk/article/1157022/labour-says-co-operative-nurseries-key-affordable-childcare

[6] Expert patients, for example.

[7] http://www.southsomerset.gov.uk/community-safety/get-involved/community-justice-panel/

[8] http://www.infed.org/schooling/extended_schooling.htm

[9] http://www.altogetherbetter.org.uk/community-health-champions

undermines their ability to be the heroes of their own lives. There is also something about reciprocal services, on the other hand, where we ask people for something back, and give them the respect that goes with being equal partners in delivery, which can turn that situation around.

There are implications of this for public services. It implies that social networks are critical to people's ability to thrive, economically, socially and mentally, and that public services can have a role in stitching them together again.

Does this 'co-production' allow everyone to feel they have a useful role, not just the articulate ones? Does it make them vital to managers because of this? Does it encourage them to reach out to others? One of the difficulties for those testing out these solutions in public services is that they often seem to conflict with the way services have been developing over the past generation. They rely on face-to-face influence when the trend has been virtual. They appeal to general skills when the trend has been increasingly specialist. They believe in ordinary skills, amateur in the best sense, when the trend has been increasingly over-professionalised.

Some years ago, my colleagues at the New Economics Foundation started the Co-production Network through the think tank Nesta, with a 'critical friends' group attached. It was in there, listening to a disabled speaker brought along by one of the friend organisations, about how grateful they were to be given a say in their daily menu, that I realised that co-production tends to get categorised as part of the 'empowerment' agenda, rather than – as it should be – a critique of it. It is, in short, a response to the *failure* of the empowerment agenda over the past decades – that, despite all the rhetoric, power has not tended to pass from service manager to service user.

So despite its widespread use, I am not sure that most of the discussion about co-production actually approaches any of these definitions. I do not say that as a challenge, because I do not believe it is possible to run a 'perfect' co-production project that ticks every one of those six boxes. It just tends to be easier to organise consultation with users and regard their co-production box as ticked. It has to be about *doing*, not just talking, because it has to involve the hardest-to-reach people – including the sickest or most difficult people – in mutual support, as part of their own recovery.

Towards a preventive infrastructure

Edgar Cahn developed time banks, initially in health services, to make co-production work in the most impoverished places (see Chapter 3).

In the early summer of 2014, the organisation that runs time banks – Timebanking UK – received a call from the Department for Work and Pensions (DWP). They wanted to know if they could borrow the time-banking infrastructure for benefit claimants. Anybody who signed on in the UK would eventually be given the chance to join a local time bank, under this scheme, and to find and provide mutual support for each other. It was a bold idea, with the prospect of a real win-win policy.

Towards the end of the year, they were drafting the joint statement, but the plan was beginning to throw up problems. Who would pay for the time-banking infrastructure to carry this extra weight of demand? Who was going to set the rules? The Benefits Agency does now direct claimants towards time banking, but it happens in a small way rather than the ambitious project originally envisaged – mainly because the jobcentre funding system changed and no money trickled down to the time banks.

The problem was that time-banking infrastructure was underfunded, delicate and informal. It could not sustain that kind of influx of demand. Yet, if only one government department paid for it, they would find they owned it and that very informality that made it work would disappear. One element that central government simply cannot provide is informality.

This dilemma goes to the heart of the co-production problem. It is known in co-production circles as the 'Parable of the Blobs and Squares' after a story retold by Cahn that he adapted from the Washington-based Kettering Foundation. The squares are the officials and the blobs are the community (Cahn, 2001). They find it next to impossible to understand each other, however much they might need each other for the official support (the squares) or the authentic energy (the blobs) they provide. You can see what comes next in a charming video narrated by Brian Blessed.[10] They train the blobs up in board and strategic management and, lo and behold, they become squares, and it still does not work.

The parable sets out the problem, but suggests no answers (although Cahn does). It does imply, though, that some of the answers may lie in intermediary organisations that have the power and resources to allow the neighbourhood to be themselves – enough anyway for the blobs to balance the squares – with a clear role and enough power to count.

---

[10] http://www.patientpublicinvolvement.com/news/the-parable-of-the-blobs-and-the-squares-2/

The trouble is that these intermediary groups, a mutual *preventive infrastructure*, are only marginal. They are social enterprises or charities, kept alive with huge effort on the fringes of the NHS and other services – when it needs to be absolutely mainstream.

It is hard for the squares to relinquish power, after all. But it may not be that they discount the potential role of the community, or friends and neighbours, as volunteers or mutual supporters – far from it. It may be a more practical consideration: that they see no clear way of organising the layer of patient or volunteer support they know they need in a systematic way. Or how to act as catalysts to encourage local people to look out for one another informally.

There are many reasons for this, of course. Perhaps professional arrogance and conservatism play a role – perhaps not. Perhaps those with the budgets are too busy or too nervous to extend their reach. Perhaps it is too difficult to measure for the technocrats, or too difficult to control. Risk aversion is a major reason, although the sheer busyness in navigating bureaucracy is perhaps the biggest problem that militates against innovation.

The problem, I believe, after years of watching this conundrum, is that this is primarily because of a paradox in organisation, which runs parallel to the blobs and squares: if the structures that form part of any preventative infrastructure are set up *inside* the NHS, for example, they become too like the NHS and lose the informality they need to be effective. Yet, if they are set up *outside* the NHS, then they waste their energy-seeking funding and find themselves hooked into a destructive biannual funding round (or worse).

This paradox effectively keeps existing power dynamics locked, thanks to the demands of accountability – monitoring and reporting back – proving value for money, efficiency of services, working with 'users' most in need, business models, ticking boxes, setting outcomes for communities, standardising outputs, scheduling interventions and so on.

Yet there is a possible way out of this dilemma – a new status, both inside and outside, which together can form a 'preventive infrastructure' between people and the services they use, dedicated to faster recovery and prevention, and primarily using the energy of service users themselves, as expert patients, volunteers, advisers, supporters, drivers and so on, and not just in healthcare. That is what I mean by a preventive infrastructure.

I am here referring to the huge number of projects and initiatives that have been tracked by Nesta and others as 'co-production', 'asset-based', 'social prescribing' or 'people-powered health'. What I am discussing here is around the question of how to spread this kind of idea wide enough to have a major impact – a question that is far from being solved.

There are two points to make about the DWP taking over time banks. First, this is a problem not so much of centralised public spending, but about what happens when one department pays for something that is actually required by all of them. I will return to this problem later in the chapter. Second, it is the imbalance of power that is important here. The key assumption here is that powerful organisations do not work easily with powerless ones without subsuming them and undermining their informality. That is the message of the Parable of the Blobs and Squares.

The preventive infrastructure needs to have an intermediate level of formality, and of regulation. It has to be formal enough to be funded in secure and sustainable ways, yet not so regulated that it ceases to be effective. That is the justification for the intermediate status being proposed here.

I am only too aware that we are living through a period where funding is extremely tight, and there will need to be direct funding of this infrastructure. So I am proposing a method whereby the preventive infrastructure can be funded partly indirectly by the savings it creates, through two mechanisms:

- **Reduce demand.** As part of their contract, all public service providers should be committed to reducing demand year on year, perhaps with each other across an area. There may be some sensible exceptions to this.
- **Contract with the preventive infrastructure.** To help them achieve this, these providers will be expected to contract with at least one unit of the preventive infrastructure.

Experience suggests that if this kind of project is paid for out of national budgets, then it will wither away when the funding runs dry (Boyle, 2013). Its long-term success depends on it being funded for cost-effective reasons at the local level. The long-term feasibility of this idea stands or falls according to whether it is worth the money at the local level – and whether commissioners and contractors are prepared to pay for it because it saves them money elsewhere.

National funding would inevitably be temporary, and would also risk sidelining the existing schemes that do so much good work now. The viability and financial benefits of the preventive infrastructure are already quite clear; the challenge is to find ways of persuading powerful local commissioners into understanding that (Horne et al, 2012). The key point here is to know *how* to prevent, aware that current statutory systems are extremely bad at forging the informal relationships that are necessary.

This is an interpretation of a complex problem, and its implication is that big solutions do not tend to work, but that small ones may not have the necessary impact. It is therefore a human-scale interpretation that asserts that small plus small plus small equals big. This also requires some very small-scale funding systems.

How to build the preventive infrastructure

It is not widely understood, even in the US, that all public housing tenants there owe eight hours a month per family in community work. Yet that was the requirement enacted under the Clinton era's Quality Housing and Work Responsibility Act 1998.

Perhaps it is hardly surprising given the sensitivities around slavery in the US that, in practice, the hours are very rarely required. Where it has been made more acceptable, in some of the big estates in racially divided Washington, the work is carried out through time banks where they can decide what they want to do, where what they do is mutually beneficial and where they get something back.

But the 'community service requirement' regulations are a good example of why central government, or centralised local government, is too blunt an instrument to build the preventive infrastructure. This is a case where a good idea gets corroded because it has been managed and imposed on people like a conquering force.

All government departments have a volunteering element, even the Ministry of Defence. It may be that only getting them around the table – as the government last did in 2000 as part of its comprehensive spending review process – will allow them to share responsibility for kickstarting a more systematic infrastructure along the lines I am proposing here. So that is the first step: a meeting, hosted by the Cabinet Office, that brings together all departments with an interest in the preventive infrastructure, to hammer out a way forward.

The next question is how to shape and plant the infrastructure on the ground. The best way may therefore be a local catalyst – one can look to the impressive way in which Community Catalysts managed to roll out micro social care enterprises in Nottinghamshire, by employing one key entrepreneurial individual around the county for two years.[11] It may be that a similar approach to getting the preventive infrastructure working across the UK might work better than top-down methods.

We need to fund one individual employed at district level for at least two years and probably three, whose task would be to seek out public service professionals interested in making things happen and working with them – and provider contractors – or raise the money to get on with it, and in whatever form local enthusiasm demands. Perhaps more effectively, these would be permanent posts within local authorities, primary care networks and integrated care systems.

But providing this by using professionals alone has disadvantages: professionals carrying out navigation, for example, have tended not to survive in mainstream services when they were there before. It may in fact be unsustainable to create another professional function in an already complex system. Any sustainable solution will have to be funded locally, on the basis of the savings it creates for local funders (Boyle, 2013). It will also need to be able to knit with, rather than undermine, existing projects that are already working well, and to be available where people are, in surgeries, hospitals, day centres and other public service settings.

There remains an issue about who should be responsible for what. The catalysts will need to be people with a background in social entrepreneurship. Those they recruit to link up with the service users themselves will need a co-production background. People with backgrounds in statutory services are often difficult to change, because they are so used to 'doing to' or 'doing for' people. Some of them understand 'doing with' (co-production), but dare not move far from controlling and coming up with solutions for people.

Any system of this kind requires both functions: the linking and doing roles – which can often be carried out by mentored volunteers – and the catalysing role. All are absolutely vital to success. The success of this approach to preventive infrastructure will also be the sum totals of very tiny individual changes. We will know it is working when people inside and outside the system feel confident that the infrastructure (and the other paraphernalia of system change) is still going to be there in three years' time. But how do we make this sense of permanence possible?

The answer could be to reverse the usual UK approach, which is to 'own' the infrastructure from the centre and micro-manage it.

---

[11] https://www.communitycatalysts.co.uk/wp-content/uploads/2014/08/Nottinghamshire-Micro-enterprise-Project-Final-Report-July-2014.pdf

Perhaps, more like the original Visa system designed by Dee Hock, the outposts of the preventive infrastructure could band together to own a central hub, which would provide training and career progression for volunteers within it, who are not able – for whatever reason – to work in the mainstream economy.[12] This could include:

- a membership system that would provide the ethics and values behind the infrastructure as a whole;
- a national branding for mutual volunteering in the public sector along these lines, perhaps as organised for the 12,000 volunteers organised locally by the National Trust – but with national training and other support for volunteers; and
- arrangements with selected higher education courses whereby the time spent by people supporting services in this way can count as credits or fees towards courses that can give them real qualifications in system change.

Four recommendations

1. Launch this programme with a series of meetings between government departments, hosted by the Cabinet Office.
2. Fund one catalyst post for three years based at every district council, charged with bringing local commissioners, service managers and professionals together to launch the missing preventive infrastructure.
3. Give local commissioners responsibility for reducing demand across their area – and expect services to contract with elements of the new preventive infrastructure to do it.
4. Make sure the central hub is owned by the local outposts, with a task of providing academic opportunities for volunteers.

References

Beveridge, W. (1942) *Social Insurance and Allied Services (The Beveridge Report)*, London: HMSO.

Beveridge, W. (1948) *Voluntary Action: A Report on Methods of Social Advance*, London: Allen & Unwin.

Boyle, D. (2013) *Barriers to Choice*, London: Cabinet Office.

Boyle, D. (2020) *Tickbox*, London: Little, Brown.

Boyle, D. and Harris, M. (2009) *The Challenge of Co-production*, London: Nesta.

---

[12] https://www.ccn.com/history-visa-probably-different-think/

Cahn, E. (2001) *No More Throw-away People: The Co-production Imperative*, Washington: Essential Books.

Daily Mail (2008) 'Doctor and kitchen fitter become paid-up pub friends of lonely pensioner after son advertised for drinking companions', *Daily Mail*, 24 April.

Goodwin, N., Harris, J. M., Nelson, J. A., Rajkarnikar, P. J., Roach, B. and Torras, M. (2003) *Microeconomics in Context*, New York: Houghton Mifflin.

Hawksworth, J. (2006) *Long-term Public Spending Trends*, London: PricewaterhouseCoopers.

Horne, M., Khan, H., and Corrigan, P. (2012) *People Powered Health: Progressing towards Co-production*, London: Nesta.

Malby, R., Boyle, D., Wildman, J., Omar, B. S. and Smith, S. (2019) *The Asset-based Health Inquiry: How Best to Develop Social Prescribing*, London: London South Bank University.

Ostrom, E. and Baugh, W. H. (1973) *Community Organization and the Provision of Police Services*, Beverly Hills, Sage Publications.

Parks, R. B., Baker, P. C., Kiser, L., Oakerson, R., Ostrom, E., Ostrom, V., Percy, S. L., Vandivort, M. B., Whitaker, G. P. and Wilson, R. (1981) 'Consumers as co-producers of public services: some economic and institutional considerations', *Policy Studies Journal*, 9(7): 1001–11.

Participle (2008) *Beveridge 4.0*, London: Participle.

Sampson, R. J., Raudenbush, S. W. and Earls, F. (1997) 'Neighbourhoods and violent crime: a multi-level study of collective efficacy', *Science*, 277: 918.

Slay, J., Boyle, D., and Stephens, L.(2010) *Public Services Inside Out*, London: Nesta.

11

Humanising health and social care

John Restakis

Sometimes it takes a pandemic to really focus the collective attention. To be sure, concerns about the decline of health and social care programmes have been ongoing for decades. The industrialised societies of Europe and North America were the first to institute what we recognise as the welfare state, a model of collective social welfare that soon became the gold standard for a modern democracy. What the pandemic has revealed is just how far that idealised notion of the welfare state has fallen. Decades of privatisation and austerity policies have hollowed out what were once established baselines for publicly funded health and social services.

Beginning in Bismarck's Germany, where the first social security programmes were established, up to the high point of public health and social care programmes instituted by the United Kingdom (UK) and the Nordic countries in the post-war era, social welfare seemed a reliable measure of progress towards greater social and economic equity. Neoliberalism and the free market policies of the Reagan–Thatcher governments put an end to that. The state, once the guarantor of public health and social welfare, became the mechanism by which public programmes – or more accurately, public *assets* built with tax money – were increasingly privatised and remade into sources of private profit.

Today, with the failures of privatised health and social care coming into full view, the state has once again been thrust into the role of guarantor of the public welfare. The COVID-19 pandemic has spurred renewed calls for bringing health and social care fully back under state control. But is this really the answer we need in the 21st century? Was it not the state itself that presided over the destruction of these very programmes by turning them over to the private sector? What would prevent the state from doing so again? Given the rollercoaster history of social welfare over the past 50 years, we are in need of alternatives.

For all the undeniable benefits that the welfare state brought to public health and welfare, it is easy to forget the deficiencies that came with it. The bureaucratisation of care brought a host of new problems, pitting the inflexible demands of centralised management systems against the individual needs of citizens and communities. State welfare presupposed anonymity and powerlessness – and poverty. The human and social factors of care were all but erased.

Social care is a *relational good* – a good or a service that is embedded in an actual relationship between *people*. In social care, it is the quality of the relationship *itself* that carries value. Relational goods acquire value through sincerity, or *genuineness* – they cannot be bought or sold or merely consumed as impersonal services. The essential quality of care – its reliance on the formation of authentic caring relationships between actual people – was eclipsed by a model of centralised administration that eliminated any role for the recipients of these services. Even more insidiously, state welfare programmes became a primary means of surveillance and control over a vast underclass.

The state-directed command-and-control model of care is a relic of the industrial machine society. It replicates the management systems – and class prejudices – of that era. And while universal programmes of social welfare greatly enhanced the security of citizens, they also displaced the traditional social bonds of mutual help that underlay previous communal models of care that were provided by friendly societies and other forms of co-operative social care (Restakis, 2010). The mass scale of the deprivation and dependence that came with the transition to a market society far surpassed the limited capacities of communal care systems.

Recently, this process of growing social precarity has accelerated. Over the past decade, working people have experienced a squeeze on wages greater than at any time in the preceding 150 years (Conaty et al, 2016). Labour market deregulation, the assault on unions and advances in artificial intelligence and automation now pose unprecedented risks to everyone who depends on a wage. Moreover, the elimination of consumer buying power through precarity, low wages and systemic unemployment undermines the very basis of the capitalist economy.

The model is unfeasible. The old paradigm of social welfare directed to the poor and unemployed people in an economy that is based on human wage labour has been superseded. We can replicate the inadequate and paternalistic systems of the past, or we can look for alternatives that actually grapple with the unprecedented changes now under way.

When social welfare programmes were first established, they were a defence against the threat of revolutionary socialism in Europe (Boissoneault, 2017). Since then, every major advance in social welfare has similarly been a consequence of political pressures arising from untenable social and economic conditions for large segments of the population. Faced with a political crisis engendered by rising inequality, the state played the role of peacemaker, enacting social reforms that ensured the continuance of the political order. Social welfare became a means of social control. Today, governments face a different kind of crisis – a crisis of legitimacy. It is no longer the case that simple reforms entrusted to the state will be sufficient to meet the economic, social and political unrest that is shaking societies from one end of the globe to the other.

The role of the state must change. Its historic role of serving and protecting power elites must come to an end. At the heart of this change is a radically different relationship that must emerge between the state and civil society. This is particularly relevant in the area where the intersection of economics and politics has the greatest potential for substantive system change – in the area of social welfare.

If the centralised, hierarchical, command–and–control model of the industrial age gave social welfare the quality of an inflexible bureaucracy dispensing welfare (and shame) to a vast class of the 'underprivileged', the fluid, atomised and hypermobile populace of the digital age has changed the context irrevocably.

Unlike previous times when social welfare focused on repairing the social wreckage of the capitalist system, social welfare in our time has a more fundamental role to play. Instead of providing a band aid for an unjust system, social care in our time must form the basis of a new kind of economic system altogether. The current trajectory of capitalism is not only unsustainable. It is also politically, socially and morally bankrupt. Its casualties are not merely the unlucky individuals of a growing underclass. The elevation of profit above all other values is undoing the very fabric of society itself. The social alienation, the toxic individualism, the collapse of trust, the death of culture, the epidemic of depression and the dissolution of the communal sense, are all a consequence of the capitalist destruction of social value.

Social care, and the broader civil society, are the foundations from which a broken and unmoored society might be rebuilt to serve authentic human needs. In an age of climate breakdown and skyrocketing social insecurity, the reconstruction of social welfare is one means of building a new kind of polity – a programme of social reformation and a chance at political renewal.

Reclaiming the 'social' in social care

Communities of the future – if they are to survive – must be based on what communities have always been based on: the communal bonds of reciprocity and the pre-eminence of social value. Social co-operatives are the most promising attempt to re-humanise social care by restoring the social and interpersonal relations that are its foundation. Social co-operatives emerged in Italy in the late 1970s following the deinstitutionalisation of psychiatric patients and the dissatisfaction of both caregivers and families with the quality of care provided by the public system (Restakis, 2010; Borzaga and Santuari 2000). Caregivers and families teamed up to create social care programmes that were owned and operated by frontline workers and the people they served. In 1981, the Italian state stepped in to pass legislation explicitly recognising the central role of social co-operatives in integrating and serving marginalised communities and expanding the range and quality of care available.

Social co-operatives reframed the traditional social purpose of co-operatives to meet the complex demands of an industrialised society in which the old, one-size-fits-all model of care no longer worked. What began as an effort to re-humanise social care and make it more responsive to the actual needs of communities, soon transformed the social care system in Italy.

Today, there are more than 4,500 social co-operatives employing nearly 360,000 people. While comprising only 20 per cent of the non-profit economy, they generate more than 40 per cent of its economic turnover. In the city of Bologna, 87 per cent of health and social care programmes are delivered by social co-operatives, providing a vast array of services under contract to municipal and public authorities. Social co-operatives began a process of democratising public services in Italy. They have offered a social alternative to the privatisation and contracting out of public services to private companies. Above all, they have shown how democratic control and reciprocity can be the basis for a system of care that is founded on the collective production of social value – not centralised control, or charity or private profit. In effect, the operating principles of the social/solidarity economy have been mobilised at scale to reconstruct the entire edifice of health and social care.

What began as a communal effort to reform services for the most vulnerable in society, has now widened to include a wide range of new services to the community as a whole. Social co-operatives provide treatment for substance users, retrain and employ ex-prisoners, provide travel and recreation services to families of disabled children, create new community services for children and families, and provide long-term care to older people. But the model is not without its problems. Chief among these is its reliance on progressive governments and public contracts, many of which replicate the efficiency and low-cost aims of private providers.

In the system of social co-operatives described earlier, while the design and delivery of social care is in the hands of care workers and end users, the economic basis of the model is still rooted in the capitalist system. The payment of these services still comes from the transfer of tax monies by the state or from the payments of individual users, which are based in turn on wages earned in the wider economy. It is a form of co-operative social democracy. Social co-operatives are dependent on public contracts, tax monies and a market economy over which they have no control. They are vulnerable to changes in public policy, to changes in government priorities and to the colonising and profit-seeking aims of capital. What is needed for such a model to thrive – beyond progressive public policy – is an autonomous market that corresponds to the communal values of the social/solidarity economy and which is capable of supporting its operations.

The social value market

Fureai Kippu is a co-operative system providing care to older people in Japan. The term 'Fureai Kippu' literally means 'Ticket for a Caring Relationship' and refers to the ticket or credit that is earned when one volunteers one's time helping older people (SWF, 1993). It is a time-bank system where members can earn time credits or points for the hours they volunteer providing physical care, home help, personal services and emotional assistance to other care-dependent members. These credits are then registered by their co-operative and saved in their personal accounts. It works on the same principle as an air miles plan. Time credit holders can withdraw and use their credits to buy care for themselves or relatives as required. The system is composed of a network of local co-operatives that track and then reimburse volunteer time on the basis of these earned credits. Credits can also be sent to other locales where the services can be redeemed to serve friends or loved ones there.

When Fureai Kippu was first created in 1995, it operated primarily as an autonomous community-based system. Since then, the model has become a key complement to the state care systems and governments at both local and federal levels have supported the model. Yokohama City near Tokyo has successfully recruited thousands of volunteers into the system by modifying the scheme to allow members to exchange time credits for services other than elder care. Young parents, for example, can use credits to pay for childcare or other services. This quality of real, interpersonal caring relationships among people who live in the same community and know each other has generated a level of trust and faith in the system that far exceeds the services provided by the state. It has also strengthened the social bonds – the social capital – that are the foundation of caring communities.

Surveys in Japan found that most recipients preferred Fureai Kippu care providers over those paid in cash. Both the relationships and the level of care received was said to be different. According to the testimony of members, Fureai Kippu created for them a personal connection and a sense of reciprocity unmatched by traditional payment systems.[1] When a network member provides a service, the person being cared for often becomes an extension of their family.

This sense of social intimacy is also evident in Japan's network of health co-operatives. More than 120 co-operatives representing nearly three million members act as a forum where locals discuss problems of health and daily life and work to resolve them with the caregivers and health professionals of these establishments. Nurses, social workers, doctors, physiotherapists and other caregivers are active partners in a community-led approach to healthcare (Restakis and Girard, 2008). This community role is reinforced by more than 40 co-operative hospitals and health clinics, which are training sites for doctors and other health professionals. In the context of disease prevention, each clinic's reputation rests on how healthy its members are, not on how many prescriptions its staff write or how many procedures they perform. Central to this disease prevention approach is the role of citizen volunteers called *Han*.

Han are cells of 10–20 citizens living on the same street or in the same neighbourhood. They agree to meet at a local hall or recreation centre for a few hours, an average of once a month, and take part in an ongoing process of disease prevention. Han undertake a wide variety of activities relating to health. Members learn how to conduct various health checks, including taking blood pressure, measuring weight and muscle mass, stool and urine analysis, and tests for diabetes. The results are then sent to a professional at the health co-operative where prompt action can be taken if the data indicate a significant anomaly.

---

[1] See https://www.youtube.com/watch?v=x7bzk3DmoGk.

During the coronavirus crisis, this community-based tracking and diagnostic capacity, as well as the close social bonds that exist inside the system, have been key to fighting the spread of the virus, and it is precisely these bonds of social trust that have been shown to be the most effective means of mobilising broad social education and compliance with prevention measures. Han also involve members in physical activity as a way to promote exercise and socialising. To strengthen the communal bonds between members, the tea ceremony offers members a time to chat and relax.

In this way, Han address a key determinant of health, one entirely ignored in conventional state and for-profit systems of care: the vital role that a social network plays in one's physical and mental health. Han lessen the isolation and loneliness that is the fate of so many people, especially older people. They are a lifeline at a time when modernisation and the growth of vast urban centres have undermined traditional familial and social bonds, not only in Japan, but everywhere. Han are an extension of the basic principle that personal wellbeing is linked to the wellbeing of one's community and the society of which one is a part. The value of this social bond is calculable in terms of overall health outcomes, in reductions to health costs and personal stress, in the high standards of care and, above all, in the sense of connectedness that individual members feel with their community.

Fureai Kippu shows that reciprocity and mutualism can be valuated in social as opposed to monetary terms. The model shows how a reciprocity-based system of community-controlled co-operatives can work with state systems to offer an alternative to the privatisation of what should remain *social* relationships of caring. The localised control that communities can exercise over their healthcare through these co-operatives, and the presence of public policies to support them, are key for the cultivation of a caring society. One can imagine a time-bank system that could be adapted to support and expand this kind of social value and to make it universally applicable across the entire field of health and social care. It is a question of design and, of course, political will.

Fureai Kippu creates a social market for the production and exchange of social value. It shows how an alternative value system can be the basis for a new kind of market – a new kind of *economy* – if the institutions are in place to give it form and effect. The credit that is earned by helping others is a form of social currency based on reciprocity. It works because people accept and stand behind its value. This, in turn, is based on the mutual trust that has been established by a specific community of users. In Fureai Kippu the practice of reciprocity is amplified and rewarded, resulting in a virtuous cycle of prosocial behaviour. It is not only individuals in the system that benefit. It is also society as a whole that benefits through the increase in social capital that is generated. Can such a system be scaled to establish a comprehensive body of goods and services not only for the provision of social welfare but as an element for the core economy itself?

Much has been made lately of the need to revive the notion of commons as an economic and social value in society. Like other forms of co-operation, commons are based on the practice of reciprocity and the notion that particular classes of activities, or resources, are not ownable but are set aside for the collective use of a community. Specific communities of users contribute to their upkeep and benefit from their preservation according to accepted rules and obligations. Commons practices have been famously documented and codified by the late sociologist, Elinor Ostrom. But whereas Ostrom was concerned primarily with the use of what she called common-pool resources such as fisheries, irrigation systems or pastures, the same principles apply to emerging forms of commons such as the new databases of knowledge on the internet, or the collective production and sharing of technical and cultural products such as software or music.

All of these activities are recognised as having a common social value. These same principles apply to health and social care if these services are valued not as commodities for private consumption but as collective goods essential for both personal *and* social wellbeing. The transition of state-operated and private for-profit care systems to collectively owned and operated systems of community-based care restores the social underpinnings of care as an expression of a community's shared responsibility for mutual welfare. And, while the state retains responsibility for ensuring that the rules governing these systems are fair and in service to the collective aims of social welfare, civil society has a far greater role in the production, administration and provision of care.

All of this, of course, is predicated on the means by which such a system can be sustained economically. The idea of a universal basic income (UBI) has been gaining increasing attention in the face of systemic inequities. To take one glaring example, 51 per cent of the working population in the United States are just one paycheck away from bankruptcy (Bach, 2019). With millions left uninsured, some form of basic income, along with universal health coverage, are inescapable options for dealing with an economic and social crisis that has now become a political crisis for the US establishment. High on the list of policy imperatives is a radical programme of wealth redistribution, starting with the reclamation of taxes from the top percentile of the population.

The question remains as to whether or not an alternative value system can be established both as a transition mechanism during the continuing decline of human wage labour, and as a sustainable model of comprehensive social welfare independently of the market economy. The great challenge for establishing a social value economy is how to assess, measure and mobilise the social value that is generated without instrumentalising the relationships that comprise it. This is over and above the usual ideological objections advanced by free market defenders to such a schema. In the past, all such models have equated the 'social' with the state and this in turn has fuelled much of the reaction to these approaches from such thinkers as Hayek, Von Mises and the Chicago School that led the assault on the state's role in the economy. Their concern was what they saw as a slippery slope to tyranny through the state's control of the economy.

We are speaking of something else. We are speaking of the *democratisation* of state systems through the direct ownership and control of essential social welfare by citizens and an autonomous social value market that sustains this essentially *civil* economy and makes it operative. Our aim is the effective sovereignty of civil society itself through its generation and institutional support of all those social relations and exchanges that have as their object the common good through the practice of citizen co-operation and mutuality.

Social care is an obvious starting place for such paradigm shift, for the reasons noted earlier. But the principle extends also to the activities of co-operative and mutual-aid enterprises that also engage in commercial markets (see Chapter 5). Moreover, it is clear that unless some kind of social valuation economy is linked also to the operations of these enterprises, they will eventually come under the influence of the dominant market economy, as shown by the phenomenon of co-operative enterprises operating indistinguishably from their capitalist counterparts. This trend has been increasing.

In Canada, Mountain Equipment Co-op – an iconic consumer co-operative with more than four million members – got into serious trouble as a result of the COVID-19 pandemic. Because of the lack of co-operative investment capital to refinance its operations, it was sold by its directors to a US hedge fund (Cecco, 2020). Canada's co-operative wheat pools were privatised years ago when they were listed on the stock exchange to raise capital. The co-op wheat pools were another instance of a major failure inside the co-op economy in large part because of a lack of co-op investment capital. The availability of co-operative investment capital is key if co-operatives are to remain true to their purposes. And this depends on the extent to which they can secure direct support from civil society through such localised contributions as time banks and volunteer services, or through the use of social investments that are linked to the social value of the health services. Instead of capitalising its operations by issuing profit-bearing shares to investors, a local health clinic could issue social value shares that raise capital on the basis of the inherent value of the health services to the investing individual and the broader community.

Co-operative health clinics, and co-operatives of all stripes, already engage in this kind of social value capitalisation and there are regulatory regimes in place to manage these co-operative investment shares. This entails an alignment with the broad public benefit as acknowledged by the state, and the institutional set-up to make such transfers universally accessible to citizens as an alternative valuation system operating in parallel with the public economy.

We need wider recognition that the social value economy is continuous with the public economy in so far as its broad social aims are concerned. This is the case with the social co-operative movement and the co-operative economy more generally, in Italy. The state's responsibility for acknowledging the social utility of co-operatives and its obligation to support them are written into the Italian constitution. Public support for social co-operatives is an extension of this principle. We can imagine a set-up where particular social economy organisations that pursue the social benefit aims and functions of the social/solidarity economy could be listed on a social value exchange where, instead of time, citizens contribute capital that is then translated into services. One can thus imagine a social value exchange operating as an investment and clearing mechanism for social value. Thousands of such social value exchanges already exist, whereby local networks allow members to invest in, and access, a wide range of services that participate in the network. Many also use social currencies to facilitate these exchanges. Japan alone has some 5,000 social currencies in use.

The risk here is that organisations that are meant to generate relationships of mutual caring can be corrupted if these services are then left hostage to the priorities of contributors, regardless of the actual needs within a community – or even a nation. Why, for example, would a young family that is in need of childcare contribute to a service for older people or for disabled people? And it is not feasible to imagine that essential services such as social security or employment insurance, or workers' compensation, can be sustained by voluntary contributions. This would be to adopt the charity model of care and public services propagated by neoliberals. What happens to the idea of universal access and equality when one community that is well off can invest in specialised services that a poor community cannot? This, of course, is the case with public education in the UK and the US, where the quality of schools often reflects the degree to which parents can subsidise their programmes. The teaching of music, theatre and art, for example, has disappeared from less-well-to-do school communities.

The role of the state and of public financing for universally accessible programmes remains essential. There is, however, no reason why these programmes cannot be democratised with respect to how they are delivered, with users having control rights in their design and in the priorities they pursue.

Can such systems be scaled to achieve the kind of critical mass that enables a social value economy to sustain itself independently of the public and private economies? A central problem is how to overcome the inevitable inequalities that will emerge from one place to another from purely localised systems. There is a reason why universal, centrally administered programmes are so valued: they safeguard the principle of equality in access to public goods. We are seeking to combine the universal access and distribution of social welfare with the localised control that will safeguard the social relations of care and the accountability that comes from user control.

One means of evaluating and managing social value has been pioneered by social media and the digitisation of social relations. Some have claimed that this mass aggregation and valuation of individual behaviour could act as a mechanism for the emergence of a new kind of 'social' – a collectivity of individuals linked through their mode of social interaction and co-operating for their mutual benefit. But this mass of individuals can also be objectified into a target of mass surveillance and manipulation – both by the state and by corporations.

One response to this fact is political. There is a growing movement arguing that wresting control of these systems from the state or from corporations such as Facebook and Google is essential to ensure that freedoms such as personal privacy may be safeguarded. At the cutting edge of these efforts is the rise of platform co-operatives that promote transparency and the fair distribution of value for the users of these platforms through democratic user control.

Apart from Fureai Kippu, there are other examples such as Buurtzorg in the Netherlands, which has created an international network of professional caregivers who work in autonomous teams to provide highly specialised healthcare to communities (Kreitzer et al, 2015). The organisation has successfully developed a platform solution for the provision of localised nursing care in 24 countries, including China, Japan and Taiwan, and employs 10,000 care workers in 900 local care teams. Each team is composed of 10–12 care workers, who are primarily professional nurses.

Through its platform, Buurtzorg provides the necessary operational and back-office functions for its local teams, including the careful measuring and monitoring of service data. However, the decisions on how to manage and deliver care services are entirely in the hands of local teams. In addition, Buurtzorg provides coaching and other support services to its frontline workers through a team of regional coaches who promote training, networking and facilitation as needed. Each coach is responsible for about 40 teams. The operating cost of this system, with the radically reduced need for management, is something like 40 per cent lower than comparable public and private services.

In key ways, Buurtzorg has pioneered the model of a highly complex service system centred on the successful operation of small, self-organised teams. The Buurtzorg IT platform (Buurtzorgweb) allows teams to act as living cells within the system and to connect with each other in ways that are normally only available through the management information systems of large corporate entities or centralised bureaucracies; and this opens the door to economies of scale, made possible by the coordination of detailed and accessible data, the sharing of experience and know-how, administrative support and the provision of advice.

In recent years, Buurtzorg has expanded from the provision of homecare to the provision of mental health services and family services. Having started in 2007 with one team of four nurses, its growth has been nothing short of phenomenal. What this points to is not only the efficacy of the model in terms of managing complex care systems at scale and at an efficient cost, but also the scale of the unmet demand for such personalised care systems on the part of the public.

The move from entirely civil and informal systems of localised social care to the creation of universal welfare programmes was the result of a continuous struggle on the part of society to establish the conditions for its own survival against the threats imposed upon it by the demands of industrial capitalism. This is the well-known dynamic of the dual movement posed by Polanyi as the driving force of historical development. But it is also more than this. It is the struggle between two opposing tendencies in the human social condition. One pertains to the need for co-operation and collective security, which is the foundation of any functional society. The other is the drive for personal and class advantage, which is embedded in competition and the urge to dominate. To put it very crudely, the rise and fall of common welfare as a primary purpose of the state is a function of this seesaw conflict. With the consolidation of corporate power and ideology at a global level, the downward slide of co-operative, collective modes of social welfare was inevitable given the aims and powers of these forces.

Ultimately, what we must speak about when envisioning what tomorrow's communities must achieve is not merely the transformation of economic and social institutions, but the reclamation of social values and social *capacities* that comes with the democratisation of social care systems. It is the actual *practice* of mutuality and co-operation that changes people's values and outlooks and establishes new norms of collective behaviour – not ideas.

What if an entire economy was based on the premise that it is the social worth of an action that generates its value? That human labour that serves a social good, such as caring for others, teaching, creating art or cleaning the environment, is acknowledged and rewarded accordingly? And what if people could determine what those social benefits could be through the control they exert in the enterprises in which they work or the services that they use? Not as disposable, exploitable and replaceable parts – as mere human capital – but as co-owners and collective beneficiaries of the value they produce in common? And finally, what if the choices we make as consumers, as investors or as citizens are similarly rewarded in proportion to the social value we create and we are taxed according to the social costs we incur?

The hoarded capital that is now operating as a vast parasitic growth on the back of the productive economy must be reclaimed and translated into the initial capital pool for a universal basic income. And, like other social security systems, it must be stewarded with a continuing stream of collective contributions from those who benefit – now and in the future. If prosocial activity can be measured and valuated it can be translated into goods, services or currency. And if a proportion of one's wage earned in a factory can be contributed to a social security plan, so too can a proportion of one's social value activity be contributed to a universal basic income. The models and mechanisms are already in place. As in the past, they have emerged as a necessary response to the widening crisis of the capitalist system. What is needed is the political movement to put them into effect as catalysts of system change.

References

Bach, N. (2019) 'Millions of Americans are one missed paycheck away from poverty, report says', *Fortune*, 29 January, https://fortune.com/2019/01/29/americans-liquid-asset-poor-propserity-now-report.

Boissoneault, L. (2017) 'Bismarck tried to end socialism's grip—by offering government healthcare', *Smithsonian Magazine*, 14 July, https://www.smithsonianmag.com/history/bismarck-tried-end-socialisms-grip-offering-government-healthcare-180964064.

Borzaga, C. and Santuari, A. (2000) *Social Enterprises in Italy: The Experience of Social Co-operatives*, Trento: ISSAN (Institute for Development Studies of Non-profit Enterprises), http://eprints.biblio.unitn.it/175.

Cecco, L. (2020) 'Shock and sorrow as Canada's best-known co-op sold to US private equity firm', *The Guardian*, 15 September, https://www.theguardian.com/world/2020/sep/15/canada-mountain-equipment-biggest-co-op-sale.

Conaty, P., Bird, A. and Ross, P. (2016) *Not Alone: Trade Union and Co-operative Solutions for Self-employed Workers*, Manchester: UK Co-operatives.

Kreitzer, M.J., Monsen, K. and Nandram, S. (2015) 'Buurtzorg Nederland: a global model of social innovation, change, and whole-systems healing', *Global Advances in Health and Medicine*, 4(1): 40–4.

Restakis, J. (2010) *Humanizing the Economy: Co-operatives in the Age of Capital*, Gabriola, BC: New Society Publishers.

Restakis, J. and Girard, J.-P. (2008) 'To Life! – Japan's model of co-operative health care and what it means for Canada', *Making Waves*, 19(1): 5–8.

SWF (Sawayaka Welfare Foundation) (1993) https://wiki.p2pfoundation.net/Fureai_Kippu.

12

Reshaping the food aid landscape

Alice Willatt, Rosalind Beadle and Mary Brydon-Miller

Charitable food aid has become a first line of response for addressing rising rates of hunger in many high-income countries such as the United States (US), Canada, Australia and the United Kingdom (UK). This can be seen in the soaring numbers of food banks, alongside other charitable projects such as community kitchens, resourced through volunteer labour and food donations from corporate retailers. In the US and Canada, food banks have been an institutionalised response to food poverty for 35 years, and in the UK they can be traced back to the introduction of economic austerity measures implemented in response to the 2008 financial crisis (Lambie-Mumford, 2019). In the UK, where 8.4 million people live in food poverty, the largest national food bank provider, The Trussell Trust, has grown its network from 65 food banks in 2011 to more than 1,200 in 2019 (Sosenko et al, 2019). Australia's largest food relief organisation, Foodbank, reports that during the 12 months leading up to 2019, the need for food relief increased by 22 per cent, with more than one in five people experiencing food insecurity. The organisation works with 2,400 charities to provide food relief but only 37 per cent reported that they were meeting the needs of those they assist (Foodbank, 2019).

Critical voices in research, policy and advocacy argue that charitable food aid forms part of the retrenchment of the welfare state, allowing governments to devolve their responsibilities onto the charitable sector and community groups (Lambie-Mumford and Dowler, 2014; Barbour et al, 2016). While alleviating the symptoms of food insecurity, food aid fails to address the structural causes, such as stagnating wages, welfare reforms and austerity policies. In March 2019, these concerns culminated in researchers and poverty campaigners publishing an open letter declaring that charitable food aid in the UK and US is 'a sticking plaster on a gaping wound of systemic inequality in our societies'.[1]

---

[1] The open letter, 'Foodbanks are no solution to poverty', was published in *The Guardian* (24 March 2019) and includes numerous international signatories: https://www.theguardian.com/society/2019/mar/24/food-banks-are-no-solution-to-poverty.

The global COVID-19 pandemic has amplified the connections between food and social inequality further. The wake of the pandemic attuned us to the dysfunctionality of a food aid system reliant on corporate philanthropy, with food aid donations dwindling due to the disruption of fragile just-in-time food supply chains caused by consumer stockpiling (Beacham and Willatt, 2020). The economic insecurities created by loss of income and employment have led to soaring rates of food insecurity. While recognising the crucial role that food aid initiatives play in keeping people alive through crisis, this also marks a critical juncture in which many countries risk further entrenching food aid as a first line of response against poverty. If we are to challenge the normalisation of food aid and the positioning of hunger as a charitable concern, we must look towards 'alternative' spaces of food provisioning that attempt to break from the mainstream of the food aid landscape.

This chapter explores the strategies of two community-based food initiatives attempting to meet immediate needs for sustenance in the here and now, while also engaging in capacity-building work that forms part of a wider social justice agenda: first, a collective of Aboriginal women, the Warburton Breakfast *Minyma* (women), who established a project to provide school breakfasts in a remote community in Western Australia; and second, a community development charity based in Gloucestershire, a county in the south-west of England, the Gloucestershire Gateway Trust (GGT). We explore how these spaces depart from regressive dimensions of the food aid landscape, and in so doing offer touchstones for how we might position a social justice agenda at the forefront of our efforts to transform the food aid system.

Touchstones towards community-based transformation

We begin by situating this chapter within a body of literature that explores the potential for alternative food initiatives to address the connections between food and social injustice. Gómez Garrido et al (2019) highlight the emergence of grassroots food banks in Spain, which arose in opposition to the formal food-bank system, aiming to empower recipients of food aid through their participation in the organisation of the project, building neighbourhood-based solidarity and activist engagements. Similarly, Levkoe and Wakefield's (2011) study describes the Stop Community Food Centre in Toronto, Canada, which evolved from a food bank into a neighbourhood hub. It provides emergency food aid alongside other advocacy and community-building activities through an explicit anti-poverty agenda, which addresses issues such as health, nutrition and housing. While these studies point towards the potential for the transformation of traditional forms of food aid, they also underscore the struggles that arise in attempting to build and sustain more life-affirming spaces of food provisioning. They highlight challenges relating to asymmetrical power relations and the potential for engagements in advocacy to limit certain channels of funding, thus jeopardising the sustainability of such projects.

The community-based food initiatives that form our case studies are sites of participatory action research projects in which the three co-authors are involved. We worked alongside these communities to co-generate knowledge that aimed to support them to negotiate the challenges involved in attempting to build more transformative spaces of food provisioning. Our collective learning across these projects informs the touchstones put forward. We do not present these as fixed or universal recommendations but rather as critical reference points for helping us to think through how we might rework the food aid landscape and challenge the ideological reluctance of governments to address the structural causes of poverty.

Our first touchstone relates to *the role of food as 'more-than-food'*. In different ways our community-based food initiatives seek to resist and renegotiate paternalistic models of service provision that adopt a narrow focus on providing access to food, which risks casting individuals as passive recipients of charity. The provision of food can create 'zones of exclusion', contributing to experiences of social marginalisation, and yet it can also foster 'zones of encounter' that give way to alternative subjectivities and politics (Miewald and McCann, 2014). Across our case studies we demonstrate how engagements with food transcend its role in just providing physical nourishment. We point towards how embodied practices and engagements with food can forge agency and cultivate alternative forms of citizenship that pave the way towards building a more inclusive and socially just society.

Second, pushing for transformation of the food aid landscape and our wider food system requires *foregrounding the voices and experiences of those experiencing social exclusion*. This touchstone is informed by our commitments to the social justice orientation of participatory action research, specifically its 'abiding respect for people's knowledge and for their ability to understand and address the issues confronting them and their communities' (Brydon-Miller et al, 2003, p 14). We argue that people with direct experiences of food insecurity and social marginalisation are experts by experience. We point towards the importance of positioning these voices at the forefront of efforts to transform our welfare structures and tackle the underlying causes of food insecurity.

Third, we underscore the significance of *cultivating deliberative engagements on the politics and practices of food provisioning*. Our case studies highlight the importance of opening deliberative dialogue relating to the day-to-day doing of food provisioning as a means to collectively navigate some of the tensions and contradictions that arise – for example, negotiating how the emergency work of meeting food needs in the here and now can be brought together with a wider long-term agenda of social transformation. Deliberation is crucial to negotiating the messiness of growing and sustaining community-based food initiatives. This also encompasses public deliberation aimed at building a wider dialogue around the connections between food and social inequalities, with the view to shaping policy from the bottom up. We point towards the generative capacity of deliberation in building inclusive and resilient grassroots community-based projects, and inspiring collective action and social change.

The Warburton Breakfast Minyma

In 2008, a group of grandmothers in the remote Aboriginal community of Warburton in the Ngaanyatjarra Lands of Western Australia (WA) responded to community concerns about school attendance. Together with the local community council, they initiated a school breakfast programme to encourage attendance and provide the children with a nutritional start to their learning day. Many children were enticed by this physical nourishment, and the comfort offered by the presence of their family members at work in the school that was typically seen as a *walypala* (whitefella) zone. This case study provides a snapshot of how '*Kurlunytjanu mapurlkarringu*' (From a small thing, [the program] grew bigger) (Lawson, 2015), and how the Minyma's (women's) initiative – grounded in their intimate knowledge of the social and cultural context – provided a platform for their informing and influencing of programmes and policies with a history of failing to meet the needs of remote Aboriginal Australians.

The women's programme emerged in a setting of very poor nutritional health, broadly attributable to a rapid shift in food systems and diet following the arrival of missionaries in the 1930s. Today, access to regular and affordable food in Warburton is made difficult by a set of complex factors that perpetuate social marginalisation within remote foodscapes. Aboriginal consumers have little control of their food security as 'outsider' non-Indigenous people manage and staff food outlets. This disempowerment is exacerbated by low food literacy, overcrowding and inadequate food storage facilities in homes, and poverty. These factors contributed to children not having access to a healthy breakfast and were the foundations for the initiation of the school breakfast programme. The food, donated from Foodbank WA (Western Australia) in Perth, was nutritious and affordable. From day one, school breakfasts were well received by the children and had a positive impact on attendance:

> Now the kids they know, 'oh ladies there' [and] they get up quick ... and they go to school ... they have good healthy breakfast so they can keep going to school and be *ninti walykumunu* (good and smart). The Family Place [the Minyma's school-based workplace] is like a magnet pulling them kids. That's making them hang about at school instead of going home. The kids all say, '*Walkumunyu breakfast pa!*' (Breakfast is good!). (Breakfast Minyma, 2012, personal communication, cited in Beadle, 2018, pp 69, 90)

As well as addressing the nutritional needs of the children, the women's programme challenged the common practices of service delivery in remote Aboriginal communities, whereby non-Indigenous staff from the outside are employed for various periods and 'apply knowledge and skills that render local knowledge irrelevant' (Beadle, 2018, p 227).

The activities of the Warburton Breakfast Minyma grew into much more than breakfast. Besides enhanced school attendance, community participation generated new connections as the Minyma were able to meet teachers and learn about the school's programmes. Their presence provided 'close family voices' (Tjitayi and Osborne, 2014) at the school, which enhanced the children's confidence to participate in formal schooling and consolidated relationships between the mostly non-Indigenous staff and the students' family members. Over time, the Minyma took over roles previously done by teachers such as catering for school events, which was received by school staff with gratitude and encouragement. Relationships between the women and the school staff provided the teachers with an insight into community life and this newfound knowledge supported them to adapt their lessons and communication to suit the needs of the Ngaanyatjarra children and their families (Beadle, 2018).

The confidence gained by the Minyma led to their programme expanding, which they named *Mirlirrtjarra Kuurl Mirrka Palyalpayi* (Making Good Food at Warburton School). It grew to include: meals on wheels for older people (previously the responsibility of the local store), a support programme for teenage girls, a range of catering services for the school and other agencies, and food-based fundraising. To manage the workload, the women recruited family members and established a pool of more than 50 Minyma, which enabled them to work while fulfilling their family and community responsibilities as mothers, aunties and grandmothers.

The Minyma adopted and celebrated their role as 'workers'; many had been previously unemployed. Importantly, they identified three significant dimensions of their work that challenged conventional non-Indigenous expectations and assumptions regarding how Aboriginal people 'should' conform to the role of 'worker'. First, they self-directed its structures; this ensured that work was meaningfully and creatively integrated into the social reality of their family and community lives. Second, they self-governed their work so that it incorporated cultural seniority and local decision-making processes. Third, they recruited their colleagues based on existing family relationships. This contrasts to non-Indigenous work cultures, are 'established to facilitate transactions among strangers' (Davies and Maru 2010, p 25). Engagement in work that aligned so naturally with their existing roles as Ngaanyatjarra women contributed to their personal wellbeing, and that of their families and the community. As a result, the Minyma collectively experienced enhanced esteem, confidence and agency.

In an arena where remote Aboriginal voices are typically marginalised, the empowerment, authority and respect the Minyma experienced as workers provided a platform from which their voices and local situated knowledge (Genat, 2009) could be foregrounded. They sought opportunities to communicate their experiences, delivering classes to local school children, presenting at conferences, and to government and non-government audiences. A range of articles, reports, posters and documentary videos were produced by the women. To address a gap in local literacy resources, they created a set of 28 storybooks about their experiences, many of which were translated into Ngaanyatjarra, the first language for most children. As well as providing engaging reading materials, the stories role-modelled the Minyma's valued and productive worker role to the next generation.

The Minyma's accounts demonstrated their passion, enthusiasm and commitment. This offers a stark contrast to the disparaging and uninformed representation by politicians and the media of remote

Aboriginal people regarding their motivation and capacity to engage in productive work (Beadle, 2018). Most service delivery programmes in the region are typically instigated, managed and run by non-Indigenous staff; in contrast, the Minyma were central to the initiation and running of their programme. In order to help sustain the Minyma's initiatives, the second author worked in collaboration with the women, drawing on non-directive, developmental practice, a solutions-based and strengths-focused model of community development that supports people to identify their own solutions to problems and build on their existing skills and capabilities (Stringer, 2013).

The suite of self-directed wellbeing activities initiated by the Minyma illustrate how programmes run by local people are more likely to result in empowerment and improve social indicators. Their reputation and stories had far-reaching effects on programmes and policies. The women became an Aboriginal reference group for the school principal, health staff and senior managers in government departments. This created a two-way dialogue with existing services about effective ways of engaging Aboriginal people in programmes and work. Their experience also encouraged groups elsewhere to adopt similar practices: a neighbouring community replicated the school breakfast programme (previously run by the school staff) and invited the Warburton Minyma to train the new workers. Foodbank WA staff also came to learn about their pursuits and took a keen interest in understanding from the Minyma how to engage local people in enhancing food security in their communities. To reduce the pattern of recipients passively receiving food aid, Foodbank WA also promoted the Minyma's stories to other food aid recipients to encourage community collaboration in the food aid space.

Counter to food security being shaped by top-down, paternalistic modes of food provisioning, the experiences of the Warburton Breakfast Minyma reveal how efforts to establish food security can be re-envisaged as something grounded in the work, experiences and knowledge of local people. In May 2017, Australian Indigenous people sought constitutional reform and a platform for shared decision making through *The Uluru Statement from the Heart*, which calls for a voice in the Australian Parliament. Reflecting the lack of recognition felt by many Indigenous people, the statement indicates the urgent need for policy makers and governments to respect, support and learn from grassroots solutions, such as the Minyma's. As well as marking a break away from the historically racist and paternalistic structures of policy and welfare, the agency and responsibility attained by the women provided an avenue for their marginalised voices to influence programme and policy development in a way that was democratic, respectful and observant of their cultural and social context. From role-modelling for their children and community members, to face-to-face conversations with state and federal Ministers of Parliament, the Minyma demonstrated that they (not policy and programme developers) hold the knowledge and relationships to affect their wellbeing, livelihoods and futures in ways that are meaningful and sustainable, and enhance self-determination.

Gloucestershire Gateway Trust

Our second case study is the Gloucestershire Gateway Trust (GGT), a community development charity based in England. It works in peripheral urban housing estates in the City of Gloucester, in neighbourhoods ranked among the most deprived 10 per cent in England.[2] The GGT aim to create communities where people feel valued, connected and empowered to influence decisions that affect their lives through the development of sustainable community-led solutions to the challenges they face. The GGT was formed by a group of local people around the idea to turn something seen as a deficit – their proximity to the M5 motorway – into an asset: a community-led motorway services station that would redirect wealth into the local area and provide secure employment.

The GGT worked in partnership with the only established family-run motorway services business, The Westmoreland Family, to open the Gloucester Services in 2014. Since this time, it has delivered employment skills training to 240 local people in long-term unemployment and provided 400 secure jobs. The GGT receives a royalty of up to 3 pence from every £1 of non-fuel sales, to fund community regeneration and build a network of local organisations working in areas relating to health, education, employment and housing, among others. This encompasses advocacy work and engaging with anchor institutions, such as local authorities, to establish citizen participation in key decision making.

The community development work of the GGT's founders spans several decades but their focus on food insecurity only emerged in the aftermath of the 2008 financial crisis and the government austerity regime that followed. The subsequent restructuring of the social security system led to substantial delays and reductions in government

---

[2] As outlined in the 2015 English Indices of Deprivation: https://www.gov.uk/government/statistics/english-indices-of-deprivation-2015.

benefit payments, which has had a profound impact on low-income areas. Over the past decade, these shifts, combined with the stagnation of wages and workforce casualisation, have resulted in a significant spike in food insecurity. A growing number of people have turned to community organisations like the GGT, and their wider network of community partners, for support. In response, the GGT has integrated a number of food initiatives into its network, which work to address emergency food needs, while also strengthening capacity and infrastructure to build community resilience in the face of these systemic challenges. While there is not the space in this chapter to develop a comprehensive analysis of this network, we provide a brief sketch of different elements to illustrate how the GGT adopts a systemic approach to addressing food insecurity that embodies the touchstones at the forefront of our argument to transform the food aid system.

The GGT brings together a network of eight 'foundational community partners', alongside other community-led groups that work across their target communities (see Figure 12.1 for a map of the foundational community partners, also identified below in italics). One of the early food initiatives, the Community Food Cupboards, was established by *GL Communities* in partnership with the GGT, alongside the local community time bank, *Fair Shares*, which supports the redistribution of surplus food from the Gloucester Services and local stores to local collection points. Once established, the ownership is handed over to community members who continue to run them today. This reflects a wider pattern in the GGT's work in which, once established, community initiatives are owned and run by community members. This community ownership has shaped the design of the food cupboards, which aim to remove the barriers and institutional gatekeeping of emergency food provisions, such as those often present in food banks, in recognition that these practices can contribute to stigmatisation. The creation of the Community Food Cupboards led to a sprouting of other food projects. There are a range of free and low-cost lunch clubs held in community centres and with partners, such as *The Venture* and *All Pulling Together*. As well as meeting basic food needs and providing a place for community connection, these initiatives signpost to other organisations within the wider network that provide advice on issues such as debt, benefits and employment, and support local wellbeing.

Over the years the GGT and partners have established a number of food provisioning projects that draw on food as a tool for capacity building in communities. In 2017, the GGT worked in partnership with *GL Communities* to establish a Community Growing Project at the

Figure 12.1: Gloucestershire Gateway Trust – foundational community partners

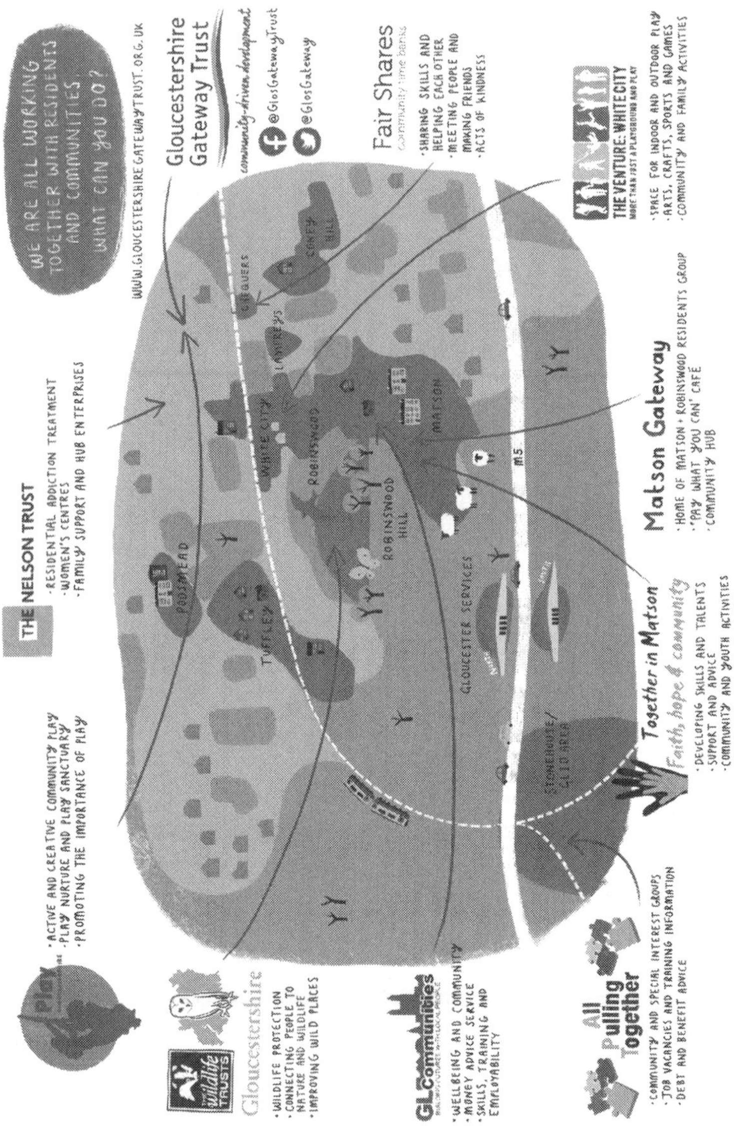

Gloucester Services. Situated on a piece of land behind the Services, this includes an orchard, fruit beds and a herb garden. While it is too early for the project to have high productive value, over time they hope to produce enough fresh produce to resource local community food initiatives. The project contributes to the local biodiversity and provides an outdoor meeting space for community partners, local schools and employees of the Services. It also serves as an important bridge to employment for the volunteers, many of whom are furthest away from the labour market. Mark Gale, founder and chief executive of the GGT, explains:

> For a lot of people, the toughest thing about getting back to work is stepping over the threshold for the first time. ... If we can get people into that growing space, just doing stuff informally, getting that communication stuff going, then they go into the [Gloucester] Services to use the facilities and get a cup of tea, and then suddenly they are over the threshold of a workplace, and can see where it is that they might work one day.[3]

Through the Community Growing Project, volunteers develop a connection to the land, the surrounding environment, and a potential future workplace, alongside building relationships with others who intermingle in the communal space, such as growers, community groups, and employees of the Services. The project forms part of a wider collection of initiatives intended to support local people into employment at the Services, such as free pre-employment training, drop-in sessions at community centres where local residents can find out about employment opportunities, alongside the prioritisation of job applicants living in target communities. With its informal approach and focus on growing food, the project provides a vital route into some of these more formal initiatives, while also building confidence and self-esteem and supporting wellbeing.

A central focus of the GGT is to ensure the voice and participation of local communities in decision making that affects their lives, which has included strategies to establish community ownership and control over elements of the local foodscape. In 2018, an independent housing association, working with the local council, announced plans to regenerate the housing estates and local retail outlets in the neighbourhoods of Matson and Podsmead. The GGT is working in collaboration with residents to ensure they have a voice in this process. Working in partnership with the first and third authors of this chapter,

---

[3] Notes from an interview Alice Willatt and Mary Brydon-Miller conducted with Mark Gale.

the GGT run annual visioning workshops and community surveys that identify community assets and explore how they can be strengthened to address local challenges. The regeneration of the retail units has been a central focus. Residents discussed the lack of affordable fresh food on offer, with the nearest supermarket being a car drive or bus journey away. Over the past year the GGT has opened dialogue with the housing association, local authority and policy makers, to push for a model of regeneration that establishes a community ownership stake in the retail units (see also Chapter 2).

Rather than letting markets dominate the regeneration process, securing community ownership would put in place a sustainable and democratic means for residents to shape their local foodscape to meet their needs, as determined by them. Residents expressed an interest in an affordable greengrocer shop and, in Podsmead, a low-cost community café with internet and computer access, and a meeting space to strengthen existing community connections and neighbourliness. While the negotiations around regeneration are still in process, this points towards how food provisioning in marginalised communities can be shaped via a process of collaboration and co-operation, rather than market competition. It highlights the role of community-led organisations like the GGT in opening spaces of deliberation between citizens and business and government bodies who often act as gatekeepers in shaping the local foodscape and determining access to healthy and affordable food.

In the wake of the COVID-19 pandemic, when the local authority struggled to address the needs of vulnerable residents, the GGT's long-embedded network of community groups meant that it could respond in a rapid and sustained way. The pandemic has led to a heightened visibility of its work, with the local authority recognising its value and potential to contribute to ongoing recovery efforts, which led to the GGT receiving a substantial grant from the Department of the Environment, Food and Rural Affairs (Defra). While the GGT has historically chosen to work independently of the local authority and statutory bodies, in recognition that alliances could undermine its autonomy and ways of working, the grant enabled it to strengthen its place-based and grassroots approach to building resilience against food insecurity and the structural causes of poverty. It also helped meet some of the shortfall in the GGT's budget, a substantial proportion of which comes from royalties of sales at Gloucester Services, which have been significantly affected by the pandemic. While the pandemic presents ongoing challenges for the GGT, it has also provided an opening to demonstrate the power and sustainability of community-owned and -led strategies for building a more equitable local foodscape. It has cast light on the limitations of institutionalised approaches to charitable food aid that start from the perspective of identifying community problems, rather than their assets, and paved the way for an approach that builds solidarity, dignity and agency.

Reworking the food aid landscape

In this final section, we bring both case studies into the discussion to consider how they contribute to the reworking of the food aid landscape in relation to our touchstones. We begin by recognising some of the challenges and tensions involved in sustaining these projects. Collaborations with food banks, local authorities and business have undoubtedly enabled both projects to sustain and grow their work, through the provision of funding and other vital resources, such as food donations. These relationships have been particularly crucial during times of crisis, such as the pandemic, during which there has been a critical need for community support and financial resources to sustain it. Yet they also present challenges and tensions, potentially compromising the agency and democratic workings of these projects. It could also be argued that such partnerships are indicative of neoliberal state restructuring in which governments withdraw social provisions and manoeuvre third sector organisations into a shadow state role. While it is important to recognise the limitations and contradictions that partnerships may bring, we understand them as indicative of the wider sociopolitical environment in which these projects exist and compete for survival. In the following discussion we illuminate how collaborations with government bodies and food charities are not one of silent acquiescence, but rather become a site of resistance in which they rework dominant narratives of poverty perpetuated through neoliberal welfare and call governments to account.

Our case studies touch on a myriad of food provisioning practices that *reach beyond the role of food in just providing physical sustenance*. They point towards the relational capacity of food, showing how embodied engagements with growing, eating and sharing food – across place, space and time – can strengthen relationships and galvanise community development. Food provisioning activities serve as a relational tool for building capacity and resilience in communities that have historically been socially excluded. We see this in the case of the Warburton Breakfast Minyma's initiative, which brought parents from Indigenous communities into school spaces where the voices and experiences of Indigenous children and families have historically been marginalised.

We also see it in the community growing project, in which the collective practices of growing food on land became a conduit into a potential future workplace. In both case studies, food was the glue that connected people together across differences, built bridges to employment and forged relationships premised on respect and an understanding of our mutual interdependence with one another and the wider living world.

We have presented the two case studies in as much detail as space has allowed because we felt it was important to provide a sense of the local context within which these projects take place, the people who make them possible and the communities they represent. However, we are aware of numerous projects around the world that also illuminate the capacity-building potential of food. The Kajoli Early Childhood Learning Centres, sponsored by Research Initiatives, Bangladesh, for example, has developed a model very akin to the Warburton Breakfast Minyma model to provide food to children attending their programmes and to promote active community engagement. Universities too can and should take an active role, as is the case with the Salikneta Farm Program at De LaSalle University Araneta in the Philippines, which provides training to local students in food production and marketing while also promoting local produce and agritourism to boost the local economy.

Transforming the food aid landscape requires harnessing the capacity-building potential of food in ways that *foreground the voices and experiences of people who are often socially excluded and marginalised*. Both initiatives cultivated place-based approaches to food provisioning, initiated by and for local people embedded in these communities, and shaped by local knowledge and experiences. In Gloucestershire, experiential knowledge and understanding of how accessing emergency food aid can perpetuate social stigmatisation, informed the design of the Community Food Cupboards as unstaffed collection points available to all without assessment of needs. Similarly, the growth of activities surrounding the work of the Warburton Breakfast Minyma was shaped by a deep-rooted understanding not only of the challenges they faced, but also the community assets they hold to address these issues. In this sense, both projects disrupt entrenched models of food aid that position marginalised people as passive recipients of charity and demonstrate that action grounded in local knowledge and experience can meaningfully contribute to enhancing food security.

Furthermore, both cases highlight the significance of *cultivating deliberative engagements* between citizens, local authorities, governments and other stakeholders to address the connection between food and social inequality. A central focus of these efforts is to carve out a place for the voices of marginalised groups in local decision making and policy. The Warburton Breakfast Minyma's engagements with food-bank workers generated reciprocal learning and instigated actions to encourage other recipients of emergency food aid to adopt community-led approaches to enhancing food security. The GGT's ongoing attempts to establish community ownership in the retail regeneration plans seek to place control and agency for shaping the local foodscape in the hands of communities, rather than governments and business. These engagements bring into political debate the structural factors that determine access to food, which is essential if we are to move away from neoliberal discourses of personal responsibility for poverty towards a recognition of how personal circumstances are shaped by the failures of state institutions and the privileging of market rationality.

Deliberation also paves the way for building progressive alliances between different community-led food initiatives, which have the potential to shape policy. We finish this chapter by pointing to the example of Cultivate Charlottesville in the US. Formed in 2018, it brings together three established projects that work collectively to build a socially just and sustainable food system in a city where one in four residents do not earn enough to cover housing, food and other basic living costs, and food insecurity disproportionately affects non-White residents.[4] The City Schoolyard Garden project and Urban Agriculture Collective work in schools and with residents living in low-income housing to develop skills in relation to food growing and share fresh produce. These projects are integrated with a city-wide Food Justice Network (FJN), which builds racial equality into the food system through education, organising and advocacy. The FJN played a central role in establishing the 2018 Food Equity Initiative, the first local appropriation bill to directly address the systemic causes of food insecurity, recently approved for a second year. Building on the integrated approach of Cultivate Charlottesville, the initiative opens dialogue with residents across eight neighbourhoods, non-profit organisations, healthcare institutions, city departments, and state and federal partners, among other stakeholders, to engage in food-system planning that places the voice, ownership and agency of local people at the heart of the local foodscape. From Charlottesville to the remote deserts of Western Australia, and the urban fringes of the City of

---

[4] You can read more about Cultivate Charlottesville on their website: https:// cultivatecharlottesville.org/.

Gloucester in the UK, these cases demonstrate how community-led practices around food serve as a vehicle for generating 'more-than-food policies' (Millner et al, 2020) underpinned by an explicitly social justice agenda.

References

Barbour, L., Rose, N., Montegriffo, E., Wingrove, K., Clarke, B., Browne, J. and Rundle, M. (2016) *The Human Right to Food*, Melbourne: The Right to Food Coalition, pp 1–11.

Beacham, J. D. and Willatt, A. (2020) 'New foodscapes', in Parker, M. (ed) *Life After COVID-19: The Other Side of Crisis*, Bristol: University of Bristol Press, pp 73–82.

Beadle, R. (2018) 'Remote Aboriginal women and meaningful work: key dimensions for Ngaanyatjarra women', PhD thesis, University of Melbourne, Victoria, http://hdl.handle.net/11343/221554.

Brydon-Miller, M., Greenwood, D. and Maguire, P. (2003) 'Why action research?', *Action Research*, 1(1): 9–28.

Davies, J. and Maru, Y. (2010) 'Living to work, or working to live: intercultural understandings of livelihoods', *Dialogue*, 29(1): 18.

Foodbank (2019) *Foodbank Hunger Report 2019*, North Ryde, NSW: Foodbank, https://www.foodbank.org.au/.

Genat, B. (2009) 'Building emergent situated knowledges in participatory action research', *Action Research*, 7(1): 101–15.

Gómez Garrido, M., Carbonero Gamundí, M. A. and Viladrich, A. (2019) 'The role of grassroots food banks in building political solidarity with vulnerable people', *European Societies*, 21(5): 753–73.

Lambie-Mumford, H. (2019) 'The growth of food banks in Britain and what they mean for social policy', *Critical Social Policy*, 39(1): 3–22.

Lambie-Mumford, H. and Dowler, E. (2014) 'Rising use of "food aid" in the United Kingdom', *British Food Journal*, 116(9): 1418–25.

Lawson, O. (2015) *Mirlirrtjarra Kuurl Mirrka Palyalpayi (Making Good Food at Warburton School)*, produced as a Parent and Community Engagement project with the support of South Metropolitan Youth Link, Perth.

Levkoe, C. and Wakefield, S. (2011) 'The community food centre: creating space for a just, sustainable, and healthy food system', *Journal of Agriculture, Food Systems, and Community Development*, 2(1): 249–68.

Miewald, C. and McCann, E. (2014) 'Foodscapes and the geographies of poverty: sustenance, strategy, and politics in an urban neighborhood', *Antipode*, 46(2): 537–56.

Millner, N., Cohen, S., Cole, T., Webster, K., Andrews, H., Cheung, M., Evans, P., Oliver, A. and the Food Working Group (2020) 'Who gets to decide what's in my fridge? Principles for transforming the "invisible rules" shaping the regulation of food habits in urban spaces' in McDermont, M., Cole, T., Newman, J. and Piccini, A. (eds) *Imagining Regulation Differently: Co-creating Regulation for Engagement*, Bristol: Policy Press, pp 85–103.

Sosenko, F., Littlewood, M., Bramley, G., Fitzpatrick, S., Blenkinsopp, J. and Wood, J. (2019) *State of Hunger: A Study of Poverty and Food Insecurity in the UK*, London: The Trussell Trust, https://www.stateofhunger.org/wp-content/uploads/2019/11/State-of-Hunger-Report-November2019-Digital.pdf.

Stringer E. T. (2013) *Action Research*, London: Sage Publications.

Tjitayi, K. and Osborne, S. (2014) 'At the heart of learning (series: paper 3 of 4): Kurunta kanyintja: holding knowledge in our spirit', *AlterNative: An International Journal of Indigenous Peoples*, 10(1): 23–32.

13

Sustainable communities for the future

Diane Warburton

Introduction

The quality of our environment shapes the quality of our lives – our health, our wellbeing, our past, our present and our future. It is what we share with other human beings and all living things. It provides our habitat and when it is beautiful, strong and healthy, we are nourished and thrive; and when it is ugly, polluted and degraded, we struggle to survive.

Environmental issues are global and complex, which can be daunting. They are also local: the slogan *Think Global, Act Local* has been around since the 1980s. However, in spite of global rhetoric and international agreements, and growing public disquiet, environmental issues are not always recognised as political priorities.

Participatory local community-led environmental action can offer one way through these dilemmas. It is not a panacea but it can make a vital contribution to tackling global environmental problems and transforming communities in two ways: creating innovative solutions for local environmental problems; and building learning and collective working as the basis for conscientisation, politicisation and wider action.

Moreover, community campaigns can draw attention to the disparities of power to own, control and access environmental assets that create the context for continued inequalities, injustice and exclusion that affect us all, especially disadvantaged groups and communities. It is the poorest people and communities who suffer the worst environmental problems – pollution, traffic, degraded neighbourhoods, flood risk, contaminated land, lack of green open space – resulting in the poorest health and quality of life. Local action can challenge the wealthiest individuals and institutions who continue to acquire, control and exploit land and buildings, depleting and damaging natural resources and privatising natural assets. Environmental inequalities, as all

215

inequalities, affect us all but it is more obvious with our environment because it is something we all share. As the song goes: 'The air, the air is everywhere'.[1]

We all know that we cannot continue to exploit and plunder the Earth's natural resources at the same pace as in the past without serious long-term damage to the health of people and the planet. We know we need to better understand and manage risks, whether from climate change or from habitat loss and species extinctions.

We have learned again during the COVID-19 pandemic how vulnerable we all are to such global forces, but also how much we can do for ourselves to help our families, our neighbours and others, and how desperately we still need good public services that go beyond what we can do ourselves. We have learnt how much healthier and more enjoyable it is to have cleaner air, less traffic and quieter streets, to walk in green spaces and to hear the birds sing without the pollution that usually surrounds us. Even locked down we have found ways to look beyond ourselves to appreciate what we share. The global and local constantly collide in the modern world and we now have some indications of what a better world might look like.

This chapter does not look at individual (important), business (crucial) or state (vital) actions. It focuses on how local community-led environmental action working within a framework of global environmental thinking can contribute to transforming communities in ways that support human flourishing within a safe and sustainable environment.

The global context

Since the 1970s, the United Nations (UN) has led international efforts to tackle the problems of the human environment – the relationship between people and the planet. The importance of communities and citizens as partners has always been recognised:

6. A point has been reached in history when we must shape our actions throughout the world with a more prudent care for their environmental consequences. ...

7. To achieve this environmental goal will demand the acceptance of responsibility by citizens and communities and by enterprises and

---

[1] The song *Air*, from *Hair, the Musical*, 1967.

institutions at every level, all sharing equitably in common efforts. (United Nations, 1973)

The concept of 'sustainable development' was created in the 1980s – the idea that we must meet current human needs (especially tackling poverty and inequality) 'without compromising the ability of future generations to meet their own needs' (WCED, 1987, p 8), especially avoiding environmental damage. Environmental, social, economic and political development were fully integrated into this thinking. Participatory community action was always recognised as essential, with the *very first* requirement in the pursuit of sustainable development being 'a political system that secures effective citizen participation in decision making' (WCED, 1987, p 65. Furthermore:

> The law alone cannot enforce the common interest. It principally needs community knowledge and support, which entails greater public participation in the decisions which affect the environment. This is best secured by decentralising the management of resources upon which local communities depend, and giving these communities an effective say over the use of the resources. It will also require promoting citizens' initiatives, empowering people's organisations, and strengthening local democracy. (WCED, 1987, p 63)

It is easy to forget how much impact the idea of sustainable development had in the United Kingdom (UK) at the time. Agenda 21 – the Agenda for the 21st century – was agreed at the UN Conference on Environment and Development (UNCED) in Rio in 1992; by December 2000, 93 per cent of UK local authorities had completed Local Agenda 21 (LA21) strategies.[2]

International agreements continue to provide the context for much local environmental action. There was already a strong movement in the UK towards local and increasingly urban community environmental initiatives (Warburton, 1998). Community environmental action has since become more ambitious and effective, as outlined in the next section, in spite of devastating cuts in public spending.

---

[2] https://publications.parliament.uk/pa/cm200102/cmselect/cmenvaud/616/2021308.htm

What does local environmental action look like?

Pollution

In the UK, the impacts of pollution on the poorest sections of the population, and particularly on black and minority ethnic communities, are well established. Studies from 1980 found that race was the most significant element in predicting the location of commercial hazardous waste facilities (Berglund, 2000). In England, the most deprived 20 per cent of neighbourhoods had higher air pollution than the least deprived, and 'the worst air pollution levels were seen in ethnically diverse neighbourhoods'.[3] Friends of the Earth calculated that air pollution caused the equivalent of 36,000 early deaths a year in the UK.[4]

Local community action can make a difference. In the United States (US), for example, the West Oakland Environmental Indicators Project in San Francisco was founded by Margaret Gordon, who was working in a school where she saw shoeboxes full of asthma inhalers, each labelled for different children. The area lies between two highways, a busy port, factories and the site of a proposed coal terminal. She monitored the number of trucks that passed through on their way to the port, learnt how to measure levels of fine particulate matter that can enter the bloodstream and cause respiratory disease and worked with scientists to collect more data. That proved what she had suspected: that the low-income minority communities in the area were far more likely to suffer the ill-effects of air pollution than other sectors of society.

The West Oakland Environmental Indicators Project (San Francisco, US) used the data they gathered to help persuade the California Air Resources Board to take action against dangerous levels of air pollution. It led to stricter regulation of trucks and the planned coal terminal has been blocked. The air pollution is 74 per cent lower than in 2008. The group also helped draft a new state law, which passed in 2017 and puts local communities at the centre of emissions planning. West Oakland has now drafted its own action plan for dealing with pollution sources, which they hope will also address the tendency for wealthy white

---

[3] https://www.imperial.ac.uk/news/163408/ethnic-minorities-deprived-communities-hardest-pollution/

[4] https://friendsoftheearth.uk/clean-air/london-smog-and-1956-clean-air-act

communities to go low carbon by offloading pollution towards poorer black and Latino areas (Watts, 2020).

The West Oakland project demonstrates the effective use of scientific data in campaigning, leading to policy and legislative change. It also shows the development from small local actions to wider political action, although many shy away from the term 'political' in talking about their work (Brodie et al, 2011).

Development of land and buildings

Local government land-use planning shapes the places in which we live – the built and natural environment in cities, towns and villages – through creating regular plans that provide the framework for all development and conservation of land and buildings. Land-use planning has increasingly used 'place making' to describe the profession, recognising the importance of 'place' to a sense of community.

Recent theories identify a new faultline in communities of place, and a difference between people who are 'Somewheres' and 'Anywheres' (Goodhart, 2017). 'Somewheres' are rooted in a specific place or community, socially conservative, often less well educated, uneasy with the modern world and nostalgic. 'Anywheres' are footloose, often urban, socially liberal and university educated, they are not nostalgic or nationalistic, and they value autonomy and self-realisation before stability, community and tradition. This theory has been used to explain new political divisions, including Brexit voting.

However, these distinctions do not have to be as tribal or divisive as Goodhart suggests. We can be both:

> [T]he desire for anchoring remains key and it is still connected to place. In spite of modern high tech communications, face to face communication remains essential to anchoring … Not necessarily my original place but some place – my flat, street, city, region, country – even if I see myself as a citizen of the world. (Landry, 2001, p 1)

Human beings may always have moved around the world, but that does not mean we never come to rest in a place; that place is where we make our home and find our community.

Since the 1960s, the UK planning system has formally incorporated community and public participation as part of plan-making and development control processes (Arnstein, 1969; Skeffington, 1969). Innovative approaches to support for community action on land and buildings include planning aid (since 1973[5]) and Planning for Real,[6] community planning (Wates, 2000) and community architecture (Wates and Knevitt, 1987). In rural areas, innovations such as local distinctiveness and parish maps, usually led by parish councils or community groups, brought creativity and flair to thinking about plan making (Clifford and King, 1993); while community-led village design statements have been adopted into the formal plan-making process and about 2,000 are now in place (Warburton, 2004; Bishop, 2019).

In spite of rhetoric to the contrary, community action on planning is very rarely simply NIMBY (Not In My Back Yard). In practice, 'people are generally not scared of development but of unpractical and unpleasant forms of it' (Krier, 2001, p 2). Indeed, all the evidence suggests that communities 'are not so intent on preserving the status quo, but are actually bubbling with ideas about how to initiate and support developments that improve quality of life', such as affordable housing (Warburton, 2004, p 264.

Some have argued that '[p]articipation is part of the "red tape" that interferes with the market and particularly the provision of housing' (Airey and Doughty, cited in Brownill, 2020, p 168). In practice, however, we know that this not the case: 'We now have, if still poorly recorded, example after example that shows clearly how good participation has saved time, has saved money, has led to better plans and projects and has raised people's confidence in the planning system and their capacity to engage' (Bishop, 2019).

The statement by the Local Government Association, in response to the UK government's *Planning for the Future*,[7] summarises the benefits of community participation in planning:

> Covid-19 has demonstrated the incredible spirit of communities as they united to support each other and fight this deadly virus. As we move forward, it should be they who drive the national recovery with the power and voice to shape their local area so it is somewhere they are proud to live, work and enjoy their time in, and where everyone has an opportunity to reach their full potential.

---

[5] https://www.rtpi.org.uk/planning-advice/about-planning-aid-england/
[6] http://www.planningforreal.org.uk/
[7] https://www.gov.uk/government/consultations/planning-for-the-future

People want their local area to have high-quality affordable homes built in the right places, supported by the right infrastructure, which provides enough schools, promotes greener and more active travel, and tackles climate change. This can only be achieved through a local planning system with public participation at its heart which enables councils to deliver resilient, prosperous places that meet the needs of their communities. It means beautiful areas and better homes. (Local Government Association[8])

Green spaces

During the COVID19 pandemic, many more people have appreciated shared green spaces. We know the health benefits:

Greener environments are also associated with better mental health and wellbeing outcomes including reduced levels of depression, anxiety, and fatigue, and enhanced quality of life for both children and adults. Greenspace can help bind communities together, reduce loneliness, and mitigate the negative effects of air pollution, excessive noise, heat and flooding. Disadvantaged groups appear to gain a larger health benefit and have reduced socioeconomic-related inequalities in health when living in greener communities, so greenspace and a greener urban environment can also be used as an important tool in the drive to build a fairer society. (Public Health England, 2020, p 11)

There is also considerable research showing the economic benefits of green spaces: such as the £2.1 billion per year that could be saved in health costs if everyone in England had good access to greenspace (Public Health England, 2020). Community-led action on green spaces takes two main forms: improving access to existing green spaces and countryside; and creating and maintaining green spaces.

Access to the nearest countryside, especially for those from the poorest communities, has deep political roots. The first modern campaign for access to land in England was the mass trespass on Kinder Scout in Derbyshire in 1932. More than 400 people took part, coordinated by the ramblers clubs, which were a part of the labour movement in

---

[8] https://www.local.gov.uk/keep-planning-local

the 1930s: 'we ramblers, after a hard day's work in smokey towns and cities, go out for rambling for relaxation and fresh air' (Allison, 2012). They found the moors and mountains closed to them by gamekeepers maintaining the land for shooting. Five of the leaders of the protest were arrested and later jailed, resulting in much larger rallies and the start of a wider movement for access. This protest is credited with leading to the creation of the national parks – the first one in 1951 in the same Peak District in Derbyshire and described as 'the lungs of the industrial north' (Allison, 2012; Barnett, 2019).

The Black Environment Network was set up in the 1980s partly to address the specific challenges for black and minority ethnic communities in accessing and feeling comfortable in the countryside. The fight to access more than the 8 per cent of the English countryside currently open for access continues, with the launch of The Right to Roam campaign in 2020 to extend the Countryside Rights of Way Act 2000 to enable more people to access open space.[9]

In spite of the warm words and cold hard economic evidence from public bodies on the health benefits of open green space, austerity has dramatically reduced local funding enabling local authorities and communities to create or maintain these areas. Nonetheless, some of the most successful projects have been run by people in the most disadvantaged communities.

Living Under One Sun in Tottenham, north London, was started in 2005 by mothers of many cultures wanting to reduce their isolation and make their much-neglected neighbourhood safer. It started with 'meet, cook and eat' activities, and grew to a local 'village square' where everyone could meet, access services and gain qualifications. In 2008, the group set up a community allotment on a vandalised site on Tottenham Marshes; the group felt people, nature and spaces were their true heritage and assets. From small beginnings, they eventually got funding from the National Lottery and in 2016 they won Best Community Group of the Year in the UK from The Conservation Trust.

More widely, community groups have succeeded in safeguarding, creating and maintaining many green spaces in cities, towns and villages through projects including:

---

[9] https://www.righttoroam.org.uk/

- community gardens;
- food growing in allotments, orchards and city farms;
- 'friends of' public parks and gardens;
- tree planting in streets and urban woodlands;
- play areas for children;
- de-paving front gardens;
- wildlife gardens, wildflower nurseries and guerrilla gardening (spreading wildflower seeds on roadsides); and
- negotiating access to private green open spaces such as garden squares and golf courses (some of which were opened to the public for the first time during the COVID-19 pandemic).

Neighbourhood quality

After years of austerity, there are many neighbourhoods where the public squalor is not just visible but also further degrades communities. Unfortunately, some local authorities see litter, graffiti, vandalism and neglect as unimportant minor nuisances or selfish middle-class concerns. They deplore communities' constant complaints even though we know that, yet again, it is the poorest communities that live in the worst environments. The broken windows research in the US in the 1980s showed that visible signs of crime, antisocial behaviour and civil disorder create an urban environment that further encourages crime and disorder and a sense of insecurity and lack of worth for many communities.

In Barnsley, south Yorkshire, budgets for street cleaning and parks were reduced dramatically and the council's workforce almost halved. There the council has recognised that lack of care and maintenance makes the area look 'tired and decayed' and 'psychologically, the population gets into a place where nothing good ever happens, and there isn't much of a future' (Stephen Houghton, leader of Barnsley Council, quoted in Harris, 2020). The poet Ian McMillan, who lives locally, says: 'You notice things kind of vanishing off the edge ... Things disappear and that becomes the norm. You notice weeds, and grass not being cut so often. It's like mood music, but all in a minor key' (Harris, 2020). In Barnsley, the council now works to support communities to tackle some of these problems.

The state of our streets is vital to the quality of our lives and to the extent to which we feel we can control our own environment – or are at the mercy of external negative forces. Success at these small but highly visible street-level actions can quickly build confidence and willingness to act on other issues.

Climate change

The issue of climate change shifts the focus of community environmental action back to the global. Environmental groups and campaigners have argued for decades that climate change is the greatest threat to life on earth. Extinction Rebellion (XR) has argued that: 'We are facing an unprecedented global emergency. Life on Earth is in crisis: scientists agree we have entered a period of abrupt climate breakdown, and we are in the midst of a mass extinction of our own making'.[10] Apocalyptic language is now a regular feature of the climate change debate.

With a few exceptions (for example, Lomborg, 2001; Lawson, 2009), there is general acceptance of the extensive scientific research that supports this view (for example, IPCC, 2018). That science remains at the core of campaigning action on climate change. It shows that increased greenhouse gases, especially carbon dioxide (CO_2) and methane, dangerously increase the heat on the Earth, with scientists being in almost total accord that global warming is due to human actions – especially as a result of burning fossil fuels (coal, oil and natural gas) for transport, electricity generation, manufacturing and so on, and by cutting down forests to clear land for commercial agriculture.[11]

Local community action on climate change is largely around two main themes: practical projects to reduce carbon emissions through energy generation from renewable sources and energy conservation; and protest and campaigning for wider changes.

Substantial national funding and support has been available for practical community-led action on climate change. One example is the UK government's Low Carbon Communities Challenge (LCCC),[12] which invested £10 million over two years in 22 community schemes to test a range of energy developments in different types of community. Projects ranged from widening the use of low-energy light bulbs to developing a 1.2MW biomass district heating system.

This programme and projects also built community organising skills and learning. Groups in the LCCC shared their experience in a series of workshops and visits by policy makers from the Department of Energy and Climate Change (DECC), as well as in wider networks. The LCCC projects not only reduced local carbon emissions (saving a theoretical 3,062,091kg of CO_2) but also created social outcomes

---

[10] https://extinctionrebellion.uk/the-truth/

[11] https://www.climateassembly.uk/about/climate-change/

[12] https://sciencewise.org.uk/wp-content/uploads/2019/05/Case-Study-1.pdf

that were seen as equally important by local people – a new residents' association, community cinemas and orchards and just 'things getting better' in the area (DECC, 2012).

The generation of energy from renewable sources (especially wind and sun) has been highly controversial at times. It can be difficult to find consensus about local solutions even within the environmental movement (for example, conservation areas versus solar panels; wildlife and landscape versus wind turbines; and electric cars versus walking, cycling and public transport). Although the scientific consensus is strong on what is happening to the climate, this is less the case on what should be done to tackle the problem. Projects to reduce energy demand and address the growth in energy consumption[13] have been less contentious. Community action here has prioritised insulation and other improvements for fuel-poor households and creating jobs and training.[14]

Initial inequality means disadvantaged groups suffer disproportionately from the adverse effects of climate change, resulting in greater subsequent inequality: 'The key here is inequality reduction, which can help to contain the adverse effects of climate change. Moreover, through the feedback effect, it may mitigate climate change itself. Thus, a virtuous circle may replace the current vicious cycle' (Nazrul Islam and Winkel, 2017). Climate justice has become a growing priority for local and national campaigning groups, alongside their longstanding work to raise awareness to increase public concern and action.

The Extinction Rebellion Together programme provided training for its local groups and supporters on diversity, including providing support for people of colour who feel uncomfortable participating in XR's tactic of civil disobedience and seeking arrest because of not feeling safe with the police, or feeling unable to take the time off work,[15] and links have been made with the Black Lives Matter movement. One of the organisers of the UK school climate strikes said: 'If you're tackling climate change while ignoring the fact that it will disproportionately impact all the most marginalised people in our society, and they are already bearing the brunt of this crisis, then you are doing them a grave injustice' (Murray and Mohdin, 2020).

---

[13] https://www.iea.org/news/global-energy-demand-rose-by-23-in-2018-its-fastest-pace-in-the-last-decade

[14] http://www.nef.org.uk/ and https://www.cse.org.uk/

[15] https://www.bbc.co.uk/news/uk-48373540

Dramatic, stylish and theatrical protests and campaigns by Greenpeace, XR and others have successfully built on scientific evidence to raise awareness of the threats from climate change. Polling in March 2020 showed that 76 per cent of the UK population were either very or fairly concerned about climate change; only 2 per cent did not believe in it.[16] By August 2020, more than half the UK's 408 principal local authorities had declared a climate emergency;[17] 282 councils according to Climate Emergency UK.[18]

It has been argued that catastrophism itself in environmental campaigning is counterproductive as people can feel disempowered by the scale and urgency of the crisis (Warburton, 2008). Catastrophism does not fit with long-term community engagement or finding solutions that gain wide acceptance, to the point where cultural, social, economic and political change is possible (Jackson, 2016). XR's call for a Citizens' Assembly on Climate and Ecological Justice suggests a welcome willingness to invest in longer-term dialogue. Local climate assemblies have already been run by UK local authorities to engage local people in identifying priorities and ways forward for local action. These have run alongside the Climate Assembly UK, commissioned by six parliamentary select committees and reported in September 2020[19] (House of Commons, 2020). Such deliberative approaches to engaging people may help support communities seeking long-term solutions.

Conclusions and ways forward

Community action, campaigns and protests can achieve remarkable changes, but community action alone can never achieve the scale of action required to transform communities. Collaborative working between the state (especially local government), communities, businesses, universities and many other institutions locally and nationally will be needed. We are not starting from a blank sheet of paper. There is a wealth of experience as well as powerful policy frameworks to build on. We can take lessons from experience in local

---

[16] https://www.ipsos.com/sites/default/files/ct/news/documents/2019-06/global_what_worries_the_world_may_2019.pdf and https://www.ipsos.com/ipsos-mori/en-uk/concern-about-climate-change-reaches-record-levels-half-now-very-concerned

[17] https://www.thersa.org/discover/publications-and-articles/rsa-blogs/2019/10/the-uk-accelerator-for-climate-action

[18] https://www.climateemergency.uk/blog/list-of-councils/

[19] https://www.climateassembly.uk/

communities to identify some ways forward that may help consolidate and build on the wonderful local work done by some amazing people.

Lesson 1: Transforming communities requires integrated environmental, social, economic and political change. Communities have found innovative ways to tackle local and global problems through practical projects to reduce carbon emissions and energy consumption, create and manage urban green spaces and open up access to the countryside, and clean up their streets. They have influenced plans for the development of land and buildings, and strategies to tackle climate change.

These are never purely environmental projects – they often start with social, economic or political objectives. Integration of these issues brings strength and resilience as interests cannot be played off against each other; separation weakens each action. Sustainable development puts social and political development to tackle poverty and inequality as a primary and overarching goal, while ensuring the environmental consequences of development (past and present) are not ignored. This provides a global ethic for sustainable community transformation, and a set of internationally agreed goals, including by the UK government.[20] Making these connections more explicit in policy and decision making, including climate assemblies and some form of green new deal, could build on and support local action.

Lesson 2: Connect practice with policy. The West Oakland project influenced emissions planning legislation, many communities influenced rural and urban land-use plans, local protest groups influenced the development of national parks and LCCC groups shared their experience with national civil servants – on-the-ground experience direct from communities can bring an otherwise missing source of local knowledge to policy and decision making.

While national voluntary organisations can speak on behalf of whole sectors and interest groups, and individuals can speak on behalf of other citizens (for example, in citizens' assemblies), the direct voice of local community activists is not often heard in town halls or Whitehall. We need to do more to connect politicians and public servants directly with community activists, including and beyond formal organisations and individual citizen participation.

Lesson 3: Use science well. Environmentalists are very good at using science in campaigning to achieve local health and social

---

[20] https://www.gov.uk/government/publications/implementing-the-sustainable-development-goals/implementing-the-sustainable-development-goals

improvements as well as environmental benefits (for example, the West Oakland project), as well as managing local and global risks. Their experience has valuable lessons for other fields.

As we recognise the increasing impacts of climate change and life-threatening pandemics, the global risks we all face have become much more immediate. It has been argued that these impacts are so significant that they have created a new geological epoch – the anthropocene – in which human beings have had a serious and lasting influence on the Earth's systems, environment, processes and biodiversity.[21]

As we tackle these global risks, it is vital that we draw on sound science. However, there are caveats. We need to understand better how to use science and research evidence (Cartwright and Hardie, 2012). Two key factors would help: following the precautionary principle[22] to ensure damage is not caused by postponing action due to insufficient scientific certainty; and greater participation to ensure there is more democracy, transparency and accountability, not less, in decision making (Stirling, 2011; Willis, 2020).

Exclusive focus on science could undermine the emotional (and, for some, spiritual) resonance of our relationship with our world: our beautiful little blue planet floating in the blackness of space – that small 'pale blue dot' (Sagan, 1994). Effective decision making will always need to take account of human values (through public engagement), and precaution, as well as sound science.

Lesson 4: Think long term. Transforming communities in ways that address climate change as well as other risks will not be achieved quickly. Long-term planning can be fatally undermined by stop/start engagement, so long-term public engagement needs to be integrated into decision-making processes. Continuing communication builds understanding, empathy and compassion as well as helping to create practical shared objectives, plans and stronger relationships between government and citizens.

Such change also cannot be achieved within one electoral cycle. Local and national cross-party working will be essential to ensure long-term commitment to agreed goals, and the specific actions needed to reach those goals. It is possible. The All Party Parliamentary Group on the Green New Deal has shown how this can work at the national level

---

[21] https://www.nhm.ac.uk/discover/what-is-the-anthropocene.html?gclid=EAIaIQ obChMIoZ6bo5PN6wIVSbDtCh2PZgbqEAAYASAAEgLsjPD_BwE

[22] https://www.un.org/en/development/desa/population/migration/generalassembly/docs/globalcompact/A_CONF.151_26_Vol.I_Declaration.pdf; Principle 15.

(Reset, 2020). At local levels, progressive politicians have begun to develop cross-party agreements on joint programmes (as in Brighton and Hove City Council between Labour and Green councillors).

Lesson 5: Provide the right resources at the right time. Nothing will change without adequate investment of money and support. Big grant-making programmes are valuable in supporting leaps forward in innovation and action. Sometimes, local groups are daunted by such large sums and by the formal organisational structures needed to access them. What most groups need are small grants that are quick and easy to access and available long term, a supportive relationship with local government and other local institutions, opportunities to find out what others are doing to share information and learning, and access to free technical advice when needed (with experts 'on tap, not on top' as Tony Gibson often said).

Cuts in local and national public spending have decimated not just local services but also support for action by communities. Funding must be restored alongside new thinking and collaborative working between communities and public bodies.

Lesson 6: Be willing to change. We live in difficult and troubling times, facing complex and frightening global threats as well as the everyday challenges of life. There are occasional turning points in human history when major change is possible, such as following a war or pandemic. Social movement theory suggests there are moments when gaps open up in the political opportunity structure, and change is possible. These gaps relate to: increasing access; shifting alignments; divided elites; influential allies; and repression and facilitation (Tarrow, 1998). Perhaps we have reached that point: what some call 'steam-engine time' (Bridle, 2018), when all the forces align and innovations from many sources coalesce. People want change, and we want the new normal to be better (Reset, 2020).

Institutions struggle with change, especially governments, despite the bubbling up of energy and innovation from communities. As Jamie Saunders from Bradford City Council has said, getting hot ideas into cold structures is always a challenge. New circumstances need new thinking. Willingness to change is the first step, then constant communication and collaboration are needed to plan and deliver change, without being rose-tinted about what is possible: pessimism of the intellect, optimism of the will (as Gramsci wrote, Hall et al, 1978).

We can only go forward together if we decide to take action on that basis. Then it becomes possible to start to transform our communities and our lives, and protect the planet that is our home.

References

Allison, E. (2012) 'The Kinder Scout trespass: 80 years on', *The Guardian*, 17 April.

Arnstein, S. (1969) 'A ladder of citizen participation in the USA', *Journal of American Institute of Planners*, 35(1969): 216–24.

Barnett, M. (2019) 'The Kinder Scout mass trespass', *Tribune*, 24 April.

Berglund, E. (2000) *Social Divisions and Environmentalism.* Paper for conference held on the topic at Goldsmiths College, London, in February 2000.

Bishop, J. (2019) 'In search of Skeffington', *The Planner*, 28 June.

Bridle, J. (2018) *New Dark Age: Technology and the End of the Future*, London: Verso.

Brodie, E., Hughes, T., Jochum, V., Miller, S., Ockenden, N. and Warburton, D. (2011) *Pathways Through Participation: What Creates and Sustains Active Citizenship?* London: NCVO, Institute for Volunteering Research and Involve.

Brownill, S. (2020) 'Planning and participation in a time of pandemic', *Town and Country Planning*, June/July.

Cartwright, N. and Hardie, J. (2012) *Evidence-Based Policy. A Practical Guide to Doing It Better.* Oxford: Oxford University Press.

Clifford, S. and King, A. (eds) (1993) *Local Distinctiveness*, London: Common Ground.

DECC (Department of Energy and Climate Change) (2012) *Low Carbon Communities Challenge: Evaluation Report*, London: DECC.

Goodhart, D. (2017) *The Road to Somewhere: The Populist Revolt and the Future of Politics*, London: C. Hurst & Co Publishers.

Hall, S., Lumley, B., McLennan. G. (1978) 'Politics and ideology: Gramsci', in *On Ideology*, Centre for Contemporary Cultural Studies, University of Birmingham, Hutchinson.

Harris, J. (2020) '"Making savings" just pushes the problems elsewhere', *The Guardian*, 22 June.

House of Commons (2020) *The Path to Net Zero: Climate Assembly UK*, London: House of Commons, Involve, Sortition Foundation and My Society.

IPCC (Intergovernmental Panel on Climate Change) (2018) 'Summary for policymakers', in IPCC, *Global Warming of 1.5°C: An IPCC Special Report on the Impacts of Global Warming of 1.5°C above Pre-industrial Levels and Related Global Greenhouse Gas Emission Pathways, in the Context of Strengthening the Global Response to the Threat of climate Change, Sustainable Development, and Efforts to Eradicate Poverty*, Geneva: IPCC.

Jackson, S. (2016) 'Catastrophism is as much an obstacle to addressing climate change as denial', *Open Democracy*, 6 September.

Krier, L. (2001) 'Planning for humanity', *Open Democracy*.

Landry, C. (2001) 'Experiencing the city anew', *Open Democracy*.

Lawson, N. (2009) *An Appeal to Reason: A Cool Look at Global Warming*, New York: Harry N. Abrams.

Lomborg, B. (2001) *The Skeptical Environmentalist: Measuring the Real State of the World*, Cambridge: Cambridge University Press.

Murray, J. and Mohdin, A. (2020) '"It was empowering": teen BLM activists on learning the ropes at school climate strikes', *The Guardian*, 11 August.

Nazrul Islam, S. and Winkel, J. (2017) *Climate Change and Social Inequality*, DESA working paper No 152, San Francisco: United Nations Department of Economic & Social Affairs.

Public Health England (2020) *Improving Access to Greenspace: A New Review for 2020*, London: Public Health England.

Reset (2020) *Time to Reset: The Public Desire for a Fairer, Greener Britain after Covid*, a report by the All Party Parliamentary Group on the Green New Deal, London: Reset.

Sagan, C. (1994) *Pale Blue Dot: A Vision of the Human Future in Space*, New York: Random House.

Skeffington, A. (1969) *People and Planning: Report of the Committee on Public Participation in Planning*, London: HMSO.

Stirling, A. (2011) 'Engineering sustainability: synergies between science, precaution and participation', *Philosophy of Engineering*, vol 2 of the proceedings of a seminar held at the Royal Academy of Engineering, London.

Tarrow, S. (1998) *Power in Movement: Social Movements and Contentious Politics*, Cambridge: Cambridge University Press.

United Nations (1973) *Report of the United Nations Conference on the Human Environment*, Stockholm, 5–16 June 1972, New York: United Nations.

Warburton, D. (1998) *Community and Sustainable Development: Participation in the Future*, London: Earthscan.

Warburton, D. (2004) 'Community involvement in countryside planning in practice', in Bishop, K. and Phillips, A. (eds) *Countryside Planning: New Approaches to Management and Conservation*, London: Earthscan.

Warburton, D. (2008) *Evaluation of WWF-UK's Community Learning and Action for Sustainable Living (CLASL): Final Report*, London: WWF Godalming and Defra.

Wates, N. (2000) *The Community Planning Handbook: How People can Shape their Cities, Towns and Villages in Any Part of the World,* London: Earthscan.

Wates, N. and Knevitt, C. (1987) *Community Architecture: How People are Creating their own Environment,* London: Penguin.

Watts, J. (2020) 'Keep it clean', *The Guardian,* 8 June.

WCED (World Commission on Environment and Development) (1987) *Our Common Future,* Oxford: Oxford University Press.

Willis, R. (2020) *Too Hot to Handle. The Democratic Challenge of Climate Change,* Bristol: Bristol University Press.

Conclusion

14

The policy agenda for community-based transformation

Henry Tam

The politics of community

We have seen in this volume how a range of approaches can help engender community-based transformation that will substantially improve people's quality of life. In this concluding chapter, we will consider how these approaches should be brought together in a unified policy agenda.

One of the first steps to take is to distinguish this agenda from others that talk up the importance of 'community' but intend to treat communities in ways that are quite dissimilar, even inimical in some cases, to the options we propose. These fall broadly into four categories:[1]

- *'Traditional' communities*: champion and reinforce selected customs and power relationships in the name of traditional values; and dismiss concerns about prejudices and oppressive structures as misguided liberal/cosmopolitan objections.
- *'Autonomous' communities*: advocate the rolling back of rules and regulations in the name of freedom for communities and their members; and dismiss concerns about harmful consequences as matters that should be left to communities to address.

---

[1] The first two categories are connected with the *Gemeinschaft* ethos of communities acting in their own ways, with minimal attention paid to any higher or external authority; and the second two categories are more linked to the *Gesellschaft* conception of people living together in a society dominated by state and market activities (see Chapter 1). As many communitarian thinkers have argued, there is a form of community life we should seek to attain beyond the *Gemeinschaft*/*Gesellschaft* dichotomy (Tam, 2019b).

- *'Supplicant' communities*: highlight the needs of disadvantaged communities and focus on helping them with centrally directed programmes; and dismiss concerns with top-down solutions as an unwarranted distrust of state intervention.
- *'Philanthropic' communities*: praise communities for helping those in need and increasingly leave them to deal with problems on their own; and dismiss concerns about inadequate responses as driven by preference for big government spending.

When political speeches and policy proposals invoking the notion of 'community' are actually based on the ideas in one or another of these four categories, they can have two potentially undesirable effects. On the one hand, people could be misled into thinking they herald support for genuine community-based transformation when their trajectories point in quite different directions. On the other hand, people might become so averse to such 'community' invocation that they assume that any agenda for community-based transformation must be more of the same of these types of ideas.

The politics of community can be interpreted in contrasting terms (Frazer and Lacey, 1993; Tam, 2019b), and unless we have a clearly formulated and articulated reform agenda, it is all too easy for the public to end up backing the wrong options, or backing away from the recommendations they ought to take on board. Recognising the importance of community life in giving people a sense of belonging and mutual support, means that we must see through the rhetoric of misleading 'community' policies.

Attempts to strengthen traditional, autonomous, supplicant or philanthropic communities are most likely to lead to the weakening of people's ability to live and work together in an inclusive, mutually supportive and collectively influential manner. The more people are diverted towards relying on the kindness of others, rather than joining forces to steer public policies for the common good, the more vulnerable they are to economic downturns and global crises. For example, there were always politicians who sought to turn the readiness of many communities to help those in need into a platform for repackaging the 'Big Society'-type advocacy of 'community resilience' by essentially asking people to spend more time doing voluntary work even as their livelihood was becoming ever-more precarious, and proclaiming that more power would be given to local people to shape their public services while the latter's remit and resources were drastically cut by central government.[2]

Having anticipated and exposed the potential misrepresentation of what the politics of empowering communities is about, we can more readily move forward with a positive agenda for engendering community-based transformation.

What have we learnt?

Communities can play a transformative role in becoming better places in which to live and work. As for how the necessary improvements are to be made, neither nostalgic pining for an imaginary past nor idealistic yearning for a utopian future can substitute for evidence-based reviews of what has worked in practice or not in enhancing people's efficacy over their wellbeing. As we have seen in the foregoing chapters, experts with considerable experience between them have identified many lessons that are invaluable in mapping out what could be done.[3] We can summarise these under the three headings of:

- the transformation of socioeconomic relations in communities;
- the transformation of collaborative behaviour with communities; and
- the transformation of policy outcomes by communities.

Beginning with socioeconomic relations, we can with confidence assert that communities can generate greater resources to meet their needs and aspirations without either totally relying on or rejecting what the public and/or private sector has to offer. The chapters in Part A of this book have pointed to at least four ways of doing this that will curtail inequalities and have more sustainable impact:

---

[2] The promotion and revival of 'Big Society'-type rhetoric has been prevalent since the Conservative Party won power in the UK in 2010.

[3] In addition to the analyses and case examples provided in this book, organisations such as the Joseph Rowntree Foundation, Esmée Fairbairn Foundation, Lankelly Chase Foundation, Community Development Foundation and many others have over decades commissioned research that produced findings reinforcing the recommendations we are putting forward.

[A1] Community economic development provides a means for funds and assets to be controlled by community-based organisations with a legally defined remit to meet the needs of the people in the area. The fulfilment of that remit requires a meaningful say to be given to the people living, working and running businesses there in relation to how those organisations will operate for their benefit. By enabling organisations rooted in their communities to grow assets, facilities and services that respond to local concerns, people can more readily secure the appropriate improvements.

[A2] Alternative mediums of exchange such as local currencies and time banking will not only promote an ethos of mutual support, but also help to make more value available by increasing the overall resources that are retained in the local economy, as well as generating services facilitated by exchanges of time commitment.

[A3] Government at all levels can put aside the false dichotomy of 'top-down control or accountability-free grants', and adopt instead the approach of genuine partnership regeneration. The greater the understanding and influence communities attain in relation to regeneration initiatives – and these factors depend critically on the robustness of arrangements to support informed deliberation and option prioritisation – the more likely communities and their elected representatives can converge on what improvements need to be made and how the impact of the available resources can be maximised in achieving them.

[A4] Both the quantity and quality of income-earning opportunities can be enhanced by the development of democratically owned and controlled enterprises in communities. Inadequate pay, job insecurity and high unemployment rates can be highly damaging for any affected area; but these problems are far more effectively tackled by businesses that are owned and controlled by the people from the area who work in them, especially with the help of platform technology.

Next, we come to collaborative behaviour, which is a key factor in determining the extent to which communities will come together in formulating and pursuing shared objectives. The chapters in Part B of this book point to a series of lessons that most people who have been at the forefront of facilitating community co-operation would endorse:

[B1] The commitment to strategic relationship building. There are many barriers to collaboration between communities and public agencies that can only be overcome if sustained efforts are devoted to developing fair and open interactions, through which all involved can be confident in playing their part in shaping collective plans for action. This requires cultural adjustment in organisational attitudes and the establishment of long-term infrastructure for inclusive dialogue.

[B2] The extension of community-based learning. In order to reverse the polarisation of communities by a mixture of deliberate misdirection and inadequate capability in assessing the veracity of major societal claims, there should be more practical support for communities to learn together, which requires trained facilitators to help people explore under conditions of civility what the real causes of the problems are that they face, what viable solutions might look like, and how to assess proposals and criticisms they may encounter regarding what should be done. Safeguarding the quality standards, impartiality and accessibility of such learning provision is essential.

[B3] The equitable sharing of power in decision making. When communities and authorised policy makers are able to consider options together as equal partners, with neither side being in a position to dictate terms to the other, they are more likely to reach agreement about what action to take. Even more importantly, the actions taken are more likely to avoid delays and costly mistakes, while leading to higher trust between partners and greater satisfaction all round.

[B4] The readiness to adjust responsively to rather than suppress uncertainties. This is to be promoted in practice through adaptive processes for goal setting, feedback assessment and open evaluation. In recognition that human experiences and external circumstances cannot be precisely predicted at every turn, allowances must be made for plans to be revised in the light of changes experienced by communities and partner organisations.

Finally, policy outcomes can more successfully reflect communities' needs and concerns if they are developed and delivered with the appropriate involvement from the communities in question. The chapters in Part C of this book show how various community-based approaches can bring about transformative results in a wide range of issues and contexts:

[C1] The co-production of public services is strengthened when service providers are incentivised to seek input from communities as a way to improve both the public satisfaction with and financial viability of their services. This can be better achieved with a form of preventive infrastructure that connects what communities and service providers can offer respectively to maximise their combined added value.

[C2] The adoption of the multi-stakeholder co-operative model can radically transform a vital sector such as health and social care. The key is to enable the people who provide care and those who need it to work out the optimal service provision, without remote shareholders or distant state officials imposing their own priorities and assumptions on what communities are to be given on what terms.

[C3] In relation to food insecurity and related social problems, the integration of community interests and contributions at the heart of planning and management arrangements has also shown how the opening up of predetermined processes to continuous reshaping by members of the affected communities can deliver not only improvement to what is provided, but also a greater sense of efficacy and dignity for those communities.

[C4] In meeting environmental challenges, from local difficulties to global threats, communities can be galvanised to make a notable difference whenever they are given real opportunities to consider the issues, help raise awareness, campaign for change, engage critically with option evaluation and selection and, most importantly, play a part in putting in place better neighbourhood designs and more sustainable arrangements for matters such as energy, transport and air quality.

By drawing on the lessons set out here, we can develop a policy agenda that will enable communities to develop the capability to work with institutional partners as well as their own members to strengthen their solidarity and transform their quality of life.

A nine-point policy agenda

Many policy makers unfamiliar with the impact community-based transformation can produce are sceptical about what should be done to aid its development. Even those who are persuaded of its potential value are often unsure as to what policies would help to bring about the most beneficial effects. The nine policy recommendations set out below provide a reform agenda that can substantially boost community-based transformation and generate wider and sustainable improvements.

(1) Promote a shared vision for a common cause

From community economic development, time banking and resident-centric regeneration, to community organising, deliberative engagement and authentic co-production, there is an underlying common cause that champions communities' potential in securing a better future. Although the focus of specialist studies on individual techniques, or practitioners' advocacy of their own preferred methods, can give the impression that these are disparate tools that may be of interest on the margins of mainstream policies, they are in fact complementary aspects of a powerful way to improve people's lives beyond what government, markets and charities can achieve by themselves. We need to put forward a shared vision of how systematic co-operation with and across communities can bring about substantial positive changes in terms of inclusion, sustainability and personal wellbeing.

Politicians, community activists and policy advisers who recognise the importance of this vision should use the language of community-based transformation to present their ideas, and make the case for, not the ad hoc adoption of one or another of the approaches we have described, but the strategic deployment of each of them wherever it is likely to have the impact sought in raising mutual understanding, community efficacy and standards of living. The vision could be consistently expressed with reference to the building of co-operative communities, and demarcated from the policy stance associated with traditional, autonomous, supplicant or philanthropic communities.

(2) Put the public at the heart of public services

When public services are disengaged from public input, they can become remote, ineffective and distrusted.[4] Even the most well-meaning politicians and officials cannot know what people in the communities affected by their decisions may think about the implications, without giving them the opportunity to consider the issues and express their views. Government institutions, at all levels, should build into their policy development and service planning arrangements the following:

- processes for the deliberative engagement of people in the areas concerned;
- sharing of power in option selection;
- examination of co-production possibilities;
- training for staff in being responsive when discussing matters with members of the public; and
- support for a representative range of people to participate in the shaping and delivery of services.

In the past, public decision makers have been attracted by the novelty of particular techniques and promoted their use for a short period before

---

[4] Some politicians prefer to see such disengagement continue, because the greater the distrust of public services, the easier it is for them to argue for cutting those services or privatising them.

looking for the next set of 'innovations'.[5] But the focus should not be on any single technique, but on how in different circumstances, the most appropriate technique – with suitably trained and experienced facilitators – ought to be used to enable the public to have an informed say about what is to be done with public funds to help solve the problems they face. The approaches to be adopted in individual cases may vary, from obtaining views from critical forums, and empowering participants to rank or choose from proposed options, to inviting community members to monitor performance or arranging joint activities to meet identified needs. It is the commitment to apply what would work best based on the evidence that should be the guiding principle.

(3) Invest in community development

The transformative impact of community development on people's lives must be recognised in terms of both integrating it into public policy making and investing in its quality and expansion. It is not enough to aspire to reach out to and engage communities in shaping public policies and services; the confidence and capacity of communities to play an influential role must be effectively cultivated. People disillusioned with being ignored, or communities weakened by economic uncertainties or torn by polarised views, are not likely to embrace community engagement offers wholeheartedly. Community development is a key discipline in providing outreach workers/advocates who can connect with diverse members of communities and help them explore how to deal with certain differences and also to reach consensus, and find ways to put forward their common concerns and agreed proposals.

Community development's role in bridge building has too often been overlooked, and suffered cuts when it is vital for underpinning community-based transformation.[6] Investment should be channelled towards securing the supply of well-trained community development workers in every large neighbourhood, town and city, with an ongoing remit to promote civil discourse, enhance familiarity and mutual understanding, advise on local connective infrastructure for casual meeting and formal deliberation, and give support for articulating shared views and priorities to decision makers. Above all, community

---

[5] These have included, at different times, small-scale citizens' juries, participatory budgeting, community organising and large-scale citizens' assemblies.

[6] The closure forced on the Community Development Foundation by the Conservative-led government's austerity programme is a typically short-sighted and counterproductive move that should be reversed.

development should receive core funding to maintain communicative relations vertically between state organisations and local communities, and horizontally across diverse sections of communities.

(4) Target support for community-based organisations

Public and private funders should collaborate in supporting community-based organisations that play a significant role in generating and/or channelling resources in meeting local needs.[7] Community enterprises, community anchor organisations, local multi-stakeholder co-operatives and others have demonstrated how they can build on investment and transferred assets to serve the social and economic interests of the communities in which they operate, and establish long-term income-earning streams, which in turn help to sustain those services. Funders should avoid directing their support towards the highest-profile organisations, or making short-term grants without planning for future investment needs.

Enabling those community-based organisations with a sound base to maintain their vitality and grow, is more important than fixating on how many new organisations the latest round of funding has helped to bring about, especially if quite a few of them will not survive with one-off funding. Funders need to develop their understanding of what these organisations need in terms of personnel training, additional investment, financial management advice and quality standards for community responsiveness, so that they can target their support to those who are more likely to utilise their support effectively and be of real benefit to local people. In the past, the loudest with demands for funds or the sharpest in running public relations campaigns have often got the most attention. It is essential for funders to shift to an evidence-based assessment of the capability and commitment of potential recipients of support.

(5) Strengthen legal protection for community interests

Just because an organisation invokes 'community' in its name or how it describes its activities, it does not mean that it will serve the

---

[7] This may include the joint establishment of an independent development agency, tasked with securing funds from a range of funders and determining how to distribute the overall funds to community-based organisations that meet the agreed criteria. One model of such a development agency can be found at https://blog.p2pfoundation. net/towards-an-open-cooperativist-development-agency-henry-tam/2015/03/04.

interests of the community in which it operates. Public or private funders may unwittingly, or even knowingly, give funds to such an organisation that may go on to spend the money primarily for the benefit of those running the organisation, or act against the interests of wider community wellbeing.[8] To prevent this from happening, it is necessary to have firm and enforceable legal protection to ensure that community interests are served when financial support is given for the stated purpose of doing just that.

The legal protection to be established will need to cover at least the following requirements:

- There must be asset locks on all assets transferred, and these should not be allowed to be sold on or gifted to any other party unless the transaction can secure comparable or greater assets that will benefit the community in question.
- There must be transparent and effective accountability arrangements in place so that members of the community can check that the stated aims of the organisation are adhered to, and mechanisms for redress can be activated if necessary.
- Above a specified financial threshold, there must be external audits to ensure there is no misuse of funds and any mismanagement is swiftly identified.
- The integrity of the organisation must be shielded from any form of privatisation or merger that will undermine the original stated intent of the organisation to serve community interests.

(6) Adopt inclusive goal setting and responsive evaluation

It has been seen that neither a rigid set of top-down targets nor a leave-it-to-whatever-a-group-may-want-to-do approach is an advisable way forward. The former shuts off responsiveness to local perspectives and changing circumstances, and the latter opens the door to prejudices and discrimination playing a part in choosing who will benefit or not. To advance community-based transformation, parameters must be clearly formulated at the outset. The goals of inclusion, mutual respect, informed deliberation and shared improvement must be

---

[8] Some may use a large share of the funding to increase payment to themselves or those close to them, and some may direct their resources to running projects that neglect those in need, or promoting distrust/animosity of certain sections of the community on the grounds of race, sexuality and so on.

built in so that they are an integral part of the funding conditions, and no group can embark on discriminatory action in the name of 'community' autonomy.

Within the set parameters, however, the process of selecting options and evaluating their impact on communities should be led by the community organisations themselves in co-operation with partner agencies and local people. Responsive evaluation means that instead of checking off quantifiable measures that may give the appearance of precision when they are not relatively important to the people concerned, what is to be examined is how the changes that have been brought about are affecting people's experience of key aspects of their lives. The interconnections of changes can mean that people's sense of priorities may alter during the course of a set of initiatives, and it is better to recognise any corresponding adjustment of action plans as a positive feature rather than cite the shift as the cause of a preconceived target being missed.

(7) Facilitate reliable information sharing

The notion that communities are better placed to work out what would protect and enhance their wellbeing is premised on the assumption that reliable information is widely shared among them without distortion. Far from taking this for granted, an effective policy agenda for community-based transformation must address the issue of responsible communication. It is long established that 'freedom of speech' is no defence against the propagation of lies, misleading reports, malicious rumours or unsubstantiated claims that can have harmful consequences. Medical treatment, engineering works, commercial transactions and many aspects of everyday life can be seriously damaged if there is no enforceable restriction on what is communicated, especially by those who intend to deceive and manipulate others. Similar standards of veracity must be applied to information sharing that can impact on policies and practices that affect communities' wellbeing. Statutory independent mechanisms will need to be brought in to provide adjudication of disputed claims and enforcement against deception.[9]

In parallel, the dissemination of reliable information should be more widely supported, as the lack of access to such information can also undermine community deliberations. Cuts to library services and adult learning, threats to public service broadcasting and failures

---

[9] See Tam (2018, chapter 8).

to ensure universal access to quality broadband have all eroded the means by which objective information can be readily obtained. To help communities enhance their understanding of the problems they face, and strengthen their ability to discover better options to improve their quality of life, the funding and support for quality assurance in all forms of public information provision must be raised to a higher and more equal level for all.

(8) Distribute power and accountability in line with subsidiarity

In line with subsidiarity, power should be exercised at the lowest possible level where it can be done effectively.[10] In practice, this means that in many cases, the power to make decisions or oversee implementation should be passed down from a higher to a lower level of governance – from national to regional, regional to local (city, county, district), local to parish/neighbourhood, down to a particular street or housing complex. How far down it should go will depend on whether the power in question can be effectively exercised at that level. For example, a city cannot handle by itself the issue of the defence of the country, but a neighbourhood group can deal with matters relating to its local park without involving the whole local authority. There will also be cases where power needs to be transferred upwards because it requires a wider perspective and capability to exercise it effectively. Despite nationalistic rhetoric, it is generally recognised that issues such as the climate crisis, global pandemics, transnational organised crime and tax avoidance – to name but a few – cannot be effectively handled without some form of international decision-making mechanism, backed by the pooling of defined sovereign authority to ensure that agreed actions are carried out.[11]

Along with the redistribution of power, accountability should also be transferred accordingly. It is ironic that though citizens have increasingly lost faith in national elections that happen every one in four or five years as an adequate accountability mechanism (Tam, 2018), elections would still be put forward as the key process to hold decision makers to account when new power structures are created at

[10] Subsidiarity is a key guiding principle for the distribution of power, without which powers might be passed arbitrarily up or down a system of governance to the detriment of the people at all levels (Colombo, 2012; Fleming and Levy, 2014).

[11] The COVID-19 pandemic has illustrated the chaotic ebb and flow of the spread of the virus on a global scale.

different levels.[12] Elections are not enough by themselves to connect people's concerns with decision-makers' actions, especially when four or five years can pass before another chance to vote arrives. We need to have robust arrangements in place to underpin ongoing scrutiny, the routine participation of decision makers in deliberative forums, the judicial administration of sanctions against misconduct and recall procedures for breaches of trust.

(9) Safeguard peaceful community challenges

Authoritarian 'populists' are known for stirring up public discontent against their political enemies, but ever ready to suppress critical views directed at themselves. Political leaders who present themselves as champions of voiceless communities are prone to deny them any voice of their own. In the United Kingdom (UK), Conservative leaders have constantly criticised independent public broadcast services such as the BBC for being 'biased' and have threatened to cut their funding further. They have brought in legislation to deter voluntary organisations from expressing any critical views about the government in the 12 months before any general election if that could influence how people might vote.[13] And in both the UK and the United States, environmental campaigners have been treated by some law enforcement agencies as posing a terrorist threat. Moving forward, all these obstacles to peaceful community challenges must be removed.

On the other hand, safeguards are also needed against disruptive and intimidatory practices to stop these from being deployed under false pretences.[14] Peaceful community challenges cannot be organised and advanced if certain individuals or groups can destabilise any meaningful

---

[12] Despite the low levels of participation in local and European elections, new public bodies were created in the UK in the name of devolution – but with the opportunities to elect unknown figures as police and crime commissioners, governors of NHS foundation trusts and directly elected city or regional mayors – as the only means to hold those new types of power-holders to account.

[13] The Lobbying Act was introduced in the UK in 2014. Its intention to restrict the expression of critical views where they might influence people's voting behaviour shows that it is precisely designed to stop voluntary and community groups from raising any concerns that might lead to voters thinking more about the merits of government actions.

[14] The routine rallying of Trump supporters to intimidate others with whom they disagree, threaten violence, not to mention assault the US Capitol itself, illustrates how the notion of 'community challenge' must not be allowed to be abused.

dialogue by using aggressive methods that are designed to end rather than promote co-operative discussions. For example, critical views from any community cannot be peacefully expressed or considered if someone can bring a megaphone to a meeting to shout everyone else down, or a group can freely threaten to cause injury or damage to other people or property if their demands are not met.

The choices for tomorrow's communities

In the face of global crises, and the increasingly severe effects they have for local communities, we will continue to hear about the importance of helping communities become more resilient. There is no question that communities can be in a stronger position to deal with the challenges they face and enable the people who live and work in them to support each other much more effectively and inclusively. In this book we have looked at a range of approaches to how transformative improvements can be made. What is striking is that they do not carry significant costs – indeed, they often save money because of their capability for avoiding errors in target setting and their greater efficiency. What they require is the grasping and sustained application of the three core principles that underpin these different approaches:

- *Promotion of mutual responsibility.* Communities need to be more inclusive, enable their members to view one another with empathy and equal respect, and help them contribute to their common wellbeing.
- *Pursuit of co-operative enquiry.* Communities need to develop shared understanding, on the basis of collaborative and objective examination, of what public claims warrant their belief, and what should be rejected as false or misleading.
- *Plan through citizen participation.* Communities need to be empowered to ensure that their members can play an informed and influential role in shaping and reviewing key decisions on what is to be done that may have an impact on them.

It is clear that no policy that treats communities as something that can be left to their own devices or steered passively by some public or private benefactors will comply with these principles or attain the transformative improvements sought. Any community initiative or programme that does little more than direct attention to particular traditional, autonomous, supplicant or philanthropic communities should be seen for what it is, and not mistaken for a genuine attempt to develop the kind of co-operative communities we have highlighted in this book.

The key is for government institutions at all levels to work with diverse communities as true partners in advancing the culture and arrangements for people to see what can better serve their common interests, and to join forces in getting the most appropriate options selected and implemented. The philosophical issues that may arise from such a vision for the development of communities, and the practical difficulties that need to be addressed in taking forward the approaches that have been set out in this book, have both been extensively dealt with by scholars and practitioners.[15] There is ample evidence and many varied examples to show that the highlighted approaches can engender community-based transformation that will make tomorrow's communities fairer, stronger and more sustainable. What remains is for political leaders, policy strategists, community activists and educators to rally around the nine-point policy agenda that has been set out in this chapter, and collaborate on making it a centrepiece of any wider reform programme in the years to come.

References

Colombo, A. (2012) *Subsidiarity Governance: Theoretical and Empirical Models*, New York: Palgrave Macmillan.

Fleming, J. E. and Levy, J. T. (2014) *Federalism and Subsidiarity*, New York: New York University Press.

Frazer, E. and Lacey, N. (1993) *The Politics of Community: A Feminist Critique of the Liberal-Communitarian Debate*, Hemel Hempstead: Harvester Wheatsheaf.

Tam, H. (2018) *Time to Save Democracy: How to Govern Ourselves in the Age of Anti-politics*, Bristol: Policy Press.

Tam, H. (2019a) *Whose Government is it? The Renewal of State-Citizen Cooperation*, Bristol: Bristol University Press.

Tam, H. (2019b) *The Evolution of Communitarian Ideas*, Basingstoke: Palgrave Macmillan.

---

[15] In addition to the foregoing chapters of this book, a summary of the critical discussion of these issues can be found in Tam (2019a, 2019b).

Index